5-16-75

Arnold Bennett
a study of his fiction

Arnold Bennett
a study of his fiction

by John Lucas

METHUEN & CO LTD
11 NEW FETTER LANE LONDON EC4P 4EE

First published 1974
by Methuen & Co Ltd
11 New Fetter Lane
London EC4P 4EE
© 1974 John Lucas
Printed in Great Britain by
Richard Clay (The Chaucer Press) Ltd
Bungay, Suffolk

ISBN hardbound 0 416 75770 7
ISBN paperback 0 416 82980 5

Distributed in the USA by
Harper & Row Publishers Inc.
Barnes & Noble Import Division

1883131

For Barry and Rita Cole

Contents

Arnold Bennett
a study of his fiction

Introduction

Arnold Bennett died in 1931. His reputation as a serious novelist was by then under siege. A few years later and it was more or less in ruins. Philip Henderson voiced the accepted attitude to Bennett when, in 1935, he described his career as 'a flagrant case of literary capitalism'. Bennett had 'dried up the springs of his own creative vitality by deliberately turning himself into a commercialised writing-machine'. There had of course been *The Old Wives' Tale*; there had even been *Riceyman Steps*, 'a belated attempt to return to the springs of his old creative vitality'. But in between had come 'an enormous mass of spurious popular novels' (*Literature and a Changing Civilisation*, pp. 107–8). And afterwards? But Henderson has nothing to say about Bennett's later work. It is hardly surprising. For his case against Bennett is little more than a rehash of old complaints decked out with reach-me-down Marxist theorizing, and it suffers from the considerable disadvantage of being quite simply wrong. Why after all should Henderson refuse to say whether *Riceyman Steps* actually succeeds or not? The answer of course is that the novel itself blows his argument sky-high. How could a novelist who had dried up the springs of his creative vitality produce so fine a work as *Riceyman Steps* undoubtedly is? Henderson has no answer to that. No wonder that he should keep quiet about *Lord*

Raingo and *Imperial Palace*. They are not novels that could have been produced by a commercialized writing-machine.

This is not to deny that Bennett wrote potboilers, even though he denied it himself. *The Regent* and *Lilian*, for example, have nothing to recommend them beyond the fact that they made their author some money. But that fact isn't sufficient to damn Bennett's career.

> In the cream gilded cabin of his steam yacht
> Mr Nixon advised me kindly, to advance with fewer
> Dangers of delay . . .
>
> 'Butter reviewers. From fifty to three hundred
> 'I rose in eighteen months;
> 'The hardest nut I had to crack
> 'Was Dr Dundas.
>
> 'I never mentioned a man but with the view
> 'Of selling my own works.
> 'The tip's a good one, as for literature
> 'It gives no man a sinecure.
>
> 'And no one knows, at sight, a masterpiece.
> 'And give up verse, my boy,
> 'There's nothing in it.'

Pound's famous study of Mr Nixon is perhaps the most damaging of all attacks on Bennett. Yet Bennett is not Nixon, as Pound himself belatedly discovered. *Hugh Selwyn Mauberley* was published in 1920. Two years earlier Pound had reviewed Wyndham Lewis's *Tarr* and remarked that it was blessedly free from the 'click of Mr Bennett's cash-register finish'. When the review was reprinted in *Literary Essays* (1954) Pound added an apologetic footnote: 'E.P. rather modified his view of part of Bennett's writing when he finally got round to reading *An* [sic] *Old Wives' Tale* many years later.'

Nor is it fair to say that Bennett buttered reviewers. In 1924 Middleton Murry, then editor of the *Adelphi*, wrote a stinging article on George Moore. The article came at a time when Bennett, in his own phrase, was something of a 'back number'. But there is nothing ingratiating or buttery in the letter he sent to Murry.

I doubt if your observations upon George Moore escape being ridiculous. They certainly do not escape bad form. For myself I think G.M. is a pretty great writer: but my opinion is beside the point. . . . All the younger generation owe a lot to G.M., who fought for a freer code & established a certain freedom which you & others now enjoy – in deplorable ignorance of how you came to enjoy it. At any rate he is now over 70; he has always been absolutely unvenal; he has cared for nothing but literature; & I think he is entitled to some respect from serious persons – even if they are young.

One might, I suppose, argue that Bennett's praise of Moore hints at the lack of critical standards which, it has been said, harm much of his journalistic reviewing of the time. But it will hardly do. For if the Bennett of the *Evening Standard* years was too ready to proclaim genius where it didn't exist, it was the inevitable penalty he paid for keeping an open mind on younger writers. Wyndham Lewis's suggestion, in *The Roaring Queen*, that Bennett was puffed up with the vanity of ignorance and stupidity is itself ignorant and stupid. *The Roaring Queen* is a thoroughly unpleasant book, vicious and whining by turns. It tells one much more about Lewis than about Bennett.

Bennett may have been generous to a fault but young writers, including T. S. Eliot, had every reason to be grateful for the time, energy and money that he spent on them. Besides, at his best Bennett was a shrewd judge of worth. One has only to look at the reviews he gathered together in *Books and Persons*, 1908–11, to see how well many of his judgements stand the test of time, and the more informal praise and criticism of his later years can be equally just. To give one example. During the 1920s Bennett read all of Lawrence's work that came his way. Much of it he didn't care for, and he said so. He disliked Lawrence's wildness, his habit of verbally assaulting the reader, of shouting rather than reasoning. But when in 1930 *The Virgin and the Gipsy* made its appearance Bennett immediately wrote to his old friend Harriet Cohen, telling her that it is '*easily* the finest of *all* recent novels. . . . Nothing else exists by the side of it. Believe me. It is marvellous, truly.' Such praise feels the more generous when one remembers that Bennett had just published *Imperial Palace*. It certainly compares very favourably with the way he himself was treated and with the sneers that Bloomsbury directed at him. Virginia Woolf's famous criticism of him is, it is true, rather more than a sneer. But her complaint that he cannot imagine what goes on inside his characters' minds is so misguided when applied to his best work that it leaves one puzzled to know just what of Bennett she had read.

She could of course have read a fair amount without coming across the best. For Bennett did write some bad novels. He also wrote novels where the good and the bad mingle; and even the best are not free from all of his faults. It is easy enough to point out what the faults are. Bennett has a bad habit of stringing together clusters of vaguely impressive words – sublime, mystical, tragic, are particular favourites – which seldom amount to much more than rhetorical gestures. His appeals to 'life' are frequently trivial. He can be tiresomely condescending and heavily facetious in his attitude to women. He will occasionally slip in and out of his characters' minds in order to give us information which he ought to supply in some other manner (I think of the moment when we are told of Sam Raingo's attitude to his friend's mother: 'Sam had completely forgotten her; had *probably* assumed that she was long dead' – my italics). And at his worst he uses up page after page in order to tell us about his characters without once giving them a chance to speak or act for themselves. Pointing out what is bad in Bennett is a simple task.

It is a good deal more difficult to show what is good. And this is not because Bennett's virtues are few and far between but because he is a genuine realist. Although there is a change of manner in some of his later novels – it probably begins with *The Pretty Lady* – Bennett is not a symbolist. Nor is he a novelist who works with a number of major or dominant themes. Nor is he a formalist. In spite of his early insistence on formal perfection, he is not really interested in the pattern and structure of his novels for their own intricate sakes. Trying to show what is good about a novel is of course always more difficult than trying to show what is good about a poem, because a novel is longer. At a practical level, therefore, one has either to make use of extended quotation or fall back on mere assertion. The latter way is obviously unsatisfactory but the former creates its own problems. Quotation means selection and selection means omission. And what is omitted may have its own importance, either for good or evil. By careful selection one can make a novel seem much better or worse than it is. But that is not what most bothers me in writing about Bennett. No, the real problem is that it is almost impossible to show how good he is, because quotation of itself won't establish his worth.

This is not, I hope, special pleading. The fact is that, faced with the question of what a Bennett novel is about, one says rather helplessly, 'Well, it's about *life*, I suppose.' Such an answer may seem uselessly vague, but I take comfort from Henry James's remark about Turgenev, which I shall quote more than once in the course of this book: ' "It is life itself", we murmur as we read, "and not this or that or the other story-teller's more or less 'clever arrangement' of life." ' Still, we can be rather more accurate. Bennett's novels aren't so much about life itself as about the lives of middle class people. In the early novels such people are provincials, in the later ones they are suburbanites or city-dwellers. The social range, however, is pretty well constant. And this is where the trouble starts. For Bennett's studies of ordinary people are built up slowly, almost unobtrusively. The impact of his novels is gradual and cumulative. His best work is always much more impressive as a whole than as a sum of its parts and what in context is a great and moving moment – as for instance Constance Baines's letter to her sister, or Edwin Clayhanger's discovery of the map which he had drawn as a child and which his father has kept for so many years – will not seem particularly moving or impressive when quoted out of context. We need to know all about Constance and all about Edwin's relationship with his father before we can see why at such moments Bennett's touch is that of a master, and this we can only do by reading the novels in their entirety and becoming aware of their slow, weighty accumulation of incident and information and the sense of time passing which they convey by reason of their dense chronicling of events. And although it is obviously true of all good novels to say that they must be read whole, it is true of Bennett in a particular sense. Only when we have turned the final page, gathered in the last detail, can we realize how deeply we have come to know and understand the lives and community he has been writing about, and how impressive a fictional achievement that is. Which is, perhaps, no more than a roundabout way of saying that

Bennett deserves to be read for himself. If this book succeeds in sending people to his fiction it will have served its purpose.

A note on texts

There is no such thing as a standard edition of Bennett's works. After each quotation I have therefore shown in brackets the chapter and, where relevant, book and section from which it comes. I have used throughout Newman Flower's three-volume selection from the *Journals of Arnold Bennett* (Cassell), and James Hepburn's fine three-volume edition of the *Letters* (OUP). All references to the *Journals* and *Letters* are given in brackets after the quotations.

I have not made much mention of other critics in the course of the book because I think it becomes tiresome if one is constantly turning aside to argue with or defer to critics X, Y and Z. But obviously I have learnt from others, even where disagreeing with them, and this is perhaps the best place to acknowledge the valuable criticism of Georges Lafourcade, Walter Allen, Arnold Kettle and, above all, John Wain.

Chapter 1

Starting out in the Nineties

I

We think of Bennett as a novelist of the Edwardian era. Rightly so. For he came to fame during the first decade of the twentieth century, and much of his finest work belongs to that period. Yet his writing career began in the 1890s; and the 1890s is where we must start if we are to see him plain. It is not simply that he published a story in the *Yellow Book*, nor that he was a professed admirer of the Goncourts and de Maupassant. These things matter, but only because they are part of a process of literary self-education which is recorded in his *Journals* and which bears early fruit in *A Man from the North*, his first published novel.

A Man from the North was written between 1895 and 1896 and published in 1898. 'The latest disciple of the Goncourts', Bennett dubbed himself in 1896, and two years later he wrote:

> As regards fiction, it seems to me that only within the last few years have we absorbed from France that passion for the artistic shapely presentation of truth, and that feeling for words as words, which animated Flaubert, the Goncourts, and Maupassant. . . . None of the (so-called) great masters of English nineteenth-century fiction had (if I am right) a deep artistic interest in form and treatment; they were absorbed in 'subject' – just as the 'anecdote' painters of the Royal Academy are absorbed in subject, and in my view they are open to the

same reproach as these. . . . The novelists cared little for form, the *science* of construction – *Composition*. They had not artistic taste; they lacked this just as Millais lacked it. Millais may have been a great painter; these novelists may have been great novelists, but neither (to use Maupassant's distinction) was a great artist in the sense in which I understand the word. An artist must be interested primarily in presentment, not in the thing presented. He must have a passion for technique, a deep love for form. . . . And so on. (*Journals*, vol. I.)

Bennett the aesthete, Bennett the assiduous student of modern French novelists and short-story writers, Bennett the attentive disciple of James and Moore in their criticisms of the inadequacies of that loose baggy monster, the nineteenth-century English novel. The passage reveals all that, and more besides. For surely it is the musing of a young, self-conscious author from the provinces, determined to show that he has absorbed the latest lessons on the art of fiction, that he is no raw ignoramus. Nor is he. I see no reason to scoff at Bennett's self-education. It is eloquent testimony, not just to his capacity for sheer hard work, nor simply to his yearning for the life of letters, but to his shrewd and innate love of literature. Reading Bennett's early *Journals* is a moving and impressive experience. If I seem to make undue use of them in this chapter it is because they help us to know what Bennett was thinking, reading, writing. In short, they tell us much about his inner life. The later *Journals* tell us much less about that life, and much more about Bennett the public man, Bennett the socialite (of sorts) and friend of men of affairs. For that reason I shall not make much use of them. They are not without interest and to any biographer they are of course indispensable. But they are not really important for the critic.

What emerges very clearly from the early *Journals* is the way in which Bennett tries out various roles for himself. The role of aesthete is very much in evidence. But so are others, and none of them taken in isolation contains the whole truth about Bennett. Of course, he was passionately interested in technical problems of the novel (what serious novelist isn't?); of course, he learned something from the French novelists. But it will not do to assume, as Walter Allen and others have done, that Bennett's attitude to life was 'essentially aesthetic'. It is true that Bennett often tried to put

a certain distance between himself and life, and reading his war
Journals one is struck by his tight-lipped refusal to mention any of
the horrors which he certainly witnessed on the Western Front.
Yet, as his friend Frank Swinnerton points out, Bennett was in
fact terribly upset by what he saw. The air of aloof indifference
that he sometimes adopts is a conscious pose, a false front behind
which there exists a sensitive, vulnerable man. And the sensitivity
comes out in his best writing. 'They inevitably went into "realism"', James remarks of the Goncourts:

> but realism for them has been altogether a matter of taste – a studio
> question, as it were. They also find the disagreeable particularly
> characteristic, and there is something odd in seeing these elegant
> erudites bring their highly complex and artificial method – the fruit of
> culture, and leisure, and luxury – to bear upon the crudities and
> maladies of life, and pick out morsels of available misery upon their
> gold pen-points. (*Literary Reviews and Essays*, ed. A. Mordell)

That brilliant and damning piece of criticism might also be applied
to de Maupassant. But it cannot be applied to Bennett. For in
spite of all the talk of 'a passion for technique, a deep love for form.
. . . And so on' (I find that last phrase both funny and reassuring –
the dots are Bennett's own, and indicate that he simply can't
continue in that vein), there is another and very different note
struck in the early *Journals*. It is sounded in an entry for 15 October 1896: 'Essential characteristic of the really great novelist:
a Christ-like, all-embracing compassion.' He has just been reading
Virgin Soil, and he remarks:

> There is no doubt in my mind that [Turgenev] is the greatest master
> of the modern novel. I can divine, even through a mediocre transla-
> tion, that his style was simple, natural, graceful, and effective.
> Probably he took no pleasure in the mere arrangement and nice choice
> of words – I mean no 'technical' pleasure in the labour itself of com-
> position – such as Flaubert, the Goncourts, Stevenson, and Pater
> found.

We need to set that entry against the much better-known one about
form and composition if we are to avoid forming a misleading
image of the young Bennett.

I may seem to be arguing against myself here. After all, if

Bennett's art isn't really to be explained in terms of an elaborate formal aestheticism, why stress that his career began in the 1890s? Two points need to be borne in mind. One, that Bennett's pessimistic reading of life – that 'illogical, indefensible and causeless melancholia' was how he described it in *The Truth About an Author* – was widely shared among the writers whom he encountered during his apprenticeship to the art of fiction. It is not merely the search for formal perfection which links so many of the novelists whom the young Bennett admired. The Goncourts and de Maupassant, George Moore and Gissing share a kinship of spirit which, however loosely, can be identified with pessimism. This is in no way to suggest that they are somehow 'like' each other; nor do I see any point in entering into a discussion of how social Darwinism, Schopenhauerian metaphysics and other related strands in the intellectual life of the 1890s variously affected writers of the decade. I wish merely to record the fact that Bennett's own tendency towards a pessimistic account of the human situation cannot be divorced from his literary beginnings. Indeed, in the very beginning it feels to be merely a literary manner. 'A Letter Home', Bennett's *Yellow Book* story, reads rather like Maupassant done into English, but with the sex left out. It is a grim little tale of a young sailor, destitute and on the point of death, who writes a last letter to his mother, and gives it to his companion to post. But the companion gets drunk, and rips the letter in half in order to make a spill to light his pipe. 'A Letter Home' is a contrived tale, and hardly a memorable one.

And yet. 'He smelt the acetic acid once more, and his thoughts reverted to his mother. Poor mother! The grandeur of her life's struggle filled him with a sense of awe. Strange that until that moment he had never seen the heroic side of her humdrum, commonplace existence!' It is marred by literariness in the bad sense, by a striving after effect which Bennett never manages to shrug off. Again and again in his later fiction one encounters those big, unearned words: 'grandeur', 'awe,' 'heroic'. Here they seem particularly obtrusive because we have no means of testing their rightness. We never see the mother. Yet the fact is that without such words to act as a justification for his chosen subjects one couldn't trust Bennett to write memorably about those humdrum, commonplace existences – which is, when all is said and done, his great and unique achievement.

This brings me to the second reason for discussing Bennett in the context of the 1890s. For if in the final decade of the nineteenth century his pessimism found soil in which to grow – and thin, acidulated soil it would often prove – so did his passion for realism. And that passion was rooted in altogether richer soil. Which is perhaps the moment to say something about *A Man from the North*.

Richard Larch is a young man who comes to London from the Potteries, determined to succeed as a writer and to discover and enjoy sexual experiences. But by the end of the novel he has failed in his attempt to become a writer, and his sexual experiences are limited to one visit to a brothel – 'he had no resistance' – a prolonged flirtation with Adeline, a girl with whom he contemplates marriage, and Miss Roberts, whom he does eventually marry though he doesn't love her. *A Man from the North* is a study of drab, unremarkable lives, and in many ways it succeeds. Bennett is able to use Richard's 'innocent' eye to record with great precision certain London scenes; there is a finely described outing to Littlehampton; and one repeatedly finds the kind of touch that is to become a Bennett hallmark: 'On one linen cuff was a stain; [the nurse] noticed this while talking to Richard, and adroitly reversed the wristband under his very gaze' (chapter 16.) Such a detail tells one a good deal about the nurse's habit of social deference, her unselfconscious care for cleanliness, and her professional deftness.

Richard becomes friendly with one literary man, Aked, who works in the solicitor's office which Richard joins. Aked had once written for the *Cornhill*, he reads Gissing, and he is now unable to write: 'I was violently dyspeptic for twenty years – simply couldn't write. Then I cured myself. But it was too late to begin again.' Aked is acutely observed, a type of the literary man who cannot reconcile himself to the minimal nature of his talent. He insists on his literary temperament: 'Do you ever catch yourself watching instinctively for the characteristic phrase?' he asks Richard, and he proposes a joint undertaking, to be called *The Psychology of the Suburbs*:

the suburbs, even Walham Green and Fulham, are full of interest, for those who can see it. Walk along this very street on such a Sunday afternoon as to-day. The roofs form two horrible, converging straight lines I know, but beneath them is character, individuality, enough to make the greatest book ever written. Note the varying indications supplied by bad furniture seen through curtained windows . . . listen to the melodies issuing lamely from ill-tuned pianos; examine the enervated figures of women reclining amidst flower-pots on narrow balconies. Even in the thin smoke ascending unwillingly from invisible chimney-pots, the flutter of a blind, the bang of a door, the winking of a fox-terrier perched on a window-sill, the colour of paint, the lettering of a name, – in all these things there is character and matter of interest, – truth waiting to be expounded. How many houses are there in Cartaret Street? Say eighty. Eighty theatres of love, hate, greed, tyranny, endeavour; eighty separate dramas always unfolding, intertwining, ending, beginning, – and every drama, a tragedy. No comedies, and especially no farces! Why, child, there is more character within a hundred yards of this chair than a hundred Balzacs could analyse in a hundred years. (chapter 12)

It is typical of Bennett at this stage of his career that Aked, with what is surely his author's approval, claims that every drama is a 'tragedy'. 'I was struck by the magnificence of a career of a *prima donna* as a theme for fiction. The old age of the *prima donna* and her death might make a superbly cruel contrast to the rest of the story – astringent, chilling, unbearably hopeless and bitter with reminiscence.' That *Journal* entry of June 1898 may stand for many others. For the young and not-so-young Bennett, the drama of life tips always towards the unbearably hopeless – which is for him the tragic (an equation over which Lawrence was later to explode).

Aked is, I think, the spokesman for Bennett's own fascination with the psychology of the suburbs, his passionate interest in the study of unremarkable lives. And though Aked's proposal does not perhaps amount to the prescriptiveness of Gissing's Harold Biffin, it comes very close – at least as stated in *A Man from the North* – to the ideals of *Mr Bailey Grocer*.

'Mr Bailey is a grocer in a little street by here. I have dealt with him for a long time, and as he's a talkative fellow I've come to know a good

deal about him and his history. He's fond of talking about the struggle
he had in his first years of business. He had no money of his own, but
he married a woman who had saved forty-five pounds out of a cat's-
meat business. You should see that woman! A big, coarse, squinting
creature; at the time of the marriage she was a widow and forty-two
years old. Now I'm going to tell the true story of Mr Bailey's marriage
and of his progress as a grocer. It'll be a great book – a great book! . . .
There'll be nothing bestial in it, you know. The decently ignoble – as
I've so often said.' (*New Grub Street*, chapter 16)

We are not meant to identify Biffin's vision of the great novel with
Gissing's. But it offers the kind of aesthetic which was common
enough in the 1890s for it to be more or less repeated by Aked.
And Aked speaks for Bennett. After all, *A Man from the North*
is itself about the psychology of the suburbs.

Or is it? For here a real difficulty presents itself. Not as regards
Richard, who strikes me as being very well done, a thoroughly
convincing study in aspiration and its gradual fading into occasional
whimperings of regret at the compromises for which he finally
settles. Bennett is good on his hero's sexual diffidence and con-
sequent frustrations, on his determination to educate himself 'he
prepared a scheme for educating himself in the classical tongues
and in French' – his discovery of painting and music (especially
the opera), his aesthetic reasons for churchgoing, that 'proceeded from a craving, purely sensuous, which sought gratification
in ceremonial pomps, twilight atmospheres heavy with incense and
electric with devotion, and dim perspectives of arching stone'
(chapter 11). This aspect of Richard is no doubt characteristic of
thousands of aspiring young men from the provinces. It was certainly characteristic of Arnold Bennett; and clearly Richard is
drawn from experiences very close to hand indeed. But in his
failure to become a writer, Richard is quite different from his
author. Although there is something of the atmosphere of *New
Grub Street* in *A Man from the North*'s study of forlorn flickering
talents, Richard is very much Bennett's own creation. There is a
particularly good section dealing with his last, despairing effort to
succeed. He decides to write a tale of adventure in modern London,
like Stevenson's *New Arabian Nights* (or, it may be, like *The Grand
Babylon Hotel*), and resolves to produce a steady 500 words a day.

The resolution wavers, comes to a halt; and Richard reads over what exists of the draft:

> He whistled as he took up the manuscript, as a boy whistles when going into a dark cellar. The first three pages were read punctiliously, every word of them, but soon he grew hasty, rushing to the next paragraph ere the previous one was grasped; then he began shamelessly to skip; and then he stopped, and his heart seemed to stop also. The lack of homogeneity, of dramatic quality, of human interest; the loose syntax; and the unrelieved mediocrity of it all, horrified him. The thing was dry bones, a fiasco. The certainty that he had once more failed swept over him like a cold, green wave of the sea, and he had a physical feeling of sickness in the stomach. . . . (chapter 29)

Bennett scarcely falters in his tracing of Richard's downward curve from would-be writer to ex-non-writer. And he is equally good at showing the sexual frustration that finally drives him into marriage and an acceptance of respectability: 'In future he would be simply the suburban husband – dutiful towards his employers, upon whose grace he would be doubly dependent; keeping his house in repair; pottering in the garden; taking his wife out for a walk, or occasionally to the theatre; and saving as much as he could' (chapter 32). The psychology of the suburbs implicit in Bennett's study of Richard Larch may not reveal a novelist of genius but its chill authenticity compares very favourably with novels of the time which cover a similar subject (*Love and Mr Lewisham*, for example).

Unfortunately, the same can hardly be said for the other characters in the novel. Indeed, we are allowed to know so little about them that one has sadly to conclude that *A Man from the North* doesn't really get much more than ankle-deep in pursuit of its own subject. When Aked lies on his deathbed, Richard discovers that life is altogether 'sublimer, more terrible, than he had thought'. But the words are absurdly too large for what we have been shown. We certainly can't think that life is sublime and terrible because of Aked's death, for the very good reason that, except for his literary ambitions, we know hardly anything about the man. Nor does Richard. True, the words actually represent an example of Bennett's indirect intervention, a device he repeatedly uses to tell us how he himself regards matters. But it doesn't help. For if

we are to accept the statement as at all plausible or even possible we need to know why the death of Aked should occasion it. And since we know so little about him we can only decide that Richard and his author are being rhetorically grandiose, injecting a thoroughly discordant note of high pathos into a drab end to a drab life.

And what is inadequate in the treatment of Aked is even more so in the treatment of his daughter, Adeline:

> Her mere existence from one moment to the next seemed in some mysterious way to suggest a possible solution to the riddle of life. She illustrated nature. She was for him intimately a part of nature, the great Nature which hides itself from cities. To look at her afforded him a delight curiously similar to that which the townsman derives from a rural landscape. Her face had little conventional beauty; her conversation contained no hint either of intellectual powers or of a capacity for deep feeling. But in her case, according to his view, these things were unnecessary, would in fact have been superfluous. She *was* and that sufficed. (chapter 21)

I would not bother with so bad a passage if I were merely trying to do Bennett down. *A Man from the North* is a first novel. It is not surprising that it should contain flaws. What is surprising is that passages such as the one just quoted can be found at any stage of Bennett's career. They are part of what, for want of a better phrase, I have to call clubman's philosophizing about the female of the species, the feminine temperament, and so on. They are distressingly condescending, a huddle of vapid generalizations; and they reveal a kind of ignorance that is a real danger to Bennett's literary programme of studying the psychology of the suburbs. If that is what he thinks of women, how can he hope to succeed?

It is at this point that we need to introduce Virginia Woolf's famous criticism of Bennett. Bennett, she protests, 'is trying to make us imagine for him; he is trying to hypnotise us into the belief that, because he has made a house, there must be a person living there'. He has laid enormous stress upon the fabric of things. And he has given us a house 'in the hope that we may be able to deduce the human beings who live there'. But, Virginia Woolf goes on, if you think that 'novels are in the first place about people, and only second about the houses they live in', then it follows that Bennett has gone about creating fiction in quite the wrong way. ('Mr Bennett and Mr Brown', *The Captain's Death-Bed* (1950), esp. pp. 101–6). He doesn't know enough, and as a result he gives us mere exteriors or, when he comes to deal with fictional women, he has to fall back on the sort of clubman's vulgarity of which the description of Adeline provides a fair example. It is true that Virginia Woolf doesn't make this latter point, but it follows logically from her argument. And as far as *A Man from the North* is concerned her argument is faultless. For we are left woefully short of information about Adeline. We never really know what kind of a person she is, and although I think Virginia Woolf wrong to imply that somehow you can separate people and houses – by which I take it she means the social contexts in which people live, and by which their lives must be at least partly shaped – there is no doubt that Richard's relationship with Aked's daughter is by far the worst feature of the novel: 'And yet, was he really, truly in love? Was she in love? Had there been a growth of feeling since that night at Cartaret Street after the holiday at Littlehampton? He uncomfortably suspected that their hearts had come nearer to each other that night than at any time since' (chapter 22). The objection to this passage must be that Bennett gives us no opportunity to weigh the rights and wrongs of Richard's questionings. At no time are we allowed to see Richard and Adeline so aware of each other's essential strangeness that Richard's question, 'Was she in love?', can have meaning. Instead, we have to make do with Richard's narration of their affair. Why? The answer is contained in Virginia Woolf's objection to Bennett's method: he is trying to make us do his imagining for him.

And because Bennett cannot or will not do the imagining, the end of Richard's affair with Adeline can be managed only by suddenly altering her, so as to make her unsympathetic and Richard's decision to leave her understandable. At one minute she is 'the very spirit of grace; she was full of aplomb and delicate tact' (chapter 22). At the next she is behaving badly to Miss Roberts: 'Adeline gazed boldly around her. They were antagonistic, these two women, and Richard, do what he would, could not repress a certain sympathy with Miss Roberts. If she had encouraged Mr Aked's glance, what of that? It was no mortal sin, and he could not appreciate the reason for Adeline's strenuous contempt for her' (chapter 23). Nor can I. From the spirit of grace and delicate tact to the bold gaze and strenuous contempt – and all in a matter of five pages. It seems very unsatisfactory. But necessary. 'He saw a little gulf widening between himself and Adeline.' In other words, the demands of the plot are too great for Bennett's control of characterization.

I have gone into the unsatisfactory presentation of Adeline at a little length partly because I wanted to show that Bennett's concern with form – by which he usually means symmetry of plot – can prove a handicap, and partly because I think it important that we note the accuracy of Virginia Woolf's criticism of Bennett. But I ought to add that it was not *A Man from the North* which she had in mind when she launched her attack, but *Hilda Lessways*. I have said that throughout his career Bennett falls back on clubman's philosophizing about women. Hilda Lessways is almost as good an example of this as Adeline Aked. But it is necessary to add that Bennett can also be quite magnificent in his treatment of women – it is a remarkable fact that many of his finest novels have women at their centre – and that if *A Man from the North* is characteristically flawed in its handling of Adeline, that flaw has to be set against something equally characteristic of Bennett, his sure and subtle understanding of many of his heroines. There are in fact two Bennetts. The Bennett of trite accounts of a man's feeling for a woman and of rotten set-piece descriptions. For example: 'Her eyes flashed mightily as she spoke, and the contempt in them added mightily to her beauty.' Admittedly that comes from *The Grand Babylon Hotel*, which scarcely pretends to be anything other than a potboiler; yet it can be matched by equally bad moments in the more serious work. But there is also the Bennett of *The Old Wives' Tale*, of *Clayhanger*, of *Imperial Palace*. And this Bennett is a very different matter.

It is of course true that towards the end of the nineteenth century male novelists began increasingly to place women at the centre of their novels. One thinks particularly of Meredith, James and Hardy in this respect. Why women should have become the focus of so many major novels of the period is a fascinating and difficult question. Partly it has to do with the steadily growing interest in the 'new woman', an interest which is implicit in most of Meredith's fiction and which has a crucial bearing on *The Bostonians* and *Jude the Obscure*. Partly it is an imaginative extension of the Brontës' and George Eliot's radical demythologizing of the conventional heroines of the nineteenth-century novel. And it no doubt partly testifies to the manner in which sensitive minds turned away from what increasingly seemed to be the objective, scientific, 'outer' world of matter and fact towards the subjective, intuitive world that would be seen as the essence of femaleness. All these elements have their part to play in Bennett's fictional concern with women. But I do not think that they can fully explain it. For Bennett is absorbedly interested in his women because they are at the centre of social groups; as lovers, wives, mothers, they are seen in a context of domesticity, of the dailiness of life – matters which are of comparatively little interest to Meredith or James, though they had certainly interested George Eliot. It is this new element which gives Bennett's fiction its unique strength (and by contrast with which Virginia Woolf's own fiction seems undernourished). Bennett is *the* novelist of the ordinary. It may sound dubious praise. But it isn't, as *Anna of the Five Towns* is the first of his novels to make plain.

II

He took his time over the new novel. We first hear mention of it as early as 1896: 'Tonight I am to begin my new novel, *Sir Marigold*, a tale of paternal authority', he records in the *Journal* on 29 September. On 18 April 1899 he notes: 'I finished the draft of *Anna Tellwright* just before Easter – having written it at the rate of eight or ten thousand words a week.' *Anna of the Five Towns* is not a long novel, so if we are to believe Bennett it is clear that the draft to which he refers in the *Journal* could have been entirely written in the first months of 1899. In that case, what had happened between September 1896 and December 1898? The clue is contained, I think, in the altered titles. The tale of paternal authority grows into a novel about a young girl and that in its turn widens into a study of the girl in her physical environment. Anna Tellwright is of the Five Towns; and as the title which Bennett eventually settled on implies, Anna cannot be understood unless she is seen in the context of the Potteries, and their social, spiritual and working life. Not people before houses, as Virginia Woolf had wanted. Instead, people *and* houses. With *Anna of the Five Towns* Bennett becomes the finest novelist of the English industrial provinces.

It is partly a matter of luck. The young novelist, keenly aware of the French realist writers and their studies of French provincial life, has ready to hand his own familiar knowledge of the Potteries; what is exotic to most of his readers is commonplace to him. But it is more than just luck. A literary programme cannot make a major novelist. Bennett's great gift is his ability to take us inside ordinary, unremarkable houses and show us the ordinary, unremarkable people who live in them – and show us these things with a passion and relish that lift his fiction far above the ignobly decent. Those overfurnished drawingrooms, dark, narrow and spotlessly clean kitchens, those cold, inhospitable bedrooms: they are set down with an almost relentless detail, yet not coldly, distantly. Bennett is not the scientific naturalist that Zola saw himself as being. But then neither is Zola.

> In a word, I had only one desire: given a highly-sexed man and an unsatisfied woman, to uncover the animal side of them and see that alone, then throw them together in a violent drama and note down with scrupulous care the sensation and actions of these creatures. I simply applied to two living bodies the analytical method that surgeons apply to corpses. . . . The human side of the models ceased to exist, just as it ceases to exist for the eye of the artist who has a naked woman sprawled in front of him but who is solely concerned with getting onto his canvas a true representation of her shape and character. (preface to *Thérèse Raquin*)

That famous defence of a novel which caused such uproar on its initial appearance is, I think, pure bluff. *Thérèse Raquin* itself contradicts Zola, and not just because within its pages artists make love to their models. The fact is that Zola is quite clearly absorbed in his subject and in his characters to a degree that goes far beyond anything that can be thought of as 'the analytic method that surgeons apply to corpses'.

The same holds true for Bennett. He is not so great a novelist as

Zola, but despite all his disclaimers in letters and the *Journals*, it is obvious that in his best work he cares passionately about the people he writes about and the lives they lead. Realism for him is not simply a matter of taste. And for all his desire to escape from his Five Towns' upbringing by moving first to London and then, in 1903, to France, it is the Five Towns which provides the setting for most of his finest work. In *A Man from the North* Richard Larch has just escaped, and that word does, I think, express how he himself regards his move south. Accordingly, the brief descriptions of the towns and their inhabitants concentrate on the tedious solemnity of their ways, the suffocating, boring, repetitious dullness of it all:

> The streets of Bursley were nearly empty as he walked through the town from the railway station, for the industrial population was already at work in the manufactures, and the shops not yet open. Yet Richard avoided the main thoroughfares, choosing a circuitous route . . . lest he might by chance encounter an acquaintance. He foresaw the inevitable banal dialogue:—
> 'Well, how do you like London?'
> 'Oh, it's fine!'
> 'Getting on all right?'
> 'Yes, thanks.'
> And then the effort of the two secretly bored persons to continue a perfunctory conversation unaided by a single mutual interest.
> A carriage was driving away from the Red House just as Richard got within sight of it; he nodded to the venerable coachman, who gravely touched his hat. The owner of the carriage was Mr Clayton Vernon. . . . He trembled at the prospect of a whole day to be spent in the company of these excellent people. . . . The Clayton Vernons were the chief buttress of respectability in the town; rich, strictly religious, philanthropic, and above all dignified. Everyone looked up to them instinctively, and had they possessed but one vice between them, they would have been loved. (chapter 8)

A Man from the North is, of course, very much a young man's novel, and Richard's distaste for his home town has elements of that self-conscious and aloof disdain common enough in someone who has just achieved independence of family and home. Nothing like something happens anywhere, but it happens particularly where you were born.

It isn't merely the dullness of Bursley that oppresses Richard, it is something worse. He changes trains at Knype: 'Two women with several children also alighted, and he noticed how white and fatigued were their faces; the children yawned pitifully. An icy, searching wind blew through the station; the exhilaration of the dawn was gone, and a spirit of utter woe and disaster brooded over everything' (chapter 8). The spirit of utter woe and misery surely owes much more to the pose of the self-conscious aesthete than it does to Bursley itself.

A Man from the North was finished in May 1896. Some sixteen months later Bennett made a journey back to the Five Towns, as Richard had done. And in the *Journal* he recorded some impressions of his home town.

> Down below is Burslem, nestled in the hollow between several hills, and showing a vague picturesque mass of bricks through its heavy pall of smoke. If it were an old Flemish town, beautiful in detail and antiquely interesting, one would say its situation was ideal. It is *not* beautiful in detail, but the smoke transforms its ugliness into a beauty transcending the work of architects and of time. Though a very old town, it bears no sign of great age – the eye is never reminded of its romance and history – but instead it thrills and reverberates with the romance of machinery and manufacture, the romance of our fight against nature, of the gradual taming of the earth's secret forces. And surrounding the town on every side are the long straight smoke and steam wreaths, the dull red flames, and all the visible evidences of the immense secular struggle for existence, the continual striving towards a higher standard of comfort.
>
> This romance, this feeling which permeates the district, is quite as wonderfully inspiring as any historic memory could be.

It is, I do not deny, self-conscious. And there is something more than a little comic – and inept – about that immense secular struggle for existence being linked to the 'continual striving towards a higher standard of comfort'. Yet for all the posturing, this entry does make plain the fact that Bennett has travelled a long way since Richard Larch, with his author's obvious approval, noted the spirit of 'utter woe and disaster' that brooded over the Five Towns. He is travelling in the direction of the *Journal* entry for January 1899: 'What the artist has to grasp is that there is no such thing as ugliness in the world. . . . All ugliness has an aspect of beauty. The business of the artist is to find that aspect.' It may sound like the credo of a pure aesthete – 'The artist is the creator of beautiful things' (thus Oscar Wilde in his preface to *The Picture of Dorian Gray*). But though Bennett's way of putting the matter is clearly affected by the kind of epigrammatic language Wilde had made fashionable, he means something very different. For in his preface Wilde had also claimed that 'The nineteenth-century dislike of Realism is the rage of Caliban seeing his own face in a glass', whereas for Bennett realism does not mean a contented mirroring of superficial ugliness. He is not a naturalist. And though in even his best novels he is far too ready to fall back on such words as beauty, romance, mystery, grandeur, sublimity, he does so because he wants to convince us of the worth of the lives he is studying; and the fact is that at his best he does convince us. We do not need the large words to be persuaded of the value of what he shows.

Admittedly, there is a price to pay for this. In the first chapter of *Anna of the Five Towns* Bennett more or less repeats the description of Burslem which he had entered into his *Journal*, and he adds to it.

Because they seldom think, the townsmen take shame when indicted for having disfigured half a county in order to live. They have not understood that this disfigurement is merely an episode in the unending warfare of man and nature, and calls for no contrition. Here, indeed, is nature repaid for some of her notorious cruelties. She imperiously bids man sustain and reproduce himself, and this is one of the places where in the very act of obedience he wounds and maltreats her. Out beyond the municipal confines, where the subsidiary industries of coal and iron prosper amid a wreck of verdure, the struggle is grim, appalling, heroic – so ruthless is his havoc of her, so indomitable her ceaseless recuperation. On the one side is a wrestling from nature's own bowels of the means to waste her; on the other, an undismayed, enduring fortitude.

At best this is specious, at worst, plain silly. For Bennett has put the struggle in wrong – and irrelevant – terms. And whatever echoes of social Darwinism underlie the notion of 'ceaseless warfare of man and nature', they are quite incapable of providing the focus for what ought to be pinpointed as the real struggle: which is not the struggle between man and nature, but the struggle between man and man. Bennett's way of putting the matter reveals all too plainly that he has no real political awareness, no feeling for the ultimate complexities and ugliness of the system in and by means of which his characters struggle to survive and sometimes triumph. It is a failing and one that has significant and damaging consequences for much of his fiction.

Yet the failing is partly offset by the fact that Bennett's readily sympathetic response to the strugglers themselves gives his fiction its especial distinction. Whatever the truth about Bennett as private man may be, there is no question of his recoiling in horror or disgust from the ugly world which as an imaginative writer he chooses to confront. On the contrary, he records it so fully and with such warmth of understanding that if we call his characteristic response to the ugliness one of acceptance we have immediately to add that such acceptance is in no way the product of complacency or ignorance. As Charles Masterman remarks in his *Condition of England* (1909), it is precisely this 'tenacious struggle [for survival] which illuminates and glorifies the monotonous streets of suburban England'. Besides, the alternative to Bennett's response is the contemptuous rejection of such lives that is sometimes to be found in the fiction of George Moore and H. G. Wells; or it results in the muddled thinking perfectly illustrated by Lawrence's remark to Forster apropos of *Howards End*: 'you did make a nearly deadly mistake glorifying those business people. Business is no good.' Bennett would never be guilty of identifying the one with the other. His position is a modest one and the rejection by other contemporary novelists of the lives he writes about with such knowledgeable acceptance is often marred by crass immodesty of tone. Of course, there are politically sophisticated and generous reasons for seeing the limitations implicit in the lives of Bennett's provincials (he saw some of them himself); and there is good cause to be distressed with Bennett's post-war complacency about the suburban lives he studies in *Mr Prohack*. But his best work demonstrates that 'it is no despicable life' – in Masterman's phrase – which his characters struggle to build for themselves.

True, his characters are mostly middle class. Bennett hardly ever does more than touch on the ugliness of working class life or the different kind of ugliness of the aristocracy, and when he does so he usually strikes a false note. But the range he covers is still formidably wide. It is a mistake to think that Bennett is somehow 'confined' to studies of middle class life. The middle class occupies by far the largest stretch of English society; and at one time or another during his thirty-odd years as a writer of fiction Bennett covers just about all of it.

But Bennett is primarily the novelist of the Five Towns. It is there that he first finds beauty in ugliness. The discovery is, I should note, a matter for the realist in paint as well as words at the end of the nineteenth century. The artist to whom George Moore gives his approval in *A Modern Lover*, paints 'housemaids in print dresses, leaning out of windows, or bar girls serving drinks to beery looking clerks. In fact, the walls were covered, not with the softness of ancient, but with the crudities of modern life' (chapter 7). Moore had encountered such 'crudities' in his years in Paris and, as the furore over Degas' famous *L'Absinthe* (painted 1876–7) had revealed, to be on the side of the realists was to be on the side of the new. *A Modern Lover* is one of a trilogy of novels which Moore published in the 1880s, each of which carried the subtitle 'A Realistic Novel'. The third of these, *A Drama in Muslin*, doesn't concern us. But the second, *A Mummer's Wife*, does, both because it was a novel which Bennett much admired – *Journal* entries of the 1890s show that he considered Moore to be the only English novelist who could stand comparison with the major French realists (an opinion which Moore shared) – and because it is set, at least in part, in the Potteries.

A Mummer's Wife is about a young woman who throws over her respectable, loveless marriage and goes off with an actor. Gradually she loses her own respectability, becomes an alcoholic, and dies. The novel is very self-consciously concerned with the crudities of modern life. It is also rather bad. And this is not simply because Moore writes badly – though much of the prose is atrocious – but because he doesn't really know enough about the life he sets out to study. Or, if he does know he doesn't succeed in getting his knowledge onto the page.

In the first place, the mummer's wife herself is not seen with any real exactness or understanding. She is, we are told, 'a child of the people' (chapter 5), and as evidence of this Moore remarks that she has a taste for sentimental romances which never leaves her, though she may put it aside for a while. The novelist comments:

> The hearts of the people change but little – if at all. When rude work and misery does not grind and trample all feeling out of them, they remain ever children in their sentiments, understanding only such simple emotions as correspond to their daily food . . . in the woman of the people there is no intellectual advancement; she never learns to judge, to discriminate. . . . The rich man changes, the peasant remains the same. . . . (chapter 8)

There is paragraph after paragraph of such nonsense. But the real absurdity is that having to his own satisfaction placed Kate among 'the people', Moore later informs us that she is middle class: 'Anecdotes of clever swindles no longer wounded her feelings; she listened and laughed at them with the rest. The middle class woman, in a word, had disappeared, and the Bohemian taken her place' (chapter 15). It is true that much later Moore tries to make amends for this gaffe by remarking that 'Kate's Bohemianism rushed away as water flows out of sight, when a sluice is suddenly raised, and she became again the middle class working woman. . . .' (chapter 29). A middle class working woman! It makes everything clear.

Needless to say, Kate not only fails to talk like a woman of the people, or like a Bohemian, or like a middle class working woman, she doesn't even talk like an inhabitant of the Five Towns: '"Yes, yes, I know you did," replied Kate: "but will you promise not to be disagreeable to him? Since we cannot prevent his coming, will you promise that whilst he is here you will attend to him just as you did to the other gentleman?"' This is a daughter of the people? Admittedly, it is a convention of the nineteenth-century novel that even working class heroines speak middle class language. Mary Barton doesn't sound much like the daughter of John Barton. But at least Mrs Gaskell makes fine use of Lancashire dialect elsewhere in her novel. Moore, the breaker of conventions, seems quite unable to handle dialect. The characters of *A Mummer's Wife* speak a pallid, anonymous language which owes everything to fictional conventions and nothing to a programme of realism.

What, then, does Moore mean by realism? Well, he certainly means frankness in dealing with matters of sex. He makes it quite clear that Kate becomes Lennox's mistress and that she ends as a prostitute, selling her body for the price of a bottle of gin; he comments on the casual sexual liaisons of the theatre people; and he more than hints that two women of the theatre company have a lesbian relationship. (It was no doubt these features of the novel which caused Mudie's and Smith's to ban it from their circulating libraries.) Second, Moore writes about a way of life that is decidedly sordid, and he takes delight in describing its more squalid aspects: the hagglings and deceptions over money, the heavy drinking, the brawling and backbiting among the actors. What this usually means, however, is that he adopts a crude and jeering tone towards his characters, as in this particularly nasty description of a pathetic woman who hopes to become a great star of the musical stage: 'With lifted face Mrs Forest recited these verses in a quailing undertone, the socket of her false eye watering profusely. She was not more than five feet high; Dick remained over six feet, dragged down as he was by the hobbling little tub at his side' (chapter 26). 'Hobbling little tub' is not the language of a realist, but of a caricaturist, and an ungifted one at that.

Third, Moore goes in for set pieces of descriptive writing: of a theatre dressing room, for example (chapter 14), of a sewing shop (chapter 2), and of the inside of a pottery (chapter 4). This last inevitably invites comparison with the marvellous chapter in *Anna of the Five Towns*, where Henry Mynors takes Anna on a tour of his pottery works. It may be that it was this particular aspect of *A Mummer's Wife* that impressed Bennett: or it may be that in general terms Moore offered him the example he needed: of a novelist prepared to write about the crudities of modern life. At all events, Moore was important to Bennett, which is why I have spoken about *A Mummer's Wife* at some length. But more important is the fact that Bennett is immeasurably the finer novelist. Merely to look at their descriptions of a pot-bank is to see why.

There are, of course, similarities. Both Moore and Bennett describe a pot-bank in great detail, and as in *A Mummer's Wife*

Lennox, who is in love with Kate, uses his tour of the bank as the pretext for being close to her, so in *Anna of the Five Towns*, Mynors conducts Anna round, eager to be at her side and to impress her. But consider the differences. Moore never really establishes the intricate process of pottery-making, nor the particular ingenuity of the arrangement of different rooms which serves that purpose. His characters wander aimlessly from room to room. At last they visit the storerooms:

> Ridges of vases, mounds of basins and jugs, terraces of plates formed masses of sickly white, through which rays of light were caught and sent dancing with a blinding brilliancy. Along the wall on the left hand side presses were overcharged with dusty tea-services. They were there as numerous as leaves in a forest. On the right were square grey windows, under which the convex sides of salad-bowls, like gigantic snow-balls, sparkled in the sun; and from rafter to rafter, in garlands and clusters like grapes, hung countless mugs, gilded, and bearing a device suitable for children. Down the middle of the floor a terrace was built of dinner-plates, the edges burnished with light, the rest being in grey tint. (chapter 4)

Obviously Moore is striving for exactness here. But the passage is clumsy. To remark that the tea-services were as 'numerous as leaves in a forest' is merely inept; and so is the attempt to get us to 'see' the mugs, hanging in 'garlands and clusters like grapes'. But one can forgive those moments. It is more difficult to forgive the fact that Moore isn't the slightest bit interested in what one would have thought was the most interesting aspect of the matter: how the storerooms strike Kate and Lennox. It is not their reactions he records, but his. Or rather, they are elbowed aside so that he can offer us a set-piece description. True, there are other moments on their tour where we hear that Kate is curious about or surprised by some feature of the pot-bank, whereas Lennox is totally bored by it and sees it merely as providing the chance to make love to her. Yet when we come to the longest and, in intention at least, most exact account of the bank, the storerooms, we know absolutely nothing about Kate's response. It is there merely as set piece, and as set piece it fails both because the language isn't precise enough and because Moore hasn't bothered to let us know about the process of potting. It is perhaps worth noting that his chapter is a

good deal less graphic and engaged than Florence Bell's chapter on
'The Process of Ironmaking', in her fine study, *At the Works* (1907).
It can of course be said that Moore is writing a novel, not a factual
report. But in that case we need to know a good deal more about
Kate than he is prepared to tell us.

Now Bennett uses Mynors's and Anna's tour of the pot-bank to
describe every stage of the process of potting in careful and attentive detail. But when they come to the storeroom he abandons
detailed description. What he is now interested in is Anna's reactions. She has seen the inside of an industrial process which ab-
sorbs the lives of thousands of her townsmen. What does she think
of it?

> Piles of ware occupied the whole of the walls and of the immense floor-
> space, but there was no trace here of the soilure and untidiness in-
> cident to manufacture; all processes were at an end, clay had vanished
> into crock: and the calmness and the whiteness atoned for the dis-
> order, noise and squalor which had preceded. Here was a sample of the
> total and final achievement towards which thousands of small, dis-
> jointed efforts that Anna had witnessed, were directed. And it seemed
> a miraculous, almost impossible, result; so definite, precise and
> regular after a series of acts apparently variable, inexact and casual;
> so inhuman after all that intensely [human] labour;[1] so vast in com-
> parison with the minuteness of the separate endeavours. As Anna
> looked, for instance, at a pile of tea-sets, she found it difficult even to
> conceive that, a fortnight or so before, they had been nothing but
> lumps of dirty clay. No stage of the manufacture was incredible by
> itself, but the result was incredible. It was the result that appealed to
> the imagination, authenticating the adage that fools and children
> should never see anything till it is done.
>
> Anna pondered over the organising power, the forethought, the
> wide vision, and the sheer ingenuity and cleverness which were im-
> plied by the contents of this warehouse. 'What brains,' she thought, of
> Mynors; 'what quantities of all sorts of things he must know!' It was
> a humble and deeply-felt admiration.

I would not defend every word of that, but on the whole Bennett
strikes exactly the right note. Anna's reactions are doubly credible

[1] By an odd and unfortunate irony, 'intensely human labour' has repeatedly
been misprinted in editions of the novel as 'intensely inhuman labour'.

to us. For we also have seen the process of potting, have been made aware of the noise, squalor and disjointed efforts that have gone to the production of calmness and whiteness (the chapter, indeed, has a very nineteenth-century feeling of sheer excitement at the human resourcefulness and ingenuity that can dream up such complicated manufacturing processes). We also know that Anna is young, innocent, and therefore will inevitably be impressed by what she sees and ready to identify Mynors as the cause of all that impresses her. Mynors, the mysterious male, is now more mysterious, more extraordinary than ever. In short, we need this chapter if we are to understand why Anna will eventually agree to marry Mynors. We also need it if we are to understand how she identifies with the energy and skills of Five Towns life; and we need it because it helps give solidity, the feel of things, to the world in which Anna lives.

It is a tough world, in which people work hard, earn good wages, acquire skills of which they are justly proud, sometimes die early, occasionally fail and are humanly wrecked. Acceptance seems the keynote of this world, but not resignation.

A huge, jolly man in shirt and trousers, with an enormous apron, was in the act of drawing the kiln, assisted by two thin boys. He nodded a greeting to Mynors and exclaimed, 'Warm!' The kiln was nearly emptied. As Anna stopped at the door, the man addressed her.

'Step inside, miss, and try it.'

'No, thanks!' she laughed.

'Come now,' he insisted, as if despising this hesitation. 'An ounce of experience—' The two boys grinned and wiped their foreheads with their bare, skeleton-like arms. Anna, challenged by the man's look, walked quickly into the kiln. A blasting heat seemed to assault her on every side, driving her back; it was incredible that any human being could support such a temperature.

'There!' said the jovial man, apparently summing her up with his bright, quizzical eyes. 'You know summat as you didn't know afore, miss. Come along, lads,' he added with brisk heartiness to the boys, and the drawing of the kiln proceeded.

There is nothing like that in *A Mummer's Wife*, with the result that Moore doesn't communicate anything of real importance about the potters' lives which he pretends to study in realistic depth and detail. When he does describe a potter it is in a tone very similar to the one he used when describing Mrs Forest.

> An old man sat straddle-legged on a high narrow table. . . . He was covered with clay; his forehead and beard were plastered with it. . . . Every one marvelled at the old creature's dexterity until he was forgotten in the superior attractions of the next room.

And that is the closest we come to an understanding of pottery workers in *A Mummer's Wife*.

I have been harsh on Moore, so it is only proper to repeat that one has to honour his campaign for fictional treatment of the crudities of modern life. I do not think he achieves this treatment himself, and in many ways his trilogy of realistic novels is marred by extraordinary clumsiness over the handling of time sequence and plot (the worst examples occur in *A Modern Lover*, though the other two have decidedly shaky moments). Yet undoubtedly *A Mummer's Wife* helped Bennett in his resolve to become a serious novelist of the industrial provinces. And that is something for which we can be grateful.

In his extremely interesting and valuable study *On Realism*, J. P. Stern quotes the following sentences from the *Mercure de France* in 1826: 'The literary doctrine which gains more ground every day and which leads to the faithful imitation not of masterpieces of art but of those originals which nature offers us . . . could well be called realism. Such, to judge by several signs, will be the literature of the nineteenth century, the literature of the true.' And Stern adds that 'At this point, then, the term is appropriated for literature – mainly in France – and the protracted (and far from helpful) literary debate begins.' But as he immediately notes, there is a sense in which the word isn't appropriated at all. It isn't and can never truly be appropriated as a technical term. 'The moment we single out the realistic aspect of a work, we are bound to be carried beyond the restriction of literary technicalities' (*On Realism* (1973), see esp. pp. 38–9). Stern's remark has an obvious bearing on my own discussion. For when Moore provided the subtitle 'A Realistic Novel' to *A Mummer's Wife* he was, I think, making what amounts to a spurious claim for the kind of novel he had written. Moore was asserting that his novel belonged to a literary form as exact as pastoral or elegy. Very clearly, the set-piece descriptions, plus the study of squalid lives and the comparative sexual frankness represent Moore's desire to feed in certain elements which will give *A Mummer's Wife* some claim to generic precision. In other words they are, odd as it may seem, literary technicalities. And because they are that they are also anti-realistic. For you cannot make out a list of prescribed parts for realistic fiction; to do so is automatically to create an arbitrariness of content in basic opposition to the 'literature of the true'. And in fact Moore's most successful realistic novel is *Esther Waters*, just because it isn't so self-consciously a novel in the realistic mode (though there are obvious modish features about it which threaten its achievement). With the possible exception of *A Drama in Muslin* it is the least 'got-up' of Moore's novels. In other words, its subject matter is not exotic to the novelist; he hasn't intruded upon it as an outsider, pencil and notebook in hand, as is certainly the case with *A Mummer's Wife*. According to Lukacs, 'Laforgue described Zola's attitude to reality as similar to that of a newspaper reporter'; and in his essay, 'The Zola Centenary' (in *Studies in European Realism*) Lukacs goes on to show how this inevitably limits Zola's achievement, makes it at its worst anti-realistic in any sense that matters. Allowing for the obvious difference in stature between the two men – for when all is said and done Zola remains a true genius of the novel – Lukacs's argument can be fairly applied to Moore.

Bennett's musings on form and presentment in the early *Journals* are also anti-realistic, because they are just as arbitrary as Moore's 'recipe' for realism. Which is not to say that the writer of realistic fiction is any less of an artist than the writer of pastoral. He shapes, he selects, he arranges, he invents. But he does so in order to be as true as he possibly can be to his chosen subject matter, 'those originals which nature offers us'. In theory this may seem an intolerable paradox. In practice it is nothing of the kind. James's response to Turgenev is the inevitable response to a successful realistic fiction: '"It is life itself" we murmur as we read, "and not this or that or the other story-teller's more or less 'clever arrangement' of life."' The point being that the novelist's arrangement doesn't draw attention to his art but to his subject. Of course, what isn't noticeable as 'arrangement' to one generation can and probably will become so to the next (as E. H. Gombrich has so brilliantly shown, our assumptions about what is 'real' are very often no more than an acceptance of purely stylized conventions of 'reality'). That is why great writers may well begin their career with a work which parodies the work of their elders. Parody – as in Dickens's treatment of the Newgate novel in *Oliver Twist* – is a way of recalling us to realities which have ossified into convention. But to say that is only another way of saying that the truly realistic novel cannot be identified in terms of a required list of contents. And having said that, it is time to look more closely at Bennett's first masterpiece.

III

Chapter 3 of *Anna of the Five Towns* is largely taken up with an account of Anna's twenty-first birthday and her father's revelation of the fact that he has built up for her a fortune of some £50,000. Ephraim Tellwright is a miserly and thoroughly mean-spirited man. His daughter's discovery of her sudden wealth might seem to open up for her vistas of promise, of a chance to escape from the drab, pinched meanness of her home. But it doesn't. On the contrary, we are told that Anna 'felt no elation of any kind; she had not begun to realise the significance of what had occurred'. Improbable? No. For Anna is a person who experiences little elation, ever. Indeed, the novel is about how she more or less misses out on life. She has no way of realizing the large possibilities that love and money might seem to offer her. In the course of the novel we see her stirring into intellectual and emotional awakening; but the awakening isn't completed. And this is inevitable, because Anna has for so long been shut up that any offer of freedom – no matter how puny or illusory – will be enough to win her gratitude and acceptance. And what makes *Anna of the Five Towns* so distinguished and moving a novel is Bennett's ability to make credible the fact of Anna's prolonged confinement and the nature of her partial awakening.

Before her father's disclosure, Anna and her younger sister, Agnes, breakfast as usual – which means in semi-silence.

The room was not a cheerful one in the morning, since the window was small and the aspect westerly. Besides the table and three horse-hair chairs, the furniture consisted of an arm-chair, a bent-wood rocking chair, and a sewing-machine. A fatigued Brussels carpet covered the floor. Over the mantelpiece was an engraving of 'The Light of the World,' in a frame of polished brown wood. On the other walls were some family photographs in black frames. A two-light chandelier hung from the ceiling, weighed down on one side by a patent gas-saving mantle and a glass shade; over this the ceiling was deeply discoloured. On either side of the chimney-breast were cup-boards about three feet high; some cardboard boxes, a work-basket, and Agnes's school-books lay on the tops of these cupboards. On the window-sill was a pot of mignonette in a saucer. The window was wide open, and flies buzzed to and fro, constantly rebounding from the window panes with terrible thuds. In the blue-paved yard beyond the cat was licking himself in the sunlight with an air of being wholly absorbed in his task.

When it comes to describing interiors Bennett has few equals. Not that this description of the Tellwright parlour is among his best – the finest being his description of Mrs Maldon's sitting room (in *The Price of Love*) – but the fact is that if you are curious about the domestic arrangements of the provincial middle class in the latter half of the nineteenth century and the early years of our own, then Bennett is the man to go to. But this isn't why the description of the Tellwright parlour really matters. The important point is that once Bennett has given us the details we are in a position to infer the monotony, dullness and grim unimaginative-ness of the way of life which Tellwright forces on his daughters. The parlour is in no way sordid or crashingly vulgar, but it lacks any spark of grace.

Unless, that is, one counts the pot of mignonette 'in a saucer'. As one inevitably does. It is the single redeeming feature of the room. It is also, of course, utterly conventional. We can be sure that there is no chance that either Anna or Agnes will be able to introduce any colour or real vitality into that awful, sterile parlour. Whatever there is of vitality is outside it. Bennett is not really a symbolist, but it is impossible not to notice the sunlight beyond the window (and while we are on the subject it seems reasonable to note that the novel begins in early summer, Anna's time of awakening, that her sudden burst of happiness takes place at high summer, and that she dips down towards near-unhappiness during the autumn and winter).

The title of the novel's first chapter is 'The Kindling of Love'. In it we are introduced to Anna herself, and to Henry Mynors and Willie Price, the two men who love her. It is a Sunday afternoon and Anna has been taking a class at the chapel Sunday school. Both men are waiting for her to appear. Both of them are potters, Mynors successful, Willie, because of his father's incompetence, on the verge of failure. As a successful potter, Mynors is socially important. He is 'morning superintendent of the Sunday school and conductor of the men's Bible-class held in the lecture-hall on Sunday afternoons'. It is a point we need to remember when we find that Anna is flattered by his paying her attentions. And it is an indication of her necessarily limited vision that she should see him as a glamorous figure, just as it is an indication of Bennett's adroit and scrupulous handling of social gradations that Mynors should seem much more attractive and worldly to Anna than Willie Price does. Willie is merely secretary of the Bible class. What could seem a finicky matter of distinction is in *Anna of the Five Towns* – and all Bennett's best work – crucial.

Equally crucial is his attention to the entertainments and diversions open to his heroine. After Sunday school Mynors walks with Anna and Agnes to Bursley's new park, to hear the band play.

The Park rose in terraces from the railway station to a street of small villas almost on the ridge of the hill. From its gilded gates to its smallest geranium-slips it was brand-new, and most of it was red. The keeper's house, the bandstand, the kiosks, the balustrades, the shelters – all these assailed the eye with a uniform redness of brick and tile which nullified the pallid greens of the turf and the frail trees. The immense crowd, in order to circulate, moved along in tight processions, inspecting one after another the various features of which they had read full descriptions in the 'Staffordshire Signal' – waterfall, grotto, lake, swans, boat, seats, faïence, statues – and scanning with interest the names of the donors so clearly inscribed on such objects of art and craft as from divers motives had been presented to the town by its citizens.

It could be any one of those countless parks that provincial towns and cities provided for their people during the second half of the nineteenth century. And as Bennett remarks, although the park is in itself unlovely, 'it symbolised the first faint renascence of the longing for beauty in a district long given up to unredeemed ugliness'. But how faint! Mynors is perfectly satisfied with it: 'In deciding that the Park made a very creditable appearance he only reflected the best local opinion.' Again, we need to note how glamorous Mynors is made to appear in reflecting the best local opinion and how that will make him even more of a splendid figure to Anna. She is, after all, Anna of the Five Towns.

She is also a tyrant's daughter. On this visit to the park, she meets her friend Beatrice Sutton, in whose eyes she sees the 'unconsciously-acquired arrogance of one who had always been accustomed to deference. Socially, Beatrice had no peer among the young women who were active in the Wesleyan Sunday-school.' Bennett's study of Beatrice is further evidence of the care and subtlety with which he notes social gradations in his provincial society. It also gives him the opportunity of showing Anna's discomfort when Beatrice refers to Tellwright's riches. Beatrice remarks that most of the land above the park belongs to Anna's father:

> 'Of course, it will be covered with streets in a few months. Will he build himself, or will he sell it?'
> 'I haven't the least idea,' Anna answered, with an effort after gaiety of tone, and then turned aside to look at the crowd. There, close against the bandstand, stood her father, a short, stout, ruddy, middle-aged man in a shabby brown suit. He recognised her, stared fixedly, and nodded with his grotesque and ambiguous grin. Then he sidled off towards the entrance of the Park. None of the others had seen him. 'Agnes dear,' she said abruptly, 'we must go now, or we shall be late for tea.'

It neatly demonstrates how Tellwright unquestioningly tyrannizes over her. Without hesitation Anna cuts short her own pleasure in order to hurry home and prepare her father's meal. And the scene tells us something of Tellwright's incalculable relationship with his daughters. He doesn't approach Anna, doesn't want to speak. He merely stares and nods.

Tellwright is a fascinating creation, and one that Bennett often repeats, especially in short stories. He is a domestic tyrant and a miser, flinty, quickwitted but utterly insensitive. He is a loveless and unlovely person, devoid of any emotion except the pleasure he allows himself to feel at other people's misfortunes or rage at his own. Any summary makes him sound thoroughly hateful, almost a caricature. The impressive thing about Bennett's handling of him, however, is that there is absolutely nothing of caricature in the study of Tellwright. Nor is he sentimentalized. Instead, Bennett sets himself to record the life of a man who is quite without music in his soul. It is the record of a pinched, humdrum, desolating existence.

> If you had talked to him of the domestic graces of life, your words would have conveyed to him no meaning. If you had indicted him for simple unprovoked rudeness, he would have grinned, well knowing that, as the King can do no wrong, so a man cannot be rude in his own house. If you had told him that he inflicted purposeless misery not only on others but on himself, he would have grinned again, vaguely aware that he had not tried to be happy, and rather despising happiness as a sort of childish gewgaw. He had, in fact, never been happy at home: he had never known that expansion of the spirit which is called joy; he existed continually under a grievance. . . . Had he been capable of self-analysis, he would have discovered that his heart lightened whenever he left the house, and grew dark whenever he returned; but he was incapable of the feat. (chapter 9)

There are novels of Bennett's in which this kind of telling you about a character is maddening, because Bennett himself becomes arch or portentous in the manner of telling, or both, so that it feels as though the characters are being condescended to by an author who has very little substantial interest in them. You are allowed to know only what he tells you. He doesn't *show* you anything about them, and he can't or he won't imagine them in action. But in *Anna of the Five Towns* Tellwright is seen with the kind of convincing accuracy that is an utterly triumphant vindication of Bennett's art. Tellwright storming at Anna over her lax attitude to debtors, Tellwright grumbling over her holiday (it is the first she has ever had), Tellwright greeting her when she returns:

> 'I see thou's gotten into th' habit o' flitting about in cabs,' he said. . . .

'Well, father,' she said, smiling yet, 'there was the box. I couldn't carry the box.'

'I reckon thou couldst ha' hired a lad to carry it for sixpence.'

She did not reply. The cabman had gone to his vehicle.

'Art 'na going to pay th'cabby?'

'I've paid him, father.'

'How much?'

She paused. 'Eighteen-pence, father.' It was a lie; she had paid two shillings. (chapter 11)

Again and again, Bennett provides us with instances of Tellwright's unthinking callousness – there is a particularly strong scene when he makes Anna write and then rewrite a letter to the Prices, demanding money from them – and in general his presentation of the mean, crimping spirit of the Tellwright household is both credible and upsetting. On one occasion Tellwright snarls and sulks because Anna has forgotten to buy the breakfast bacon.

> At dinner the girls could perceive that the shadow of his displeasure had slightly lifted, though he kept a frowning silence. Expert in all the symptoms of his moods, they knew that in a few hours he would begin to talk again, at first in monosyllables, and then in short detached sentences. An intimation of relief diffused itself through the house like a hint of spring in February. (chapter 6)

It is a measure of Bennett's success in catching the atmosphere of the Tellwright household that we should understand the girls' relief at the scarcely perceptible thaw in their father's anger. And Anna's response to it is very nearly one of acute pleasure. Happiness is not easy to come by in Tellwright's house. It is that fact which does so much to explain why she should be dazzled by Mynors.

Mynors is a popular man. More to the point, he is likeable. Even Tellwright grudgingly responds to his charm. He respects Mynors as an acute man of business, and is slightly awed by the other man's tactful but firm refusal to defer to him. Mynors is not to be bullied.

Anna also is awed by Mynors. At the sewing meeting she goes to, 'He talked gaily with Beatrice and Mrs Banks: that group was a centre of animation. Anna envied their ease of manner, their smooth and sparkling flow of conversation. She had the sensation of feeling vulgar, clumsy, tongue-tied; Mynors and Beatrice possessed something which she would never possess' (chapter 7). She is also im-

pressed by Mynors's religious convictions, which she finds she
cannot share. There is nothing finer in *Anna of the Five Towns* than
Bennett's treatment of the revival meeting and Anna's reluctant
involvement in it. The episode could so easily become the opportunity for satire or polemic. Yet Bennett never wavers in his acceptance of the genuine and deep seriousness of these people and
the cause which brings them together. And even the famous re-
vivalist himself, keen though he is on money – 'He played the
cornet to the glory of God, and his cornet was of silver' – isn't
mocked. Bennett's control of tone is steady as a rock.

> Mynors' prayer was a cogent appeal for the success of the Revival.
> He knew what he wanted, and confidently asked for it, approaching
> God with humility but with self-respect. The prayer was punctuated
> by Amens from various parts of the room. The atmosphere became
> suddenly fervent, emotional and devout. . . . Anna felt, as she had
> often felt before, but more acutely now, that she existed only on the
> fringe of the Methodist society. She had not been converted; tech-
> nically she was a lost creature: the converted knew it, and in some
> subtle way their bearing to her, and others in her case, always showed
> that they knew it. (chapter 4)

But she will not submit. There is an account – far too long for me
to be able to quote it – of the anguish that grips her when she sees
Mynors persuading a young man to join the converts. She becomes
tense with a sense of guilt, but cannot persuade herself to join the
'saved'. Instead, she sits alone, muttering ' "I believe, I believe" . . . .
Nothing happened. A doubt whether the whole affair was not after
all absurd flashed through her, and was gone.' And then, after a
night of agony, she goes down to the chapel, determined to seek
'salvation', only to discover that the early morning prayers are
being conducted in the lecture hall, a cold, inhospitable place, and
that the minister is 'vapid, perfunctory and fatigued'. 'He gave out
a verse, and pitched the tune – too high, but the singers with a
heroic effort accomplished the verse without breaking down. The
singing was thin and feeble, and the eagerness of one or two voices
seemed strained, as though with a determination to make the best
of things' (chapter 6). And so out of the lecture hall and back to
her father and the discovery that in the stresses of the night she has
forgotten his breakfast bacon. Set down here the episode no doubt

seems trivial, even absurd. Yet it is nothing of the kind. What must strike anyone reading Bennett's novel is the care and considerateness with which he follows Anna's shifting states of mind. There is no other novelist who so fully and uncondescendingly illuminates a whole area of experience of provincial life in the latter half of the nineteenth century. Those forlorn chapels of Nonconformism still stand in Midland towns – just. But the way of life that supported them is almost gone. Bennett alone can tell you what it was like to be a part of that life.

It is the same with Anna's delight at being taken on holiday by the Suttons. They go to the Isle of Man, accompanied by Mynors. And on the last night of their stay he proposes to her: 'They walked home almost in silence. She was engaged, then. Yet she experienced no new sensation. She felt as she had felt on the way down, except that she was sorely perturbed. There was no ineffable rapture, no ecstatic bliss. Suddenly the prospect of happiness swept over her like a flood' (chapter 10).

The next day they return home:

> Mynors' face expressed the double happiness of present and antici-
> pated pleasure. He had once again succeeded, he who had never failed;
> and the voyage back to England was for him a triumphal progress.
> Anna responded eagerly to his mood. The day was an ecstasy, a bright
> expanse unstained. To Anna in particular it was a unique day, marking
> the apogee of her existence. In the years that followed she could
> always return to it and say to herself: 'That day I was happy, foolishly,
> ignorantly, but utterly. And all that I have since learnt cannot alter it –
> I was happy.' (chapter 11)

For she isn't in love with Mynors. Dazzled, awed, happy to be chosen by him, happy above all to be given the chance of escaping from her grim, joyless home – but not in love with him: 'Anna thought to herself: "Is this love-making?" It could not be, she decided: but she infinitely preferred it so. She was content. She wished for nothing better than this apparent freedom and irresponsible dalliance. She felt that if Mynors were to be tender, sentimental, and serious, she would become wretchedly self-conscious' (chapter 10). This moment of introspection occurs when they are still on the Isle of Man, and it typifies Bennett's discreet handling of Anna's gradual awakening to the true nature of her feelings for Mynors. *Anna of the Five Towns* isn't the saddest story, but there is a good deal of sadness in the fact that only when it is too late does Anna realize that she is in love with Willie Price, and he with her. For how could she love him? He is her social inferior, in debt to her, fawning on her father, pleading for time to pay off moneys owed.

At first, her attitude to him is one of near contempt: 'The idea of being in debt was abhorrent to her. She could not conceive how a man who was in debt could sleep at nights' (chapter 3). Her morality is purely that of the lower middle class; it is based on a respect for solvency. 'After all, she said to herself, a debt is a debt, and honest people pay what they owe' (chapter 6). When she goes to see Willie's father, Titus Price, to ask him about his settling his debts with her, there is a 'flinty hardness in her tone'; and when Price offers her £10: '"Liar! you said you had nothing!" her unspoken thought ran, and at the same instant the Sunday-school and everything connected with it grievously sank in her estimation' (chapter 3). For Price is a senior member of the Sunday school staff and tries hard to keep up appearances. But poverty makes him devious, ignoble. '"Come inside, Miss Tellwright," he said, with a sickly, conciliatory smile.' And later, when Willie begs her for more time in which to find the money to pay off their debts, Anna tells him that her father won't allow for any more delays.

> 'Yes,' she said, tapping her foot on the rug. 'But father means what he says.' She looked up at him again, trying to soften her words by means of something more subtle than a smile.
> 'He means what he says,' Willie agreed; 'and I admire him for it.'
> The obsequious, truckling lie was odious to her. (chapter 9)

Moments like that make one realize just how good Bennett can be. There is no dignity in poverty – it corrupts and warps both the poverty-stricken and the observers of it. And it is built into the Five Towns world. Anna can no more escape its effects than the Prices can.

Where I think Bennett goes wrong is in his comments on Titus Price's suicide – to which the old man is driven by Tellwright's implacable demands for money.

Here was a man whom no one respected, but everyone pretended to respect – who knew that he was respected by none, but pretended that he was respected by all; whose whole career was made up of dissimulations: religious, moral, and social. If any man could have been trusted to continue the decent sham to the end, and so preserve the general self-esteem, surely it was this man. But no! Suddenly abandoning all imposture, he transgresses openly, brazenly; and, snatching a bit of hemp cries: 'Behold me: this is real human nature. This is the truth; the rest was lies. I lied; you lied. I confess it, and you shall confess it.' Such a thunderclap shakes the very base of the microcosm. (chapter 11)

Somewhere in among that portentous rhetoric a good idea is struggling to escape. The trouble is that Bennett won't allow himself to focus on the real rottenness that forces Titus Price to take his own life – the struggle of man against man which, as I earlier remarked, Bennett always turns away from. Price's suicide doesn't really do anything to the microcosm (if by that Bennett means the society which produced him, and if he doesn't mean that then I don't know that he can mean anything at all). Society simply goes on forcing people into 'decent sham'. It is hardly too much to say that one feels Bennett to be uneasily aware that Price's suicide cannot really be justified or accepted on the grounds that it uncovers 'real human nature'. 'Such a thunderclap shakes the very base of the microcosm' is a forlorn attempt to ease a troubled conscience.

Having said that, I must add that Bennett's handling of Anna's relationship with Willie Price is well-night faultless. Her initial contempt for him modulates naturally into pity, and finally develops into a love which she can never feel for Mynors. For Mynors condescends to her 'He kissed her lovingly. But, beneath the feeling of a reassurance, which by superior force he had imposed on her, there lay a feeling that she was treated like a frightened child who must be tranquillised in the night' (chapter 11). With Mynors, Anna is merely submissive; she has no chance to assert herself or to come fully alive. He takes care of everything. But with Willie it is the other way round. She treats him as her child, loves him with a maternal passion that is otherwise thwarted (indeed, we are told at the end of the novel that her marriage will be a childless one).

Mynors is her surrogate father. She hastens her marriage to him when her father finally rejects her (which he does after discovering that she has burned a forged bill of credit of Price's to save Willie from public humiliation). And Mynors buys the Price house for Anna and himself. Mynors succeeds. The surrogate child, Willie, fails and like his father commits suicide.

Between both men moves Anna of the Five Towns. 'She had sucked in with her mother's milk the profound truth that a woman's life is always a renunciation' (chapter 14). That may seem perilously close to clubman's philosophizing. It is saved from being so by the fact that Anna's life is plainly one of renunciation. She renounces her own deepest feelings and instincts – is barely conscious of them – because in the social, moral and domestic patterning of the Five Towns, women have no opportunity fully to express themselves. 'Something is pushing them to the side of their own lives' – Philip Larkin's line might almost have been written with Anna in mind. And the something that pushes her is, of course, the Five Towns themselves. When her father discovers that Anna has been seeing Willie, Bennett remarks, 'The miser was wounded in the one spot where there remained to him any sentiment capable of being wounded: his faith in the irreproachable, absolute chastity, in thought and deed, of his womenkind.' As far as Tellwright is concerned, Anna is now 'sneaking, creeping – like any brazen moll' (chapter 11). He speaks there as a man of the Five Towns.

One of the saddest figures of the entire novel is Sarah Vodrey, the Price's housekeeper. As she lies dying, she tells Anna that for two years she has received no wages from Titus Price, but that she has saved enough to be able to pay for her own funeral.

> '. . . and Willie must have what's over. There would ha' been more for the lad, but *he* never paid me no wages this two years past. I never troubled him.'
>
> 'Don't tell Willie that,' Anna said impetuously.
>
> 'Eh, bless ye, no!' said the dying drudge. . . .
>
> The next day Sarah Vodrey died – she who had never really lived save in the fetters of slavery and fanaticism. After fifty years of ceaseless labour, she had gained the affection of one person, and enough money to pay for her own funeral. (chapter 12)

It is uncompromisingly bleak, and rightly so. Because for all Bennett's passionate involvement with the 'romance of the Five Towns', he knows well enough how its spirit oppresses women, and in various ways thwarts their energies. He is terrific on the sewing party (chapter 7) and its pallid pleasures. Mrs Sutton, at whose house the meeting is held, could so easily be treated in a dismissive manner. She is a complacent sectarian, utterly conventional, incurious, amiably dull. Bennett shows this side of her with easy authority. But he also shows her kindness, sincere friendliness, her desire to be and do good. Mrs Sutton typifies his unwavering gaze at Five Towns society. He is neither sentimental about her, nor cynical.

It is true, of course, that in later novels he will sometimes present women's lives as 'renunciation' in ways that seem contrived, procrustean or plain silly. And it is relevant to note that Bennett is rarely able to deal convincingly with sexual passion. But his study of Anna, and of her relations with her father, with Mynors and with Willie, seems to me fastidious, searching and truthful. To take one last example.

Anna is out walking with Mynors one evening shortly after Titus Price's suicide and the final collapse of his business. Suddenly, she is aware of feeling a 'cold melancholy', and is

> apprehensive of vague sorrows. 'Why am I so?' she asked herself, and tried in vain to shake off the mood.
>
> 'What will Willie Price do if the business is sold?' she questioned Mynors suddenly.
>
> 'Surely,' he said to soothe her, 'you aren't still worrying about that misfortune. I wish you had never gone near the inquest; the thing seems to have got on your mind.'
>
> 'Oh, no!' she protested, with an air of cheerfulness: 'But I was just wondering.'

They continue with their walk, and Mynors tells her how much she fascinates him. 'His warmth made her feel sad.'

> In the dark he seized her with such violence, and kissed her so vehemently, that she was startled out of herself.
>
> 'Oh, Henry!' she exclaimed.
>
> 'Call me Harry,' he entreated, his arm still round her waist; 'I want

you to call me Harry. No one else does or ever has done, and no one ever shall, now.'

'Harry,' she said deliberately, bracing her mind to a positive determination. She must please him, and she said it again: 'Harry; yes, it has a nice sound.' (chapter 12)

It is so tactful, so touching, the way her sadness increases at Mynors's warmth. Her mind is on Willie and her love for him – as the sudden question, which finely catches the unconscious movement of her thoughts, shows; but she also feels genuine regret that she can't love Mynors. It is regret, quite as much as resignation, that makes her brace her mind to a positive determination to please him. And in its implied generosity of spirit that determination also makes her of the Five Towns.

Chapter 2
The Professional

I

It is typical of Bennett that in 1902 he should have published not only *Anna of the Five Towns* but also *The Grand Babylon Hotel*. A minor masterpiece sits on the shelf beside an 'entertainment'. And in the next few years there were to be more such entertainments. I use this word as a way of avoiding the harsher though perhaps more accurate term 'potboiler' (Bennett himself came to use the term 'Fantasia'). *The Gates of Wrath, Teresa of Watling Street, Hugo, The Loot of Cities, The City of Pleasure* – they were all written with an eye to the market; and none of them seems to have made him much money. Nor did the plays he was busying himself with, often in collaboration with Eden Philpotts.

It was money that Bennett was after. By 1903 he had crossed to France, determined to succeed as a professional writer; and the *Journals* of the time show him absorbedly totting up output and income. They also reveal the pride he took in his industry. On 5 February 1904 he noted:

> I finished the play. All that remains to be done to it now is Eden's revise. In 3 weeks exactly, we have written, between us, (1) the play, (2) 2 short stories, (3) 3 articles, (4) a long chapter of my novel [*A Great Man*]. This is what may be called the industry of genuine craftsmen. Nothing has been scamped except this journal, which doesn't count.

And almost a year later, he remarked in the *Journal* that 'Idleness is a very bad thing for me in every way'.

There is no doubt that the amount of work Bennett produced in the opening years of this century was simply prodigious. Quite apart from the fiction and plays, there is an unceasing flow of articles, essays, reviews, journalistic bits and bobs. Confronted with the fact of such industry one is compelled into a kind of awe. Such colossal determination, such energy, such resourcefulness! And there is something very moving about Bennett setting himself to master the French language, trying various recommended cures for his stammer – none worked – reading voraciously and according to plan, and grittily pursuing his ambition to live well by his writing.

Yet the doubts crowd in. Was the industry really a good thing? In particular, do the entertainments amount to anything worthwhile? Is nothing ever scamped? The first question cannot really be answered. Bennett's unceasing toil helped him to become better known so that more commissions came his way (and of course he was popular with editors because he never missed a deadline); and that eventually came to mean more money. There is no way of telling whether all this was harmful to his creativity. 'As for literature', Mr Nixon is made to say, 'it gives no man a sinecure.' Bennett might well have said or thought that. But he would not have spoken the words which follow and which have so often been quoted against him:

> And give up verse, my boy,
> There's nothing in it.

Bennett never gave up art, even if there were to be times when he came perilously close to it. But it could perhaps be argued that art came near to giving him up as a bad job, simply because he wasted so much of his talent on trivia. Perhaps. For the fact is that the early entertainments are worthless, and the mechanical ease with which they were written may have induced bad habits. Bennett was proud of the fact that he scarcely ever rewrote. Such pride may have been misplaced. There is a feeling of mere mechanical competence about some of Bennett's later works. They are novels in second gear. Bennett learned the use of that gear in his early entertainments, and it may be that the very ease with which he could move along in it dulled his ambition to shift out of it. But then one might up-end this argument and say that because of his professional competence Bennett was always able to write, and that his training helped him create his masterpieces. It is an old-fashioned view of art and the artists, but not necessarily the worse for that.

There is no point in spending much time on the entertainments. But a word or two is in order. *The Grand Babylon Hotel* is the first and best known of them. I do not know why it should have proved so popular. Perhaps because it reveals that fascination with the working of hotels which Bennett puts to such good effect in *The Old Wives' Tale*, *Hilda Lessways* and *Imperial Palace*. Perhaps because the hotel itself reappears or is referred to in several later novels. And perhaps because of Bennett's obvious delight in his hero, Theodore Racksole, the American multimillionaire around whom the plot stiffly revolves.

> 'I have a private car on the New York Central, and I have a two-thousand-ton schooner-yacht – though it isn't on the Hudson. It happens just now to be on East River. And I am bound to admit that the stables of my uptown place are fitted with marble,' Racksole laughed.
>
> 'Ah!' said Hazell. 'Now I can believe that I am lunching with a millionaire. It's strange how facts like those – unimportant in themselves – appeal to the imagination. You seem to me a real millionaire now.' (chapter 25)

There is a good deal of this sort of thing in the book. There is also a disagreeable, calculated snobbishness, as when Mr Sampson Levi, moneylender, converses with Prince Eugen.

> It was a scene characteristic of the end of the nineteenth century – an overfed, commonplace, pursy little man who had been born in a Brixton semi-detached villa, and whose highest idea of pleasure was a Sunday up the river in an expensive electric launch, confronting and utterly routing, in a hotel belonging to an American millionaire, the representative of a race of men who had fingered every page of European history for centuries, and who still, in their native castles, were surrounded with every outward circumstance of pomp and power. (chapter 20)

It might almost be out of W. H. Mallock. But whereas Mallock would believe in it, my guess is that Bennett's tongue is firmly in his cheek. *The Grand Babylon Hotel* is so obviously a novel in search of an audience. It combines the thriller novel of Conan Doyle with the faintly exotic high-life romance of Elinor Glyn. And it is to Bennett's credit that it should fail. He simply doesn't believe in what he is doing, with the result that he doesn't work hard enough to avoid some very implausible plotting and thoroughly unconvincing characterization. 'An old imitator', Lawrence called him. In fact, like all truly creative artists Bennett is genuinely original. It is only in his entertainments that he is an imitator. Not a very good one, either.

The Gates of Wrath, 'A Melodrama', was published in 1903. It is a not inefficiently told tale of a young man tricked into marrying the stepdaughter of an evil and scheming woman who knows through her equally evil doctor friend that the man is due to inherit an enormous fortune. The young man himself doesn't know this because he is illegitimate, and the apparent heir is a friend of his who turns out to be mad (the madness shows particularly in his dropping golden guineas from his bedroom window into the water butt below). Much of the action takes place in the apparent heir's vast and lonely house in Staffordshire, and includes a butler called Sims who is the evil servant of the evil doctor. *The Gates of Wrath* is dull but at least it is competent, which is more than can be said for *Teresa of Watling Street* (1904). Indeed, Bennett was so ashamed of this sub-Buchan story that he even thought of consulting H. G. Wells to discover whether its publication might be prevented. Yet it is not much worse than *The Loot of the Cities* (1905). The title story of this collection is about a Raffles-like, devil-may-care American, Cecil Thorold, who enjoys living in expensive hotels and solving mysteries. *The Ghost* (1907) is just as bad. Its heroine is a *femme fatale*, an opera singer who has a literally deadly effect on men. She belongs to a mode made better use of by Marie Corelli. Finally, there is *The City of Pleasure* (1907), a comic-macabre tale, whose worth Bennett himself summed up when he noted in his *Journal* for 2 June 1905, 'I finished *The City of Pleasure* on Tuesday morning, being heartily sick of it.'

All these novels were written between 1900 and 1905, and the last of them was published in 1907. Bennett was to write later entertainments but never again would he attempt detective fiction or the macabre thriller. He turned instead to comedy, and the first of his comic entertainments came out at this time.

II

A Great Man was written between 1903 and 1904 and published in May 1904. 'I finished *A Great Man* at 11.30 this morning', Bennett notes in the *Journal* (13 March 1904), and he adds: 'I am more satisfied with it than I thought I should be. I began it with an intention merely humorous, but the thing has developed into a rather profound satire.' When it was published, he noted:

> I read through most of it in the evening. I thought one or two parts were too technical in detail; but on the whole it amused me well enough. I was struck by the ease and virtuosity of the writing (on that plane of writing) and by the sound construction. I don't fancy holes can be picked in these aspects of the book. But humour is often a matter of opinion.

A Great Man is certainly not a rather profound satire. It is, however, extremely funny, and Bennett was right to be struck by his own accomplishment. For in writing the novel he fashions a comic style which seems to me peculiarly his own: it is a style at once bland, laconic, matter-of-fact. *A Great Man* does not use or depend on extreme situations or characters. On the contrary, it feels disarmingly low-key, even flat. The style reappears at moments in all Bennett's major works and it can become gratingly insensitive – especially in *Mr Prohack*. But it also lifts such otherwise minor works as *The Card* and *The Price of Love* into a class of their own. And it points to a fact about Bennett which is too often forgotten – that he can be a very funny writer.

A Great Man is about an utter mediocrity, Henry Knight, who cannot avoid converting into gold everything that he touches. In particular, he succeeds as an author. From birth, indeed, he has had the suspicion that he might be destined for greatness as a writer. His father, a draper's manager whose middle name is

Shakspere, writes letters to the press under such pseudonyms as:

> A British Citizen, Fiat Justitia, Audi Alteram Partem, Indignant, Disgusted, One Who Knows, One Who Would Like to Know, Rate-payer, Taxpayer, Puzzled, and Pro Bono Publico – especially Pro Bono Publico. Two letters, to a trade periodical, were signed A Draper's Manager of Ten Years' Standing, and one, to the *Clerkenwell News*, bore his own name. (chapter 1)

At school Henry wins a prize for his essay on 'Streets', – part of which is declaimed by his irreverent cousin, Tom, who is a genuinely talented artist: 'Some streets are longer than others. . . . Very few streets are straight. . . . But we read in the Bible of a street which is called Straight. . . . Oxford Street is nearly straight. . . . A street is what you go along. . . . It has a road and two footpaths' (chapter 5). Tom turns up from time to time, always mocking, needling and troubling Henry. But Henry is no fraud. He is entirely innocent. It is simply that he lacks any kind of talent and cannot help succeeding because of it. His first work is written while he is ill in bed, recovering from a mild bout of measles, watched over and tended by his anxious mother and aunt (as is to be expected, Bennett is marvellously funny over the exact and intricate details of the sickroom, Henry's bath, the sealing of doors and windows prior to fumigating the room, and so on). Henry's thoughts have been engaged on 'analysing the detrimental qualities of the Stream of Trashy Novels Constantly Poured Forth by the Press', when suddenly he has an idea for a novel. It is to be called *Love in Babylon*, and is in fact a spoof on the kind of romance which at that time was bringing Elinor Glyn so much money and fame. Not that Henry thinks of his novel as a spoof. He is convinced of its worth and not at all surprised when Mr Onions Winter accepts it for his Satin Library. *Love in Babylon* is published. The critics trounce it. It becomes a bestseller.

Henry is now famous. He is interviewed by *Home and Beauty* and has an entry in *Which is Which*, 'a biographical annual of inconceivable utility'. Then he finds himself in difficulties. He cannot think up the plot for another novel. Eventually, however, he manages to produce a story called *A Question of Cubits*. It is even dafter than *Love in Babylon* and makes even more money. Henry becomes an international celebrity, goes to Paris, is seduced, gambles in Monte Carlo, and an article devoted to him appears in a monthly review. 'The article explained to him how wonderful he was, and he was ingenuously and sincerely thankful for the revelation' (chapter 26). A third book follows, in which a victim to the passion of gambling 'is redeemed by the love of a pure young girl'.

Then comes the theatre. A former acquaintance, Doxey, collaborates with Henry, and between them they turn *Love in Babylon* into a curtain-raiser for 'old Johny Pilgrim', and Henry finds himself interviewed by the great actor-manager (Beerbohm Tree? Henry Irving?).

Mr Pilgrim greeted Henry as though in a dream.

'What name?' he whispered, glancing round, apparently not quite sure whether they were alone and unobserved.

He seemed to be trying to awake from his dream, to recall the mundane and the actual, without success.

He said, still whispering, that the little play pleased him.

'Let me see,' he reflected. 'Didn't Doxey say that you had written other things?'

'Several books,' Henry informed him.

'Books? Ah!' Mr Pilgrim had the air of trying to imagine what sort of things books were. 'That's very interesting. Novels?'

'Yes,' said Henry.

Mr Pilgrim, opening his magnificent chest and passing a hand through his brown hair, grew impressively humble. 'You must forgive my ignorance,' he explained. 'I am afraid I'm not quite abreast of modern literature. I never read.' And he repeated firmly: 'I never read. Not even the newspapers. What time have I for reading?' he whispered sadly. 'In my brougham, I snatch a glance at the contents-bill of the evening papers. No more.'

Henry had the idea that even to be ignored by John Pilgrim was more flattering than to be admired by the rest of mankind.

Mr Pilgrim rose and walked several times across the room; then addressed Henry mysteriously and imposingly:

'I've got the finest theatre in London.'

'Yes?' said Henry.

'In the world,' Mr Pilgrim corrected himself.

Then he walked again, and again stopped.

'I'll produce your piece,' he whispered. 'Yes, I'll produce it.'

He spoke as if saying also: 'You will have difficulty in crediting this extraordinary and generous decision: nevertheless you must endeavour to do so.'

Henry thanked him lamely.

'Of course I shan't play in it myself,' added Mr Pilgrim, laughing as one who laughs at a fantastic conceit.

'No, naturally not,' said Henry.

'Nor will Jane,' said Mr Pilgrim.

Jane Map was Mr Pilgrim's leading lady, for the time being. (chapter 27)

But of course both of them act in the play and it is a howling success. After that, Henry decided to turn his third novel into a play, and has to accept Pilgrim's censoring of all long speeches. 'The blue-pencilling of the play proceeded. But whenever John Pilgrim came to a long speech by Hubert, the part which he destined for himself, he hesitated to shorten it. "It's too long! It's too long!" he whispered. "I feel it's too long. But, somehow, that seems to me essential to the action. I must try to carry it off as best I can."' A little later, he objects to Hubert calling himself a silly fool.

'Now, I don't think that's quite in the part. You must understand that when I study a character I become that character. Perhaps it would not be too much to say that I know more about that character than the author does. . . . Shall we strike that out?'

A little farther on Henry had given Veronica a little epigram: 'When a man has to stand on his own dignity, you may be sure that his moral stature is very small.'

'That's more like the sort of thing that Hubert would say,' John Pilgrim whispered. 'Women never say these things. It's not true to nature. But it seems to fit in exactly with the character of Hubert. Shall we – transfer –?' His pencil waved in the air. . . . (chapter 28)

By the end of the novel Henry is making increasingly vast sums of money, and he is happily married. 'Upon the whole the newspapers and periodicals were very kind to Henry, and even the rudest organs were deeply interested in him.' He even becomes president of the Anti-Breakfast League. True, cousin Tom remains ruthlessly sceptical, but then as Henry points out, for all that Tom may be admired and honoured as a sculptor, he can't pay his creditors.

A Great Man is a highly professional novel. It is clearly and crisply told. Bennett moves the story forward at a splendid pace, cutting just the right number of corners, feeding us just the right amount of information. It may lack the exuberance of Wells's *History of Mr Polly*, but it is very much better written. It isn't of course a satire on the literary life, since Bennett's stance of wry, stoical acceptance, his acknowledging that this is the way things are, goes quite against any satiric bitterness of feeling for how things might be. (The stance is thoroughly characteristic of him. In his *Journal* for 27 May 1904 he notes: 'My new series begins to appear today in the *Windsor*. My name is not on the front cover. Anthony Hope's stands there alone. And I am 37. Comment is needless'.) But the novel is certainly comic and informative about the poseurs, frauds and sharks with whom Henry Knight comes into contact. Those parts of it which deal with the flotsam of the literary world are done very much from the inside.

With Henry himself, however, one feels twinges of unease. He is done very much from the outside, and although it would be quite wrong to make too much of this, since *A Great Man* isn't one of Bennett's major fictions, there is a *kind* of implausibility about Henry that is carried over into novels which Bennett himself seems to have intended as altogether weightier works. I say 'seems', because anyone reading through Bennett's work soon discovers that a very odd tone plays over some of his fiction. At moments more than one of his novels develops an air of diffident self-mockery, as though Bennett himself isn't always quite sure how serious he wishes to be. Such a tone makes itself very strongly felt in *A Great Man*, and indeed much of the novel's charm depends on it. Yet it also produces false moments. I think, for example, of the episode where Henry discusses his new novel with his wife.

'What do you think I'm going to call it?' he demanded of her once, gleefully.
'I don't know,' she said.
'*Red and Black*,' he told her. 'Isn't that a fine title?'
'Yes,' she said. 'But it's been used before;' and she gave him particulars of Stendhal's novel, of which he had never heard.

'Oh, well!' he exclaimed, somewhat dashed. 'As Stendhal was a Frenchman, and his book doesn't deal with gambling at all, I think I may stick to my title. I thought of it myself, you know.'

'Oh yes, dearest. I *know* you did,' Geraldine said eagerly.

'You think I'd better alter it?'

Geraldine glanced at the floor. 'You see,' she murmured, 'Stendhal was a really great writer.'

He started, shocked. She had spoken in such a way that he could not be sure whether she meant, 'Stendhal was a really *great* writer,' or, '*Stendhal* was a *really* great writer.' If the former, he did not mind, much. But if the latter – . . . he perceived again, and more clearly than ever before, that there was something in Geraldine which baffled him – something which he could not penetrate, and never would penetrate. (chapter 26)

But could he really be such an idiot? Surely, Henry would at least have heard of Stendhal, even if he hadn't read him? Marie Corelli, it is true, thought herself the equal of Shakespeare. But she also took good care to show herself well informed about literature and writers. Her novels are laced with references to the great dead. And then one reflects that after all Bennett tells us hardly anything about Henry's mental life. It isn't of course of much consequence in *A Great Man* and it would be wrong to make heavy weather of the matter. But I think it important at least to note Bennett's readiness to leave us in a state of ignorance about his character's inner life, because it can become decidedly irritating in such a novel as *Buried Alive*. *Buried Alive* is *A Great Man* turned upside down. It is about a painter of real genius who decides to seek anonymity. But as with Henry so, and much more damagingly, with Priam Farll: we know far too little about him to find Bennett's fiction at all convincing.

A Great Man is interesting for two reasons. On the credit side, it employs a comic manner which seems to me one of Bennett's important achievements. But against that, it exhibits a curious tactlessness in the handling of its main character. Bennett, one feels, is quite ready to make fiction out of lives about which he knows and can imagine nothing. I do not think that such tactlessness is the product of professional cynicism, a determination to go through with a 'well-made fiction', and hang the artistic consequences. On the contrary, it stems from an innocence that is really remarkable in so shrewd, intelligent, sensitive and critically astute a man. The fact is that Bennett often seems not to have the least idea of when he is writing badly or inadequately. Or perhaps any tremor of doubt is to be disarmed by self-mockery. The point applies particularly to the more serious and considered works of the period under present discussion.

III

Leonora (1903) is interesting, in many ways very good, but in the last analysis it fails to be fully satisfying. *Sacred and Profane Love* (1905) is a total disaster, and probably the silliest book ever written by a good novelist. *Whom God Hath Joined* (1906) is in some ways as good as *Anna of the Five Towns*, and perhaps even better. All three novels are about crises in sexual relationships, with *Leonora* and *Sacred and Profane Love* told from the woman's point of view. Writing about d'Annunzio in 1910, Bennett remarks:

> How adult, how subtle, how (in the proper signification) refined, seems the sexuality of d'Annunzio after the timid, infantile, barbaric sexuality of our 'island story!' People are not far wrong on the Continent when they say, as they do, that English novelists cannot deal with an Englishwoman – or could not up till a few years ago. They never get into the same room with her. They peep like schoolboys through the crack of the door. D'Annunzio can deal with an Italian woman. He does so in the first part of 'Forse che si forse che no.' She is only one sort of woman, but she *is* one sort – and that's something! . . . There is nothing to modern British taste positively immoral in the first part, but it is tremendously sexual. It contains a description of a kiss – just a kiss and no more – that is magnificent and overwhelming. You may say that you don't want a magnificent and overwhelming description of a kiss in your fiction. To that I reply that I do want it.

That comes from an essay, 'Unfinished Perusals', published in *Books and Persons, 1908–11*, and reading it we are entitled to feel that Bennett not only wanted sexuality in English fiction, but that he had provided it. 'Up till a few years ago' English novelists (I take it Bennett means male novelists) could not deal with women.

And now? And now there is Bennett and George Moore (*A Drama in Muslin*), and almost certainly Wells's *Ann Veronica*, which had been published in 1909. Bennett, Moore and Wells all undertake to show 'people on the continent' that they are wrong about English novelists. They deliberately set out to give their fictional women sexual feelings and desires, to show them trapped in provincial, bourgeois marriages or relationships from which, with various degrees of success, they struggle to free themselves; and in every case the women choose 'real' love rather than the conventional matches which they are offered.

Leonora is about a woman of the Five Towns respectably married to a businessman who is shady in his professional affairs, secretive and careless of other people's feelings, and who excludes Leonora from much of his life. She is approaching middle age, has three grown daughters, and feels that her life is more or less over. Hearing her daughter Millicent singing, Leonora is beguiled

> into a mood of vague but powerful melancholy. It seemed tragic that that fresh and pure voice, that innocent vanity, and that untested self-confidence should change and fade as maturity succeeded adolescence and decay succeeded maturity; it seemed intolerable that the ineffable charm of the girl's youth must be slowly filched away by the thefts of time. 'I was like that once! And Jack too' she thought. . . . She had a glimpse of the significance of Nature's eternal iterance. Then her mood developed a bitterness against Millicent. She thought cruelly that Millicent's magic was no part of the girl's soul, no talent acquired by loving exertion, but something extrinsic, unavoidable, and unmeritorious. . . .

Her thoughts drift from Millicent to her other two daughters, Ethel and Rose: '"Ah, well!" she reflected finally with an inward sigh, as though to whisper the last word and free herself of this preoccupation, "they will be as old as me one day." "Mr Twemlow," said the parlourmaid' (chapter 'The Call'). Arthur Twemlow is an American acquaintance with whom Leonora is to fall in love and whom she eventually marries. Her sadness will be overthrown by a fresh start in life.

On the whole, Bennett tactfully and sympathetically communicates Leonora's melancholy – except for the moment when he intrudes the remark about her glimpse of 'the significance of

Nature's iterance'. Speaking of a similar moment in *The Old Wives' Tale*, Wayne Booth remarks that 'there is, throughout the novel, much too much of the narrator, who is clearly Bennett himself. 'Whenever I find myself disagreeing with him, either in his explicit commentary about the meaning of life in the Five Towns or in the implicit judgement conveyed by all the less obvious forms of the author's voice, the book suffers in my eyes' (Wayne C. Booth, *The Rhetoric of Fiction* (1961), p. 147). It is a proper objection and it points to an element in Bennett which is both portentous and banal, a readiness to use phrases that imply vast and reverberative judgements without in any sense coming clear about what they actually mean. Such phrases nearly always invoke the melancholy of the universe, speak of the defeat of happiness, the fading of hope with the passing of time; they enlist on the side of sadness. Philip Larkin has remarked that Hardy's best poetry has about it the 'authority of sadness'. So does much of the best of Bennett's prose. But so also does much of the worst. Or rather, it has about it a sadness that aims for authority. Often enough it is associated with women. When Anna is made to recognize that woman is born for renunciation Bennett can get away with it because we sense that Anna is thinking as a Five Towns' woman. But when the same idea is trundled out in novel after novel we begin to realize that we are down among the clubmen. Bennett likes to air the topic of 'the nature of women', and often in a distressingly vulgar way. (In one of his *Journal* entries he recalls asking two Cambridge graduates 'Don't you think women are the most interesting thing in the world?') So Leonora is made to perceive 'the vital inferiority of women to men – that quality of callousness which allows them to commit all cruelties in the name of self-sacrifice, and that lack of imagination by which they are blinded to the wounds they deal' (chapter, 'The Refusal').

Yet in spite of this kind of silliness *Leonora* is good because for the most part the social situation is shown to be one where women are trapped in a life of stultifying dullness and unfair discrimination. John Stanway not only relegates Leonora to the suburbs of his good pleasure, refusing to discuss even domestic matters with her – when he has to mortgage her house 'By an effort she conquered the impulses to ask why, why, why; and to suggest economy in the house' (chapter, 'The Chance') – but he treats her very much as a doll (an attitude underlined by his calling her Nora. Nobody reading *Leonora* in 1903 would have been likely to miss the significance of *that* name). He is also a tyrant. Not histrionically or violently. It is merely that he determines what shall and shall not happen. Millicent wants to go on the stage, but Leonora knows that her husband will forbid it.

> It seemed to her that her children, though to outward semblance they had much freedom, had never listened to anything but 'No,' 'No, dear,' 'Of course you can't,' 'I think you had better not,' and 'Once for all, I forbid it.' She wondered why this should have been so, and why its strangeness had not impressed her before. She had a distant fleeting vision of a household in which parents and children behaved like free and sensible human beings, instead of like the virtuous and martyrised puppets of a terrible system called 'acting for the best.' (chapter, 'The Departure')

In that passage we hear for the first time a note which is to be struck with increasing frequency in Edwardian fiction. I think, for example, of that moment in *A Room With a View* when Miss Bartlett whisks Lucy away from the dangerous presence of George Emerson, and about which Forster comments that 'She had worked like a great artist; for a time – indeed, for years – she had been meaningless, but at the end there was presented to the girl the complete picture of a cheerless, loveless world in which the young rush to destruction until they learn better . . .' (chapter 7). And I think, too, of the row between Ann Veronica and her father about whether she shall go to a fancy dress ball:

> 'Why shouldn't I go?'
> 'It isn't a suitable place; it isn't a suitable gathering.'
> 'But daddy, what do you know of the place and the gathering?'
> 'And it's entirely out of order; it isn't right, it isn't correct; it's impossible for you to stay in an hotel in London – the idea is preposterous. I can't imagine what possessed you, Veronica.'
> He put his head on one side, pulled down the corners of his mouth, and looked at her over his glasses.
> 'But why is it preposterous?' asked Ann Veronica, and fiddled with a pipe on the mantel.
> 'Surely!' he remarked, with an air of worried appeal. (chapter 1)

Forster's and Wells's novels are of course much more concerned
with the issue of parents and children and 'respectability' than
Bennett is in *Leonora*; but it is characteristic of the good Bennett
that he should see it as a matter of real importance to Leonora
herself. Wells and Forster are on the side of the young: their
novels are frontal attacks on the hypocrisy of middle class values
and the restrictions placed on youth by crabb'd age. Bennett, on
the other hand, is much more conscious than either of the complex
tangle of claims and relationships that enmesh people. There is a
real weightiness of social reality in *Leonora* that both *A Room with
a View* and *Ann Veronica* manage without. This is not to criticize.
I admire both novels. But the fact is that Bennett can do things that
Wells and Forster can't. Above all, he is unerring in the way he
renders Leonora's sense of being confusedly in love with and
contemptuous of her husband. 'His terrible lack of frankness, that
instinct for the devious and the underhand which governed his
existence, struck her afresh and seemed to devastate her heart'
(chapter 'A Death in the Family'). That isn't merely rhetoric,
because again and again we are given instances of conversations
between the pair which demonstrate the lies, the suppressions,
the evasions and half truths that they are forced to make do with,
he contentedly, she desperately. I am not going to give an example, because no one instance will seem particularly impressive if
lifted out of context. One of the facts about Bennett which any critic
must bow to is that it is the *entire* presentation of events and characters in his novels which makes them so good. His best work gets its
wonderful concreteness and air of reality (to borrow James's
phrase) from the slow accumulation of incident and gradual
revelation of individual lives and relationships. To pick here and
there would be to divest the moments that one chooses of their
essential strength.

It is true, however, that you can easily quote from Bennett when
he is at his worst. The strengths are overall, the failures tend to be
local. The overwriting that goes with Bennett's pondering the
nature of woman is an obvious case in point. But so is something
which is much more damaging to *Leonora*. For Bennett does not
seem to me to be very convincing when he comes to present Leonora's love for Twemlow. This is partly because Twemlow is such

a shadowy figure, little more than a cliché of handsome, cheerful considerateness (and why, oh why call him Twemlow? Hadn't Bennett read *Our Mutual Friend*?) It is also partly because Bennett makes the awakening of Leonora's love depend on a single scene, a dance which Twemlow unexpectedly attends – Leonora thinks that he is still in New York, to which he has returned after their earlier meetings – and the dance is described in a manner considerably closer to Ouida than to d'Annunzio.

> Her entire being was absorbed in a transport of obedience to the beat of the music, and to Arthur's directing pressures. She was happy, but her bliss had in it that element of stinging pain, of intolerable anticipation, which is seldom absent from a felicity too intense. 'Surely I shall sink down and die!' said her heart, seeming to faint at the joyous tides of the music, which rose and fell in tides of varying rapture. Nevertheless she was determined to drink the cup slowly, to taste of every drop of that sweet and excruciating happiness. (chapter 'The Dance')

'English novelists cannot deal with an Englishwoman.' The words return to plague the inventor. Defending *Leonora* in a letter to a woman friend of his – she had told him she thought it inferior to *Anna* – Bennett wrote:

> That women of forty, generally, do regret the past, is an undoubted fact. That they long to be young again is an undoubted fact. That they are particularly, peculiarly, & specially passionate & prone to sexual excitement is an undoubted fact. It was the discovery of these piquant truths which led me to write *Leonora*. (*Letters*, vol. II, pp. 186–7)

To which one can only reply that Bennett manages the regret and the longing perfectly well, but not the sexual excitement.

Besides, he partly evades his own subject. Leonora doesn't go away with Twemlow. What makes their marriage possible is that her husband kills himself after the final downfall of his business affairs. This is not a clumsy piece of plot manipulation, since much earlier in the novel we see him contemplating suicide. 'Story-tellers born and accomplished do not tell poor stories,' Bennett wrote in 1908. 'A poor story is the work of a poor story-teller' ('The Novel of the Season', reprinted in *Books and Persons*, *1908–11*). He was thinking in particular of clumsy construction. His own novels are singularly free from such clumsiness, and *Leo-*

nora is no exception. Stanway's suicide isn't awkwardly contrived. It does, however, mean that there is no real crisis for Leonora to be confronted with. The novel has seemed to be driving towards the question, what will she do? how will she choose? But in the end she doesn't have to choose. Admittedly, Bennett tries to manufacture a crisis for her by having her agonizedly decide to renounce Twemlow and look after her two unmarried daughters, who live in London. But the uneasiness of this becomes clear when one notices the technicolour prose in which it is described: 'She was uplifted by the force of one of those tremendous and invincible resolutions which women alone, with their instinctive bent towards martyr-dom, are capable of making' (chapter, 'In London'). And anyway the instinctive bent proves weaker than her love for Twemlow. They marry.

It is obvious, of course, that had John not killed himself, Ben-nett would have been forced to place Leonora in a much more interesting social, moral and physical dilemma. Yet before we condemn him of cowardice in fudging his own subject we should recall the probable reception of a novel in which a wife left her husband for a lover and was neither condemned by the novelist, nor doomed to retributive disaster. *Leonora* comes almost midway between the outcry that had greeted Grant Allen's *The Woman Who Did* (1895) and the one that was to greet *Ann Veronica*. It may well be that Bennett was chary of upsetting reviewers and public when it wasn't necessary. In other words, he could imply the shockingness of what Leonora proposed without overstepping the bounds of acceptability. And though the consequence of this is that *Leonora* cannot be the novel which establishes an English-man's 'adult, subtle, and refined' treatment of sexuality, there is much in it that demonstrates Bennett's sensitivity to and imagina-tive sympathy with his heroine. Much too, that could only have been written by a novelist with his soberly realistic understanding of English provincial life.

The same can hardly be said for *Sacred and Profane Love*, Bennett's novel about a woman who also did, and in ways that are as embarrassingly awful as those of Grant Allen's heroine, Her-minia Barton. In *The Woman Who Did* Herminia has a 'free' re-lationship with her lover, Alan Merrick, who dies just as their

daughter, Dolly (Dolly!) is born. Herminia finally commits suicide because the grown-up Dolly wants to marry a young man
whose family is shocked by the disclosure of her illegitimacy. Dolly
is equally shocked, in spite of the fact that 'she had known authors,
artists, socialists, the cream of our race; she had been brought up in
close intercourse with the men and women who are engaged in
revolutionising and remodelling humanity' (chapter 19). She has
even had the opportunity of studying at close quarters 'the little
groups of advanced London socialists who call themselves Fabians'
(chapter 16). Given the sexual goings-on of the Fabians – it was
about the only way in which they *were* advanced – one is inclined
to be on Dolly's side. But Allen of course does not see it that way.
Dolly's chief crime is wanting to marry at all. Herminia is in the
right of it when she insists that love must be free. Marriage, she
tells her lover, is '"an assertion of man's supremacy over women.
It ties her to him for life; it ignores her individuality; it compels
her to promise what no human heart is capable of performing. . . .
It is full of all evils, and I decline to consider it. If I love a man at
all, I must love him on terms of perfect freedom"' (chapter 3).
Bennett's heroine, Carlotta, might have spoken these words. But
she is meant to be a much more passionate woman than Herminia,
whose dedication to the cause of freedom is indeed so total that it is
very difficult to know how Dolly was ever conceived. Carlotta has
read and been much influenced by *Mademoiselle de Maupin*, that
novel which W. H. Mallock had some years earlier described as
'the foulest and filthiest book that ever man put pen to. It is the
glorification of shameless and nameless vice' ('A Familiar Colloquy',
The Nineteenth Century (August 1878)). Carlotta is certainly shameless. She sees nothing wrong with sexual passion.

And such passion. *Sacred and Profane Love* is in three parts. The
first, 'In the Night', is about Carlotta's seduction by a famous
pianist, Diaz, interpreter of Chopin, whose playing carries her 'to
the dizziest heights of which passion is capable', and which shows
her that 'each moment of life, no matter what its import, should be
lived intensely and fully'.

When we next meet her in 'Three Human Hearts', she has become a famous novelist and poet, author of *Burning Sappho*.
She is now involved in an affair with her publisher, one Ispenlove.

But he commits suicide because his wife, knowing of his love for Carlotta, leaves him. In the third section of the novel, 'Victory', she meets Diaz once again. Ten years have elapsed since their night of passion and he is now an alcoholic. Carlotta decides to live with him, restores him to health so that he is enabled to compose a brilliant opera for which she has written the libretto, and dies of peritonitis just as she is to join him in New York for a triumphal tour.

Sacred and Profane Love could well have been written by Henry Shakspere Knight. How it came to be written by Bennett I cannot for the life of me understand. When Diaz seduces Carlotta she tells us that 'I was proud and glad that he was not clumsy, that he was a master. And at that point I ceased to have volition.' However, reflecting on the experience, she decides that 'I have learnt the secret meaning of existence'. No worst, there is none.

The really staggering fact is that Bennett appears to have been perfectly serious about *Sacred and Profane Love*. Certainly, there is nothing in the *Journals* to suggest that he was writing it tongue-in-cheek, or merely in the hope of turning a dishonest penny. On 22 November 1904 he notes: 'Today I began to plan out in detail the first part of *Sacred and Profane Love*.' It is, he promises himself, 'to be entirely magnificent'. In July 1905 he records that the novel is finished and that 'I wrote the third part of the book with less verve than the other two parts, and was doubtful of it several times, but when the thing was quite done it seemed to me all right.' And when he came to reread it in 1910, he remarked that 'I found it very young. It seemed to contain some good stuff, but also a proportion of cleverly arranged effects – effects of which the real difficulties had not been met. Still, it interested me.' Such comments seem all the more peculiar when one thinks that in the same year he was writing a hugely funny, deadpan review of Elinor Glyn's new novel, *His Hour* – 'It is magnificently sexual. . . . this noble, daring, and masterly work' (*Books and Persons*) – and that two years earlier he had performed a hatchet job on the heroines of Mrs Humphry Ward.

Gladstone, a thoroughly bad judge of literature, made her reputation. . . . Gladstone had no sense of humour – at any rate when he ventured into literature. Nor has Mrs Humphry Ward. If she had she would not concoct those excruciating heroines of hers. She probably does not know that her heroines are capable of rousing temperaments such as mine to ecstasies of homicidal fury. (*Books and Persons*)

When Ispenlove kisses Carlotta she reports, 'we shut our eyes for an eternal moment, and the world was not.' How could the one man say what Bennett does of Mrs Humphry Ward and at the same time not notice how excruciating his own heroine was? The only possible answer to the question is that at this stage of his career Bennett simply couldn't imagine a woman sexually alive. But why, then, should he try to? The answer to that must be that as an Edwardian, alert to the 'new woman', and as an ardent Francophile, it was inevitable that he should attempt to write a novel of sexual passion, seen from the woman's point of view. But since he was also Arnold Bennett, it was equally inevitable that the novel should fail.

To be fair, I don't know of any Edwardian novelist who can be said to succeed in creating the passionate woman so many of them write about. Mary Justin, of Wells's *Passionate Friends* (1913) is not much better than Carlotta; and Helen of *Howards End* is merely embarrassing. The point is, I think, that the idea of the 'passionate woman', as it is invoked in novels of the period, is purely that – an idea, an airy theorem as generalized and vague as the earlier image of the 'pure woman' or 'angel in the house' which, in the interest of truth, it was intended to replace. If *Ann Veronica* seems to me the most successful of the novels that take the idea as starting point it is because Wells convinces us that for Ann freedom means much more than the freedom to be passionate: it includes the freedom to study, have ideas, find social companionship. Whereas the casual pretence that Carlotta is a deservedly successful writer is merely an insult to the reader's intelligence. Whatever the weaknesses of Ethel Snowdon's *The Feminist Movement*, she is surely in the right to protest that the charges of immorality brought against feminists are either ignorant or malicious. Of course, feminists believe in freedom, 'but the freedom the feminist stands for is not freedom of passion, better called licence, but freedom to develop, freedom to achieve, freedom to serve'. True freedom, she adds, 'is of the spirit and of the intellect rather than the flesh'. No doubt she should have said 'as well as' instead of 'rather than'. But her point is valid.

It is a just rebuke to the kind of thinking which produced such heroines as Carlotta, Helen Schlegel, and Mary Justin, where freedom is reduced to 'fearless passion', and thus allows for an essentially condescending attitude (woman thinks with her body).

It is a complicated subject. At one extreme one has the sneering suggestion of George Dangerfield that all feminists were really lesbian. (*The Strange Death of Liberal England*, see his chapter on 'The Women's Rebellion'.) At another, one has Lawrence, at his best aware that the various equations of freedom, feminism and passion are all reductions of vast subtleties to manageable and life-less proportions (though Lawrence at his worst is just as ready to make use of the equations as any of the other novelists I have mentioned). And somewhere in between one has Bennett, wanting to be sympathetic to the passionate woman, failing hopelessly, and not even noticing. 'They like his best work almost as much as they like his worst', Randall Jarrell once remarked of Frost's admirers. The same might almost be said of Bennett's attitude to his own fiction. Certainly there is no evidence that he thought *Sacred and Profane Love* in any way inferior to *Whom God Hath Joined*.

I hold *Whom God Hath Joined* in high regard. But I am bound to admit that there is something wrong with it. Not so much the occa-sional overwriting, nor the moments of heavy-handed jocularity, especially when Bennett is writing about women. These faults are typical but in this novel they do not count for much. There is, however, a disturbing loss of focus in the treatment of one of the two relationships on which *Whom God Hath Joined* is built. As a result, the novel seems at least partly blurred. I am not at all sure how much this matters, in view of what Bennett succeeds in doing, but that it matters to some extent cannot be denied.

Whom God Hath Joined is about the collapse of two marriages. Lawrence and Phyllis Ridware's marriage breaks up when she goes off with another man, Emery Greatbatch, who dies. Much of the novel is concerned with the Ridware divorce proceedings. These are handled by the lawyer, Charles Fearns, a womanizer who se-duces a French governess. Unknown to him, his daughter finds out about the affair, tells her mother, and Mrs Fearns decides to sue for divorce. By the end of the novel the Ridwares have gained their divorce while the Fearns are reunited (Charles is still a woman-izer, but he has learnt enough discretion to pursue his subsequent affairs away from the Five Towns).

Bennett's handling of the Fearns side of the story seems to me fine and on occasions quite masterly. It is the Ridware relationship that bothers me. It seems as though we are required to be equally sympathetic to both of the Ridwares, but because we hardly ever see them together we can never quite understand just why their relationship has proved unsatisfactory. The root of the trouble is Lawrence Ridware. A good deal of Bennett has gone into Lawrence and some of Bennett's own confusions about 'woman' are discern-ible in him. He is seen as both sensitive to and understanding of women and also utterly insensitive to and ignorant of them. Or so I think. But let us have the text before us. In this passage he has gone to see Mrs Fearns.

> A *morceau de salon* of Chaminade's stood on the open piano, and lying on a small table was a reprint of Alexander Smith's *Dreamthorp*. Not in Lawrence's house would such examples of the brilliant second-rate have been found conspicuous, and his highly sensitive taste recoiled from them. Nevertheless, he said to himself that Mrs Fearns' sheer goodness and the personal distinction that she exhaled were worth more than all the artistic taste in the world. He would, at that instant, have sacrificed his whole intellectual and aesthetic equipment in exchange for the assurance of passing the rest of his life in the atmosphere he was breathing then. Mrs Fearns had good blood and a kind heart; the two things that Phyllis lacked. And he, the grandson of a potter's fireman, possessed emphatically the aristocratic temper. When he was differentiating between a masterpiece, and an imitation of a masterpiece, you could see that he had the nostrils of an aristocrat. (chapter 5)

I do not really know how to take this. It seems reasonably clear that Bennet is endorsing Lawrence's highly sensitive taste. But can he really be serious when he speaks of the 'nostrils of an aristocrat', or is he derisively indicating Lawrence's vanity and ignorance? Or remarking that, like Cecil Vyse, Lawrence is only any good with things, books, pictures, but kills when he comes to people? That would help explain why Phyllis, with her 'bad blood' (passion?) left him. Yet Lawrence is shown to be highly sensitive to Mrs

Fearns's 'sheer goodness and personal distinction'. But yet again the phrase 'personal distinction' may imply a snobbishness that is meant to tell us more about him than about her. Isn't it matched by his noting that she has 'good blood'? These questions cannot be resolved by saying that Bennett is showing us a complex man. The fact is that one isn't at all clear how we are to take Lawrence in this passage. Is he giving himself away? Or does Bennett mean to present him in a favourable light? And if so, isn't Bennett giving himself away? In short, what is Bennett's attitude to Lawrence? The question prompts another and inevitable one. To what extent does the state of Bennett's own emotional life at the time he was writing *Whom God Hath Joined* intrude into his novel?

The facts are these. Bennett began the novel in November 1905, and on the 16th he was able to record in his *Journal* that he had completed the first chapter: 'It seemed to me rather original and rather good, and quite unlike anything I had done before.' By the following May he had written at least half the book. On 24 May he notes, 'I finished another section (10,000 words) of the divorce novel on Monday night, having written it in eight days.' And he adds, 'I spent this afternoon with Eleanor Green.' The next entries are as follows.

Friday, June 15th.
   At 5 p.m. on this day in the forest of Fontainbleau I became engaged to marry Eleanora.
Friday, August 3rd.
   At 11 a.m. on this day, at Caniel, my engagement to Eleanora was broken off.
   In the meantime I had, with the utmost difficulty, finished my novel, *Whom God Hath Joined*.

'In the meantime.' If that phrase means anything mustn't it surely mean the engagement had been an unhappy one? And everything we know about it – which isn't much – suggests that it was. It was also distinctly odd. In the first place, Eleanora's real name was Eleanor. Presumably Bennet added the final letter in order to give his girl added distinction (in letters to Violet Hunt and Wells he spells her name Eléonora). When he wrote to Wells to inform him of the engagement he gave her age as twenty-five. In fact, she was younger. Reginald Pound says she was only eighteen, James Hepburn thinks she was older than that, but both agree that Bennett was revising her age just as he had revised her name (Reginald Pound, *Arnold Bennett, A Biography* (1950), p. 160, and James Hepburn, *The Letters of Arnold Bennett*, vol. II (1968), p. 207). I imagine that he didn't want his friends to think that there was too great a disparity in their ages or that she was a young chit who didn't know her own mind. But Bennett himself didn't know it. For the oddest feature of all is that according to Eleanor Green's own account she didn't even know that she and Bennett were supposed to be engaged. Bennett might be writing to Wells to inform him that 'I am – I mean, we are – thinking of being married at a registry office in Folkestone, this being the handiest', but according to Pound Miss Green was later to insist that she

> knew nothing of these arrangements for the disposal of her future. Her family had protested because she continued to leave his numerous letters lying unopened about the house and finally her mother, deploring what she insisted was a discourtesy, pressed a paper knife into her daughter's hand and made her slit open each envelope in a considerable pile even if she did not propose to read the contents. Miss Green says that she was never in love with him and, so far as she knew, had never given him cause to believe that his feelings for her were reciprocated beyond the terms of ordinary friendship. (*Pound*, p. 163)

How to make sense of this? My own guess is that Bennett more or less invented the engagement. We know that he was determined to marry; and I suspect that he simply set about the task of finding himself a wife who would accord with his preconceived image of what the wife of Arnold Bennett should be (it is not irrelevant here to recall his delight when, much later, Beerbohm told him of his cartoon of the Two Bennetts, Young and Old, the older saying, 'Everything has gone according to plan', the younger replying '*My* plan'). So Eleanor becomes Eleanora or Eléonora, her age is improved; and Bennett plans a marriage. Plans it alone, too, if the slip in the letter to Wells is anything to go by: 'I am – I mean, we are . . . .'

How does all this bear on the 'divorce novel'? Chiefly, I think, in the oddly unbalanced study of Lawrence and his wife, a study in which it becomes increasingly difficult and finally impossible to make out where Bennett stands in relation to either of them.

Whom God Hath Joined is not really a divorce novel. It is a marriage novel. That is to say, it is about the complicated, shifting relationships between men and women who are married to each other. Lawrence, we are told, can't understand his wife. The trouble is that Bennett doesn't understand her either. Or rather he doesn't present her clearly enough for us to have any chance of understanding why her marriage to Lawrence is the appalling misalliance that we are meant to see it as being. As a result, we have only Lawrence's word to go on, and the trouble with *that* is that we don't know how we are supposed to take Lawrence. What might have been a properly speculative study of a broken marriage becomes merely baffling. Because Bennett is baffled? One can't, of course, say, but I am certain that there is much more of Bennett in Lawrence than is good for the novel. I think here not so much of Lawrence's book collecting, although that is clearly modelled on Bennett's bibliophilia, as of his cool, level behaviour, the air he has of being almost incapable of emotion. Bennett was capable of emotion, but he often has the appearance of being three parts iced-over (his favourite philosopher was Epictetus), and in his *Journals* he cultivates an aloof detachment from the human scene. Bennett was a shy, vulnerable man who did not want to be hurt. How hurt he could be comes out in a letter to George Sturt. Sturt wrote to Bennett about *Anna of the Five Towns*: 'You refuse to be emotional yourself: you are unimpassioned, will not take sides, and all that – which is quite right. But, you seem unwilling to let the reader be emotional. You refuse to ask him to sympathise: you simply call upon him to observe.' To this, Bennett replied:

> The book is impassioned & emotional from beginning to end. . . . I might have been seriously perturbed by your opinion on my novel (since I regard you as, potentially, one of the most distinguished writers now living), had I not remembered that you said just the same things about Turgenev when you first read him. It is a singular surprising thing, but your taste in imaginative literature is crude & unreliable. I don't believe you have any genuine critical standard. (*Letters*, vol. II, pp. 172 and 175)

It is clear enough that Bennett was sorely wounded by Sturt's criticism, 'You refuse to be emotional yourself.' It is true, though. Throughout his life Bennett kept his emotions tightly buttoned up. Consider, for example, this letter to Wells: 'I have never been in love. Sometimes the tears start to my eyes, but they never fall. . . . I reckon I am above a passion for justice. Here we come to the "difference between our minds". I look down from a height on the show & contemplate a passion for justice much as I contemplate the other ingredients' (*Letters*, vol. II, p. 197). It is not to be taken at face value, as the letter to Sturt shows, but it does make one thing plain: that Bennett was profoundly unsure of himself, and frightened of giving himself away. And this comes out in his presentation of Lawrence. In particular, it comes out in the fact that Lawrence's apparently indifferent attitude to his wife is really prompted by a fear of inadequacy, a deep, uneasy sense of possible rejection. How else explain the extraordinarily odd moment when Lawrence attempts to tell his brother, Mark, about Phyllis's departure?

'But I always thought you and Phyllis got on awfully well together!' cried Mark, naïvely.

'Did you?' snarled Lawrence, in a tone so dry, sarcastic and acrid that not another word was needed to indicate to Mark the disaster that his brother's married life must have been.

'I certainly thought so,' he repeated weakly.

'My wife has been nothing to me for four years,' Lawrence proceeded. 'She hates me. I believe that woman positively hates me, and I—'

'But she's so —'

'My dear fellow, you know nothing about women.'

Mark smiled sheepishly. (But his soul said: 'Oh, don't I?') (chapter 1)

I take it that Lawrence is not meant to be particularly sympathetic here. I also take it that we are meant to realize that he doesn't know about women. But are we meant to notice what is surely a pretty odd slip? 'My wife has been nothing to me for four years. She hates me.' Oughtn't he to have said 'I have been nothing to my wife . . . she hates me'? As it stands, his remark is decidedly peculiar. On the one hand he's saying that he feels nothing for his wife, doesn't care about her. On the other, he is revealing that he *does* care: 'She hates me.' It is the cry of a grievously hurt man insisting that he can't be hurt. And it takes us to the heart of the deep question that, whether Bennett knew it or not, underlies his treatment of Lawrence: is this man fit for marriage?

To such a question the answer would seem to be, no. But it is clearly so painful an answer to have to return upon yourself (for that is what it amounts to in Bennett's case, so I think) that he occasionally puts it aside by suggesting it is all Phyllis's fault – 'she hates me' – and then undermines that suggestion by ironies of tone that themselves contradict or throw doubt on what is being said:

> He knew now exactly how to treat Phyllis, and how to avoid future quarrels. The secret lay in one's tone, he said. Phyllis was decidedly an inferior creature (though often delightful) and she must be treated as such. Useless to appeal to her reason, to her sense of justice! Useless even to appeal to her good-nature! She was not good-natured – this was the dreadful pill he had to swallow. She must be humoured. Yes, he now thoroughly understood women. (chapter 2)

The irony there is obvious enough. But its force is dissipated because we are never allowed to see Lawrence's attitudes to his wife being put to the test and because one has the nagging suspicion that Bennett half agrees with Lawrence (as clubman he is capable of saying much the same sort of thing). It is almost as though Bennett uses an ironic tone to guard against taking Lawrence seriously and yet also shows him to be deserving of serious attention. For isn't the scene with Mrs Fearns meant to suggest that he *does* thoroughly understand women? Well, no. And yet. . . . And so we come back to the unanswerable questions, irresolvable ambiguities.

Only after the death of her lover do we see Phyllis and Lawrence together, in a brilliant little scene which exactly catches the feeling of those mutual misunderstandings and suspicions that lacerate them both. Lawrence goes to visit her:

> 'I was very sorry,' he began. But he did not know what he had meant to say. As a fact, he had never defined his intention.
>
> Mrs Capewell's winking eyes dropped tears behind her gold-rimmed spectacles. 'I'd better leave you,' the old lady muttered, rising.
>
> 'Stay where you are, mother. Do, please!' Phyllis commanded her sharply. 'What do you want, Lawrence? What have you come for?' Her voice was frigid, scornful, acrimonious; a voice he knew well, out of several voices she possessed. He cursed himself.

'I read about the death,' he recommenced, crestfallen, striving to conceal his anger.

'Do you think I want your sympathy?' Phyllis asked, and her tones were clear and terrible against the background of her mother's smothered sobbing. 'Do you think I want your sympathy, now? You've slandered me. And you've slandered Emery Greatbatch. And now he's dead you think you'll get me back, do you? What if it was you that really killed him? . . . I don't want your sympathy.'

'Then there's nothing more to be said,' he replied with forced bravado. He was blushing. (chapter 8)

It is a powerful moment, but it comes too late. It doesn't really help us to know Phyllis – or rather, it cannot make up for the earlier shadowiness of her presence. The only previous glimpse we have had of her is when she tends her dying lover: 'The whole of Phyllis's bearing was changed in his presence. Her beauty grew softer, and lost its enigmatic quality. Her mouth and eyes ceased their disturbing and challenging mockery' (chapter 7). Which is all very well, but we have never been shown Phyllis's mockery. In the scene with Emery we see only her rage of hatred against Lawrence as the divorce papers are served.

And while Emery's mind had room for a shameful sympathy with his old friend Lawrence, while Phyllis could only think of Lawrence with an almost virulent hate, the conclusion here was that this Lawrence, that distant and threatening figure, once so mild, once so ignored and flouted, would inevitably crush them in the battle that was to ensue.

Again, we have to ask why we haven't been shown something of the way in which the mild Lawrence has been ignored and flouted and to protest that elsewhere it is Lawrence who ignores Phyllis, who won't take her seriously – 'she must be humoured.' Lawrence suffers 'cruelly' from Phyllis, but only because she is 'his', a possession rather than somebody loved. It is true that we are told that 'he yielded in disputes far more often than his sense of justice could approve. But he forgot that she, the creature whom he could not treat as an equal, had not his interior resources, and it did not occur to him that she was not temperamentally cold. He never so much as suspected that he had innocently ruined her life' (chapter 2). Innocently? Once again, the question can't be answered be-

cause we are shown too little of Phyllis's temperament to know
whether Lawrence can be excused for his treatment of her.

Is this man fit for marriage? The answer now seems to be yes
but he's made the wrong marriage. At the end of the novel we are
told that Lawrence is not altogether unhappy: 'He had probed life.
He had attained calm', and he is 'intellectually and morally free'.
He realizes that he is drawn to Charles Fearns's daughter, Annunciata, and wonders whether he should try to marry her:

> But the notion vanished whence it came, even as he gazed at her
> placid features. Why trouble her career, why trouble what was left of
> his, letting loose again that force, terrific and ravaging, which through
> the agency of others had already embittered and poisoned their
> existence? Why awaken desire, which destroys calm – the most
> precious thing on earth, as it seemed to him. Why not be content with
> the fact that Annunciata lived, a beautiful activity on which all that
> was most pure in his soul might dwell.
>
> He was sick of love. And she, he reflected, might have the good
> fortune never to know it. And so he allowed the notion of wooing her
> to vanish whence it came. And for him and for her it was best.
> (chapter 12)

It is difficult not to seem heavy-handed in challenging these sentences, with their irritatingly vague appeals to life and love, and their
ready acceptance of Lawrence's point of view. There is no critical
or distanced view of him in this passage – 'he had probed life' –
nor is there any saving irony about it. If we ask why this should be
so the answer must surely be that Bennett is really talking about
himself, or at least using Lawrence as a way of ruminating about
his own recent disastrous love affair. To say this is in no way to
justify the novel's ending, but it does explain why the study of
Lawrence and Phyllis should be so off balance; and I think that a
certain amount of tactful forbearance is in order when we come to
criticize it. Then why, it may be asked, should I spend so much time
on it? Because, I suppose, flawed though it undoubtedly is, there
is still much to admire in Bennett's presentation of Lawrence and
belatedly, Phyllis.

Besides, one part of it comes off triumphantly. Bennett handles
the actual divorce proceedings in masterful fashion. He is good
on Lawrence's agonized reading of Dixon's *Law and Practice in*

Divorce and the Matrimonial Causes: 'It was Chinese in its laconic impassive indifference to the possibilities of emotion . . . On every page were terse sentences that ripped the tissue of the heart' (chapter 2). And he is superb on the divorce court itself. Chapter 9, 'Matrimonial Division', displays most of Bennett's considerable virtues: attentively accurate dialogue, the exact feel for a place, relentless control of the pace at which the proceedings unfold. And how good he is at catching the squalor and hypocrisy that are inevitably part of the court, and its cold and brutal nastinesses.

> 'Now, Mrs Ridware,' [Lawrence's Counsel] piped. 'Do you mean to state seriously that you have never given your husband just cause for suspicion? Is it not a curious thing that these visits to the late Emery Greatbatch, which you wish us to believe were perfectly innocent, took place exactly at the time when your husband was away in London?'
> She made no reply.
> Lawrence leaned forward and pulled Wray's arm. 'She said I left her alone in the house,' he whispered fiercely. 'The fact is she was asked to go to London and refused. My brother here can prove that. Get that out of her.'
> Wray nodded, with a touch of impatience, and then put the question to Phyllis.
> 'Yes,' Phyllis said cautiously. 'He did leave me alone in the house. It was true that I was asked to go to London with him, but I did not feel well enough. I begged him not to go, but he went.'
> 'What an awful lie!' Lawrence muttered. 'She wasn't well enough to go to London, and yet she could walk ten miles home from Manifold.'
> 'As to cause for suspicion,' Phyllis went on, not in response to a further question, 'in the relations between the sexes my husband was always extremely suspicious. You see, he himself is an illegitimate child.' She spoke deliberately, in her low, clear voice, playing the while with the glove that hung on the rail. And she faintly smiled.

Admittedly, this cruel and lacerating moment would cut even deeper if we had seen more of the Ridware marriage. But as it stands, 'Matrimonial Division' is impressive testimony to Bennett's powers as a realist, his uncanny feel for the way things are.

Yet the sucess of this chapter cannot possibly justify my claim that *Whom God Hath Joined* is in some ways as good as *Anna of the*

Five Towns. The real achievement of the novel lies in the study of the Fearns marriage. There are shaky moments. Overblown descriptions of the daughter and occasional near-hysterical denunciations of the adulterous husband, for which Bennett's own situation can perhaps be held to blame. Such moments stand out because on the whole Bennett is so successful in getting onto paper the sheer ordinariness of the marriage. He fashions art out of the mundane. And it is a fashioning. The story glints with ironies. Charles Fearns resolves not to meddle with the governess. In a moment of weakness – vanity, lust – he pats her cheek and his action is seen by his daughter, the one person he loves. Later, he takes the governess into his bed – Mrs Fearns is away for the night – and then decides she must go before his wife returns. But Annunciata, who knows what has happened, has already wired for her mother. The governess is dismissed, Fearns's wife leaves him, he is sued for divorce. In the end the action fails because Mrs Fearns won't let Annunciata suffer the ordeal of giving evidence in public. Married life is resumed.

From the first, that married life is seen as utterly conventional in its placid, low-keyed, apparent happiness. Like John Stanway, Fearns is a domestic tyrant: unthinking and complacent:

> For more than twenty years he had been the petted and pampered god of the household. His wife or his daughter, or both, were continually thinking of his convenience and satisfaction. Never did he eat alone. 'Some one must be in to keep father company.' It was all father, father. They lived for him. As the state of the tide is always at the back of a mariner's mind, so were his moods at the back of their minds. (chapter 6)

But Bennett also makes plain the fact that Fearns has vitality and charm. He is attractive to men and women; and he has a real sensuality about him. Fearns is not a wicked man, he is merely an average, easygoing, morally insensitive person. He is not unlike Henry Wilcox of *Howards End*, for example. But Fearns is a more convincing creation because Bennett is much better than Forster at knowing about the furtive kind of sexual encounters that both men go in for. The adulterous liaison between Wilcox and Jackie Bast is, when all is said and done, pretty absurd: part of the novel's pattern ('only connect') yet otherwise incredible. But Fearns's seduction of Renée is altogether credible because Fearns himself is so fully realized. The seduction is, however, nearly incredible to his daughter, who inevitably has a much simpler view of him than we have, and for whom Fearns now changes from hero to villain. And here it should be said that Bennett's handling of events is that of a very good novelist indeed. We watch while the four people involved take up simple attitudes to each other which we cannot share. We know too much about them.

For Annunciata, Fearns's seduction of Renée makes him an altogether foul man. The pages which describe her lying awake at night, pondering the significance of her father's patting the governess's cheek, hearing him return from his club, come upstairs, then the later sounds which make her tiptoe into Renée's room and find the bed empty – these are masterly. Bennett is astonishingly tactful in his presentation of Annunciata. Forgive a few silly moments, and she is brought touchingly alive, never more so than in her hazy, confused, priggish and yet decently bewildered sorrow for her mother, shocked hatred for her father, care for her younger brothers. I do not know of any other English novelist who could have imagined the scene where she takes the young twins out for a walk on the morning after her terrible discovery:

> At half-past ten she returned home with her brothers. The boys were tired, tired of swans, of little brown swans, of flowers, of gravel pies, and even of chocolate from the slot-machines in the park shelters. And Annunciata was exhausted utterly. She had tasted nothing but bits of chocolate, which had nauseated her in the hot morning sun. The scullery maid was cleaning the front steps. It was quite wrong that the scullery maid should have been cleaning the front steps at such an hour . . . (chapter 4)

Who else but Bennett would have told you that the time was half past ten? Yet it matters, because it suggests a disordering of the household. And *that* matters because it means a shattering of Annunciata's universe of agreed and responsible domesticity. So her mind has an almost hysterical edge to it when she discovers the scullery maid cleaning the steps at the wrong hour. It is part of the crumbling of her world which is also implicit in her having to eat bits of chocolate (she can't face her father at breakfast, the meal she has always before shared with him).

What Annunciata doesn't know is that Fearns had struggled against involving himself with Renée. But we know. It prohibits the rehearsed response. Yet Fearns himself is guilty of such a response. Shame follows the seduction, and panic follows shame. He leaves home early and Renée phones him at his office. He agrees to see her and she shows him a note Annunciata has written her, telling her to leave the house. Hiding under a canal bridge, Fearns and Renée talk, and we discover that Renée cares for Fearns. She is not the calculating whore that Mrs Fearns and Annunciata think her. She agrees, however, to go away. She will make no trouble, doesn't even want money from Fearns. He begins to brighten:

> he must enlist his wife's aid against Annunciata; that was the plan. Alma was extremely clever, and had tremendous influence over her daughter. Alma was also an angel, capable of forgiveness to an indefinite extent. He would appeal to her; he could not appeal in vain, for the future of the children was at stake. He would confess to Alma, and then persuade her of the necessity of convincing Annunciata that, whatever the girl had seen or had not seen, her conclusions were wrong. The matter would require the nicest delicacy, coupled with firmness, but Alma would succeed. Of course his relations with his wife, while remaining normal on the surface, would for a long time be secretly painful. But he could win her back. He was sure that he could prove to her that at last he had learnt his lesson. (chapter 6)

But unfortunately for Fearns Annunciata has already wired her mother; and the two women are to combine against him. He thinks his wife will not return for another day and plans to go to Liverpool for the night on the pretext of business but really so that he won't have to face Annunciata. He outlines his plan to Renée. They kiss farewell. '"Goodbye, little girl," he said, and his voice broke.' Sentimentality mixed with relief. Then, waiting for his train, he sees his wife get out of another one. He hides. Annunciata must have telegraphed. 'He was powerless. He was conscious of an abject fear of his wife. He knew that he could not meet her eyes.'

And then comes one of the most authentically imaginative moments in all of Bennett's fiction. Still in hiding, he feels a touch on his shoulder. He turns. It is Renée.

He was trapped and helpless. At once it seemed to him that if she had not sprung herself upon him, he would, after all, have had the courage to go to his wife. And now Renée was audacious enough to seize his coat. She was bent on his ruin; he could see that, and he anathematized her with the savage sincerity of desperation. . . . Dividing his frightened glances between the platform and the woman, he gasped:

'What do you want?'

'I missed the train,' she stammered, boldly clutching at the lapels of his coat. And then, abandoning herself to emotion, she cried aloud. 'No, no! I did not miss it. I could not leave you, *chéri*! Forgive me! I could not leave you. I have waited for you.' And she sobbed as freely as if they had been locked up in some secret chamber, secure from any possible interruptions.

He was furious with anger at her deceit, at the calculated comedy she had played under the canal bridge. He was sure it was comedy she had played. And this too, though real tears rolled from her eyes – this too, was a comedy. She did not mean to lose him. She had got him, and no scruples would prevent her from keeping him.

He decides that she is trying to blackmail him, and tells her that it won't work:

'I may be ruined, but I'm not an absolute mug. Do you hear?'

'Yes,' she answered, stifling her sobs.

'That's good. Did you get your ticket for London?'

'No, I had no money.'

'Then why in God's name did you tell me you had money?' he demanded with uncontrolled passion.

She shrank away. 'I was too proud,' she said.

'That be damned! That be damned!' he shouted. He did not care who heard him.

He thrusts money at her, buys her a second class ticket to Euston (typical of Bennett to let us know it was second class) and eventually he is rid of her. It is simply terrific, this revelation of Renée's emotional involvement with Fearns, his utter refusal to see it or credit it, and his desperate, mean, selfish and entirely credible wish to have seen the last of her. Chapter 6 of *Whom God Hath Joined* is a very remarkable piece of writing, scrupulous and intensely dramatic in its unfolding of ironies, convincing and

imaginatively sympathetic in its study of the man and women who
are at its centre.

What follows is, of course, the crash. Fearns's wife leaves, and he
decides that he must get her back, even though divorce proceedings
are under way. He goes down to Sandgate, where she and the children are staying, determined to make her change her mind, convinced of his power over her and of the rightness of his reading of
her character. And so the fourth member of the quartet is now seen
in some depth, and again simple judgements on her turn out to be
inadequate, even absurd. She is not an angel, capable of forgiveness
to an indefinite extent. Chapter 10, in which Alma Fearns proves to
be a strange, new and unknown person to her husband, is further
evidence of Bennett's sure and imaginative grasp of irony; and the
dialogue between husband and wife is as good as anything he has
as yet attempted. Because it stretches over several pages one can't
quote from it and hope to do it justice, but perhaps the following
gives some impression of its rightness. Bennett doesn't miss a
trick. Fearns tells himself that Alma is still his wife, 'the same woman who had lived in subjection to him for twenty years'. Accordingly:

> 'There's something I must say to you,' he muttered awkwardly. Cer-
> tainly the situation was infinitely more delicate than he had antici-
> pated. He simply could not use the phrase which his brain had formed
> in advance.
> 'What?'
> 'Look here, Alma, this action must stop. It really must. You are
> bound to regret it afterwards.'
> 'I don't think so.'
> 'But surely anything is better than the scandal?' he argued.
> 'No,' she said. 'I don't think anything *is* better than the scandal.
> That's just the point that I really have settled in my own mind.'

Alma Fearns is a conventional woman, behaving conventionally
over her husband's discovered sexual peccadillo. But she's also
tough-minded and determined on independence, suddenly aware
that she doesn't after all need Fearns, doesn't need to act out her
role of subjection; doesn't like it, doesn't want it. It is this discovery
of hers which her conventional and complacent husband cannot
grasp. He tries another tack.

'You know I think the world of you. Don't you?'

'Yes,' she admitted, 'I believe you do.'

He was pleased. He had scored a little advantage. And he continued with a slight access of confidence:

'And then there are the children. I'm just as attached to them as you are, every bit. I never get as much pleasure as I get in my own home.'

'Evidently!' she ejaculated. And he detected in her voice a note of callous bitterness – that was startlingly new in his experience of her. He had said something stupid, something that left him open to an obvious and extremely cruel retort. And she had not hesitated to fling the dart. He was wounded. . . . She was destroying his ideal of her.

The indirect account of Fearns's feelings there perfectly brings out his self-pity, hurt complacency, male vulgarity. 'She was destroying his ideal of her.' One is reminded of Cecil Vyse's regretful discovery when Lucy Honeychurch loses her temper with him that 'she had failed to be artistic'.

Fearns tries again. '"But to see Annunciata in the witness box will simply kill me." "Yes," said Alma coldly, but always gently. "It's yourself you're thinking of."' And then she tells him why she wants a divorce. She can't trust him, and she means by that not merely that he'll always be running after other women but that, given his complacency, lack of interest in her as a person rather than as some sort of ideal, there is no chance for an honest relationship between them: '"You say that anything will be better than the scandal. I say that anything will be better than not being absolutely free of a man like you. No! You must not try to mind me talking in this way. You came to me, and I'm bound to tell you."' But Alma Fearns isn't a Nora Helmer. She is still bound by her conventionalities: '"All the humiliation is mine. Oh! Charles I don't believe you will ever guess what the humiliation was!"' This isn't a flaw. Alma's conventionality is inevitable, is how she is expected to be, is what she has been educated for. But she is striving to break free of her bonds: '"And here you come and ask me to forgive you! Well, I do forgive you. But I must have my freedom. I will have it. It's my right. No woman ever suffered more than I've suffered. I'm the mother of your children, but I'm just a woman too."' There is nothing of set speech about this, except in so far as Alma has clearly to nerve herself to say the words ('I'm bound to tell you'). She isn't suddenly and dramatically making the case for wronged women. There is no suggestion of a door slammed shut. The moment of excusable self-pity sees to that – 'No woman suffered more than I've suffered.' But Alma is certainly made intensely alive in a way that is hopelessly baffling to her husband.

Why, then, does she finally go back to him? Partly because she finds that she cannot after all escape her own conventionality. But, more important, when she is faced with Annunciata's distress in the witness box she decides that the price of freedom is too high. This neither affects her credibility nor demeans her. It is utterly convincing. The irony of her capitulation doesn't mark an important defeat for her, it rather shows her acceptance of responsibility to Annunciata, her kindly and commonsensical refusal to sacrifice other people to her freedom – as her husband would unthinkingly have done (and did indeed do, when he bundled Renée onto a London train).

In this quiet, sober-toned study of a conventional marriage in crisis, Bennett achieves a triumph that has no equal of its kind in Edwardian fiction, and not many outside it.

Chapter 3

'Absolute Realism'

I

In 1907 Bennett published *The Grim Smile of the Five Towns*. It
was his second collection of short stories, and a considerable improvement on *Tales of the Five Towns*, which had appeared in 1905.
Tales of the Five Towns is filled with bread-and-butter stories,
teased-out anecdotes of little worth. The title is misleading, for not
all the tales are of the Five Towns. But whether Bennett is writing
about Hanbridge and Bursley or London and Vienna there is the
same lacklustre slightness. It is not that the tales are incompetent
or botched. There is simply nothing to them. They read like space-
fillers. And one can see why. The period 1900–14 was the heyday
of weekly and monthly magazines specializing in the short story.
Bennett was a professional writer who could be relied on to meet
editorial deadlines and to produce any number of words to order.
No wonder, then, that he should write short stories. But it isn't his
natural medium. Nearly all his stories rely far too heavily on anecdote, and while his worst faults glare out heavily from them his
special virtues have very little chance to show themselves. Bennett
needs elbow room to be at his best. The short story rarely allows
him that. Even the most successful story in the first volume – 'His
Worship the Goosedriver' – is little more than an extended anecdote and is marred by a ponderous jokiness and thinness of detail.

We don't really know anything much about the characters, and this weakness is even more marked in the other tales. Anyone reading through *Tales of the Five Towns* would be perfectly justified in concluding that as a short-story writer Bennett had very little talent.

But *The Grim Smile of the Five Towns* is a different matter. The same faults recur, and in abundance. The flat-footed humour of 'The Nineteenth Hat' (apparently built out of an incident involving Eleanor Green), and of 'Vera's First Christmas Adventure'; the trivial anecdotage which is all that 'The Lion's Share' and 'Baby's Bath' amount to; the unsatisfactory, external view of 'The Silent Brothers'. There are compensations, however. In the first place this collection feels much more authentically about the Five Towns than the first one had. There are deft touches of comic observation, as where the hero of 'Beginning the New Year' 'climbed into a second-class compartment when the train drew up, and ten other people, all with third-class tickets, followed his example'. There is the perception on which 'From One Generation to Another' depends, that in the Five Towns 'families spring into splendour out of nothing in the course of a couple of generations, and as often as not sink back again into nothing in the course of two generations more' (a perception that has much bearing on *The Old Wives' Tale* and the *Clayhanger* trilogy). There is also the grim smile itself. Bennett's Five Townspeople are vividly evoked in that phrase. Laconic, tough, rueful, gritty, quick to seize the main chance, generous without grace, towards which, indeed, they profess indifference or scorn, and proud in a way that blends in shifting proportions the boorish and the decent. The collection as a whole is shot through with the kind of observation and incident which justifies Bennett's title. And there is one story, substantially longer than the rest, where the grim smile is seen at its fullest and in which Bennett fashions a masterpiece.

John Wain has called 'The Death of Simon Fuge' the most delicate product of Bennett's art, and I would not want to disagree with that judgement (*Arnold Bennett*, Columbia Modern Writers, 1967). Indeed, what he has to say about the story rings so true that there is not a great deal that can be added to his account. But let me give the tale in outline. It is told us by Loring, a southerner and

aesthete, whose professional work – he is an expert on ceramics –
brings him to the Five Towns. On the train journey down he reads
of the death of Simon Fuge. Fuge had been a painter of some
genius. He had also been born in the Five Towns, though he had
long ago left them for a cosmopolitan existence. Loring recalls a
tale Fuge had once told of a night he had spent boating on a lake
with two beautiful Five Towns girls. Will he be able to discover
more about this romantic episode? The question is much in his
mind when he gets out of his train to be met by his host, Brindley.
So is the shock of his first encounter with the Five Towns:

> as I stood on that dirty platform, in a *milieu* of advertisements of soap,
> boots and aperients, I began to believe that Simon Fuge never had
> lived, that he was a mere illusion of his friends and his small public.
> All that I saw around me was a violent negation of Simon Fuge, that
> entity of rare, fine, exotic sensibilities, that perfectly mad gourmet of
> sensations, that exotic seer of beauty.

Loring's way of putting things mustn't be thought to cast doubt on
his opinion of Simon Fuge. It does, however, clearly indicate why
he is so shaken by his first view of the Five Towns and of his host
who 'although an architect by profession . . . appeared anxious to
be mistaken for a sporting squire'.

Much of 'The Death of Simon Fuge' is about Loring's gradual
realization that for all the outward appearance of meanness and
dirt, the Five Towns are not the haunts of barbarians. Installed at
Brindley's house, he discovers that his host is a discriminating
book collector. Brindley's friend Colclough drops in and the two
men play Richard Strauss and Mozart. Throughout the evening
there is a constant whirl of activity and drinking, and it ends with a
visit to the house of a doctor friend of Brindley's, who turns out to
have an even finer collection of books than Brindley's own. Loring
passes from hostility through bewilderment to a reluctant admiration for Five Towns life and the sheer happiness of the people with
whom he comes in contact. And Bennett, of course, manages quite
effortlessly to give us the feel of this life. He packs so much in, and
so casually. The bleak, dirty station, muddy, greasy streets and
cobbled ways, Brindley's house with its ingenious heating arrangements and large, comfortable rooms, supper accompanied by

bottles of ale, electric trams like large boxes of light on wheels, the warm, male-dominated pubs: all these are seen through Loring's innocent and wondering eyes, so that the details spring before us, fresh and alive.

But what of Fuge? And what of his tale of the night on the lake? Gradually Loring discovers that Fuge's version of the story bears little relation to the facts. He also discovers that nobody has anything much to say about the dead artist. It is not that they dislike him, merely that they have dismissed him as he dismissed them when he left them for the larger worlds of London and Paris. In the Bursley Museum Loring sees a small painting by Fuge. He knows it to be a work of genius:

> It *was* Simon Fuge, at any rate all of Simon Fuge that was worth having, masterful, imperishable. And not merely was it his challenge, it was his scorn, his aristocratic disdain, his positive assurance that in the battle between them he had annihilated the Five Towns. It hung there in the very midst thereof, calmly and contemptuously waiting for the acknowledgement of his victory.

Loring asks Brindley if the painting isn't by Fuge.

> 'Which?' said Mr Brindley.
> 'That one.'
> 'Yes, I fancy it is,' he negligently agreed. 'Yes, it is.'
> 'It's not signed,' I remarked.
> 'It ought to be,' said Mr Brindley; then laughed. 'Too late now!'
> 'How did it get here?'
> 'Don't know. Oh! I think Mr Perkins won it in a raffle at a bazaar, and then hung it here.'

The local papers are every bit as indifferent to Fuge's death as Brindley has proved to be. It may make headlines in the national press, but the *Staffordshire Signal* devotes its headlines to the fact that Knype F.C. have signed a new centre-forward. Brindley defends the *Signal*: ' "You don't understand these things. If Knype Football Club was put into the League Second Division, ten thousand homes would go into mourning. Who the devil was Simon Fuge?" ' That question hangs over the entire story. For Loring, Fuge was an artist of genius. But for Brindley and his friends Fuge was a boaster, a loudmouth and a deserter. Besides, he hasn't any relevance to their lives, he isn't materially important. We have to take this last point seriously or we will soften and sentimentalize the story. Through Loring's eyes we are allowed to see that Brindley and his circle are cultivated and sensitive people. But there are inevitable limits to their sensitivity, limits placed on them by the Five Towns, by their grim smile of acceptance of a life which is a compromise between contradictory elements. Brindley accepts the Five Towns. He is proud of his own moneymaking abilities. He is tough, abrasive, hard-headed. He likes books and is genuinely and passionately devoted to music. But if it came to a choice between them or the Five Towns – well, who the devil was Simon Fuge? Brindley is lucky, of course, for there is no need for him to choose. He can enjoy both Bursley and books. But the limitations in his own way of life are implicit in the very fact that Fuge left. Bennett does not criticize Brindley. There is no shadow of disapproval in the way he shows him to us, and the use of Loring is crucial here, because if anyone were to disapprove of Brindley it would be him, and he finds that he cannot.

And yet – who the devil was Simon Fuge? The plain answer is – an artist who left for the good of his art. Inevitably one feels that the question came from somewhere deep inside Bennett. 'The Death of Simon Fuge' holds the Five Towns in perfect equivocal poise. But we know that Bennett, like Fuge, chose to leave. He is their critic and their champion. He knows what is good about the place, but its grim smile is not for him. Except, that is, as an artist who can draw on it for his art. And when he next writes about the Five Towns his view of it will be darker, gloomier than in his fine story. It will also produce his greatest novel.

II

But before I speak of *The Old Wives' Tale*, I need to say a little about *Buried Alive*. At first called *The Case of Leek*, this novel occupied Bennett during January and February of 1908. It was published in June and by July he was noting in his *Journal* that the reviews 'have been simply excellent'. Yet *Buried Alive* is not very good. In fact it is no more than a faintly humorous anecdote spun out to novel length. A famous English painter with the very un-

English name of Priam Farll arrives back in London from foreign parts, unannounced and unaccompanied except by his valet, Leek. Leek dies suddenly and the doctor attending takes him for Farll and Farll for his own valet. The artist sees in this confusion a chance to escape into welcome anonymity. He marries a working class woman, Alice Challice, lives in Putney, and for a while gives up painting. But he begins again and subsequently finds himself called upon to prove his identity in court (the reason for this being that an art-dealer recognizes his new work as that of Priam Farll, buys and sells it as such, and is then accused of false dealing since Farll is officially dead, has indeed been given a burial in Westminster Abbey).

As a short story *Buried Alive* would do well enough. Stretched out to novel length it becomes tedious, at least until the court scenes, when it picks up considerably. There is also an odd wavering of tone throughout the novel which suggests that Bennett wasn't sure just how seriously he should take his own idea. For Priam Farll to be buried alive in Putney is, I think, a reasonably knowing joke (Bennett was, after all, aware of Swinburne's semi-incarceration); and the notion of a famous artist marrying a working class woman might seem to be a spoof on the habit, which had started up in the 1890s, of the artist seeking love and life in the music hall and pub. Even the name, Alice Challice, hints at this, just as it reminds us of the Edwardian fondness for using religious imagery in a secular context, in order to insist on the 'holiness of the heart's affections' (I use the phrase which Forster borrowed from Keats and used so fervently in *A Room With a View*). Bennett wants us to see Alice as comic in herself and doubly comic because Priam thinks of her as perfection: 'She had a large mind: that was sure. She understood – things, and human nature in particular. . . . She was balm to Priam Farll. She might have been equally balm to King David, Uriah the Hittite, Socrates, Rousseau, Lord Byron, Heine or Charlie Peace' (chapter 5). I don't find that particularly funny, but I think it is a bit distasteful. Oddly so, for Bennett would never adopt such a dismissively jocular tone for any character in a Five Towns novel. But it is a fact that his London novels are often marred by this leaden facetiousness. *Buried Alive* certainly is, though not consistently so. For Bennett also wants us to take Alice seriously. We are told that she gives Priam new joy in life. Because of his marriage 'all life gave him joy; all life was beautiful to him'. As for Alice: 'She lived. She did nothing but live. She lived every hour. Priam felt truly that he had at last got down to the bed-rock of life' (chapter 6). But for this to be anything like convincing we would need to see a good deal more of Alice than Bennett is prepared to show us. Instead, he reports – and very cursorily at that.

Indeed, with the honourable exception of the court scenes, *Buried Alive* is nearly all report. As such, it becomes tiresome. We know nothing about Alice, and we know precious little about Farll. He is typical of what happens to a Bennett hero when the author isn't greatly interested in his own subject. Priam Farll is merely sketched in, and so are all the other characters. We see them in hazy outline, and such a view is woefully incomplete. It is also irritating, because both Farll and Alice are little more than clichés. Compared with *The Horse's Mouth*, a novel which flirts with clichés about the unworldly artist and 'life', but which blasts through them to something altogether more convincing, *Buried Alive* is poor stuff.

The question arises, why did Bennett write it? Partly, of course, because he was Bennett, the professional craftsman, able to turn his hand to any kind of tale. And without doubt *Buried Alive* is neatly told. The very unlikely plot hasn't any loopholes in it and as a whole the novel is mechanically competent. The best one can say for it is that it is a distinct improvement on those early entertainments to which it looks a likely successor, though Bennett never classified it as one. But that is to say very little.

It is, however, important to realize that *Buried Alive* was an act of interruption. It was written while Bennett was on holiday, one might say, from the exhausting labour of *The Old Wives' Tale*. We know how long the plan for his great novel had been maturing in his mind; and it is obvious that the strain of actually writing it, of finally and irrevocably putting into print the fiction on which he was prepared to stake so much, must have been very great. Not that Bennett is prepared to give a great deal away, either in his *Journals* or in letters of the time. But the *Journals* supply hints enough:

Friday, May 29th:

I worked well at *Old Wives' Tale* yesterday, but indifferently today.

Tuesday, June 2nd:

Gradually got involved in one of my periodic crises of work, from which I emerged last night, having written the first chapter of Part III of *Old Wives' Tale.* . . .

Sunday, July 19th:

I don't know when I wrote the last entry.

I finished the third part of the *Old Wives' Tale* on Tuesday last. Everything else gave way before it, and I simply did nothing but that book. It meant the utter defeat of all other plans.

Writing *Buried Alive* during the opening months of 1908 must have been a welcome rest. It is true that very few people would consider that the writing of a novel, however slight, is the most satisfactory way of taking a rest. But then Bennett wasn't ordinary. If he had been we should not now be in possession of *The Old Wives' Tale*.

III

But why should *The Old Wives' Tale* have meant so much to him? Perhaps there is no way we can confidently answer that question. Yet I think it reasonable to suggest that Bennett saw the novel as a vital test of his worth as an artist. He would stand or fall by its success or failure. Reading between the lines of the *Journals* and letters, one has the strong impression that despite his show of calm certainty in himself and his career, Bennett was liable to the doubts and uncertainties that trouble all creative men. There is something close to self-parody in his presentation of himself as Artist: book collector, bon vivant, adopted Parisian, opera-goer, dandy, lover: it is as though he takes on various roles in order to convince himself, or others, or himself through others, that he is, after all, the genuine article. Speculation? Yes, indeed. But inevitably one speculates about the painfully shy, sensitive man with the protective carapace of tough stoicism and invulnerability – 'I began to try to explain to Marriott the philosophy of the Stoics, the inferiority of ambition as a motive and of glory as an end, etc. But I doubt if he understood what I meant by the control of the mind and

its consequences.' (*Journals*, August 1907.) I do not blame Marriott
for his incomprehension. How could anyone who knew Bennett at
all well really believe in him as a convincing disciple of Epictetus?
Apart from anything else, Bennett was an ambitious man. All
through the planning of *The Old Wives' Tale* he kept vividly in mind
'the example and challenge of Guy de Maupassant's *Une Vie.* . . .
Une Vie relates the entire life history of a woman. I settled in the
privacy of my own head that my book about the development of a
young girl into a stout old lady must be the English *Une Vie*'
(preface to *The Old Wives' Tale*). One is reminded of another, later
novelist who was determined to take on the best: 'I started out very
quiet and I beat Mr Turgenev. Then I trained hard and I beat Mr
de Maupassant. I've fought two draws with Mr Stendhal, and I
think I had an edge in the last one.' But where Hemingway is
boastful and absurd, Bennett is merely truthful. He *did* want to
write the English *Une Vie*. Yet if he had settled for beating 'Mr de
Maupassant', *The Old Wives' Tale* wouldn't be the fine novel that
it is. Its flaws do perhaps come from the French writer, or from
something that was deep in Bennett himself and which attracted
him to de Maupassant. But the novel's strengths are uniquely
Bennett's. And they prove him to be a rare and genuine artist. At
his truest, Bennett is not to be compared with de Maupassant but
with another writer whom he much admired, and who largely
replaced de Maupassant in his affections:

> As you read him you fancy that he must always have been saying to
> himself: 'Life is good enough for me. I won't alter it. I will set it
> down as it is.' Such is the tribute to his success which he forces from
> you.
>
> He seems to have achieved absolute realism. . . . His climaxes are
> never strained; nothing is ever idealised, sentimentalised, etherialised;
> no part of the truth is left out, no part is exaggerated. There is no
> cleverness, no startling feat of virtuosity. All appears simple, candid,
> almost childlike. (*Books and Persons*)

Bennett on Chekhov. The words might be applied to *The Old
Wives' Tale*. Almost. One has to add the qualification because the
shade of de Maupassant undoubtedly hangs over the novel; its
dark influence shows itself in the pessimism which Bennett
felt himself to share with the Frenchman – though in de Mau-

passant's case it is closer to cynicism – and which occasionally distorts the 'absolute realism' at which *The Old Wives' Tale* aims.

It is a point to come back to. For the moment I need to sketch in the development of the novel, from the moment when the first idea for it lodged in Bennett's mind to its final flowering. We first hear of it in a *Journal* entry, for 18 November 1903. Bennett has gone to dine at his usual restaurant, and discovers that the seat opposite to his has been taken by a 'middle-aged woman, inordinately stout and with pendant cheeks'. The fat woman is annoyed that Bennett should sit opposite her, moves all her belongings to another seat, then to another and yet another, until everyone in the restaurant is secretly laughing at her odd behaviour.

> The fat woman was clearly a crotchet, a *maniaque*, a woman who lived much alone. Her cloak (she displayed on taking it off a simply awful light puce flannel dress) and her parcels were continually the object of her attention and she was always arguing with her waitress. And the whole restaurant secretly made a butt of her. She was repulsive; no one could like her or sympathise with her. But I thought – she has been young and slim once. And I immediately thought of a long 10 or 15 thousand words short story, *The History of Two Old Women*. I gave this woman a sister fat as herself. And the first chapter would be in the restaurant (both sisters) something like tonight – and written rather cruelly. Then I would go back to the infancy of these two, and sketch it all. One should have lived ordinarily, married prosaically, and become a widow. The other should have become a whore and all that; 'guilty splendour.' Both are overtaken by fat. And they live together again in old age, not too rich, a nuisance to themselves and to others. Neither has any imagination.

And there, in the outline of a short story, is the beginning of the 200,000 word novel. It might well be the outline for a story by de Maupassant. 'She was repulsive; no one could like her or sympathise with her.' The sisters are to be 'a nuisance to themselves and to others'. Something of this remains in the novel; something, too, of the 'sketch' of their lives, from infancy to grave. But is that all? According to E. M. Forster, yes:

> Our daily life in time is exactly this business of getting old which clogs the arteries of Sophia and Constance, and the story that is a story and sounded so healthy and stood no nonsense cannot sincerely lead to

any conclusion but the grave. It is an unsatisfactory conclusion. Of course we grow old. But a great book must rest on something more than an 'of course,' and *The Old Wives' Tale* is strong, sincere, sad, it misses greatness. (*Aspects of the Novel*)

But *The Old Wives' Tale* does rest on something more than an 'of course' (whereas the proposed *History of Two Old Women* certainly doesn't). For Bennett's novel isn't simply about Constance and Sophia; it is about a whole family, its successes and eventual failure and disappearance; and because the Baines family is in trade in Bursley, *The Old Wives' Tale* is also and inevitably about the Five Towns. In 'The Death of Simon Fuge' Brindley tells Loring that 'there's practically no such thing as class distinction here. Both my grandfathers were working potters. Colclough's father was a joiner who finished up as a builder.' Families rise, families fall. And though of course there *is* class distinction in the Five Towns it is maintained only by that ceaseless movement from success to failure, failure to success which characterizes Five Towns life.

The Old Wives' Tale opens in the 1860s and comes to a close in the 1900s. By the time it has ended the Baines family has ceased to be the principal haberdashers of St Luke's Square in Bursley, St Luke's has 'gone down' in the social scale, and Bursley itself has been replaced by Hanbridge as the economic centre of the Five Towns. This is not to say that *The Old Wives' Tale* is primarily about these matters; but they are very important to the novel, and they explain why at least some of the many deaths which the novel records can be set down so matter-of-factly, made into an 'of course'. Mr Baines dies, Mrs Baines dies, Constance's husband, Samuel Povery, dies, and Constance reflects that 'Her career seemed to be punctuated by interments. But after a while her gentle commonsense came to insist that most human beings lose their parents, and that every marriage must end in either a widower or a widow, and that all careers are punctuated by interments' (Book 2, chapter 5, i).

Deaths occur, careers continue. Time subjects those careers to different experiences. The young Samuel Povey is funny, grows into a splendidly conscientious manager-proprietor of Baines's and good husband and father, dies a bit absurdly. Cyril, his son, declines from glittering promise as an art student to contented acceptance of his mediocrity. Dick Povey, his cousin, rises from self-pitying ineptitude to become an energetic and successful businessman. And so on. The novel is threaded through with these different careers, and manages effortlessly to give the feeling of a community 'set down as it is', in a manner which 'appears simple, candid, almost childlike'.

The Old Wives' Tale is equally successful in its feeling for place. This isn't something that can be demonstrated by quotation, because although there are one or two sustained descriptions – as for example, the Baines's kitchen – the real success comes from the way in which Bennett slowly builds the solidity of the world he is writing about. The result is that, as Arnold Kettle has said, 'we come to *feel* every stairway and passage, to relish every piece of furniture in that stuffy house on the corner of the Square in Bursley' (*An Introduction to the English Novel*: vol. II). Bennett is supreme among English novelists in his ability to communicate this sense of place, of domestic interiors, streets, squares, parks, railway stations, shops, pubs, chapels, theatres. That may seem faint praise, but I intend no damnation. It is the achievement of a very considerable novelist to be able to convince one about the texture of his characters' lives. And we are interested in and sympathetically responsive to Bennett's characters because of the dense particularity with which they are socially placed.

Nor does this mean that Bennett's view of Bursley is either myopic or uncritical. In 'The Death of Simon Fuge' he had discovered a way of using a double perspective on the Five Towns; and he pushes this further in *The Old Wives' Tale* through his use of Sophia. Sophia wants to get away from Bursley. She yearns for the world beyond the Five Towns, and Bennett makes her ache of rebellion against her family and Bursley thoroughly plausible and sympathetic. When, years after her flight, she returns to her home, we suddenly see St Luke's Square through her eyes and not those of the stay-at-home, contented Constance, for whom the square is more or less the world:

> Several establishments lacked tenants, had obviously lacked tenants for a long time; 'To Let' notices hung in their stained and dirty upper windows, and clung insecurely to their closed shutters. And on the

sign-boards of these establishments were names that Sophia did not know. The character of most of the shops seemed to have worsened; they had become pettifogging little holes, unkempt, shabby, poor; they had no brightness, no feeling of vitality. And the floor of the Square was littered with nondescript refuse. The whole scene, paltry, confined, and dull, reached for her the extreme provinciality. (Book 4, chapter 2, iii)

Bennett makes no attempt to arbitrate between the two views: Constance's devotion to the square is as authentic and proper as Sophia's sense of revulsion from it. And any temptation we may have to identify with Sophia's way of seeing things is prevented by Bennett's way with Constance. We find ourselves sympathizing just as much with her choice of 'career' as we do with Sophia's.

It is of course true that the sisters' lives are essentially those of middle class women, and this might seem to undermine my suggestion that Bennett is concerned with a community. What, for example, of the servants? Well, there is Maggie, the Baines's maid-of-all-work.

Maggie had been at the shop since before the creation of Constance and Sophia. She lived seventeen hours of each day in an underground kitchen and larder, and the other seven in an attic, never going out except to chapel on Sunday evenings, and once a month on Thursday afternoons. 'Followers' were most strictly forbidden to her; but on rare occasions an aunt from Longshaw was permitted as a tremendous favour to see her in the subterranean den. Everybody, including herself, considered that she had a good 'place,' and was well treated. (Book 1, chapter 1, ii)

It looks from this as though Maggie is to be treated with typical middle class complacency, Bennett's every bit as much as the girls'. Maggie is to be a figure of fun.

But when, much later, Constance is to be married and take over the shop, Maggie hands in her notice.

Constance looked at her. Despite the special muslin of that day she had traces of the slatternliness of which Mrs Baines had never been able to cure her. She was over forty, big, gawky. She had no figure, no charms of any kind. She was what was left of a woman after twenty-two years in the cave of a philanthropic family. And in her cave she had actually been thinking things over! Constance detected for the first time, beneath the dehumanized drudge, the stirring of a separate and perhaps capricious individuality. Maggie's engagements had never been real to her employers. Within the house she had never been, in practice, anything but 'Maggie' – an organism. And now she was permitting herself ideas about changes! (Book 2, chapter 1, i)

And later still, Constance is made to realize how deeply offended Maggie is by not having been invited to Samuel's funeral: 'Constance perceived that by mere negligence she had seriously wounded the feelings of Maggie. . . . The truth was, she had never thought of Maggie. She ought to have remembered that funeral cards were almost the sole ornamentation of Maggie's abominable cottage' (Book 2, chapter 6, i). I have traced something of Maggie's 'career' in order to show that Bennett has no intention of letting us settle complacently into a single – middle class – view of her life, and that he takes every opportunity to unsettle the 'fixed' or simple view that we may think ourselves encouraged to take of her. It is true that most of what we see is through the eyes of Constance and Sophia, but Bennett refuses to endorse any one point of view. As the two sisters see St Luke's Square very differently, so they can be made to change their views about people. Bennett establishes a many-sided view of the community, not by exhaustively tracing each career, but by showing the sisters occasionally having access to views which customarily they are denied.

But here we come to a difficulty. For if Maggie represents an aspect of Bennett's successful way with community, it has to be admitted that other characters show where he can go wrong. Miss Insull, for example. She works in the Baines's shop and she is, we are told, 'honest, capable, and industrious'. There speaks the novelist-creator. And he goes on:

beyond the confines of her occupation she had no curiosity, no intelligence, no ideas. Superstitions and prejudices, deep and violent, served her for ideas; but she could incomparably sell silks and bonnets, braces and oilcloths; in widths, lengths, and prices she never erred; she never annoyed a customer, nor foolishly promised what could not be performed, nor was late nor negligent, nor disrespectful. No one knew anything about her, because there was nothing to know. Subtract the shop-assistant from her, and naught remained. Benighted and spiritually dead, she existed by habit. (Book 2, chapter 7, ii)

This is not how one of the sisters sees Miss Insull, it is how Bennett himself sees her. Yet later we learn that, married to the ancient misogynist, Critchlow, who has taken over the Baines's business after Samuel's death, the former Miss Insull has tried to kill herself and has been committed to an asylum. She is surely more interesting than that earlier account suggests? But Bennett offers no explanation for why she should at one point have been 'Benighted and spiritually dead' and at another possessed of enough imagination to hate the life she leads with Critchlow. The inevitable result is that we feel cheated. Why can't we know more about her?

It is a feeling that extends to other characters. Arnold Kettle says that because Bennett

> for all his sympathy with the poor and servants, conveys across to us nothing of the other side of the coin, the beginnings to trade union organization for instance, the total effect of his picture of the Potteries is bound to lack something in vitality, is bound to give a certain sense of life running down like a worn-out spring.

This seems to me less than fair to Bennett. It is not only that his sympathy with Maggie has nothing of pathos about it; not only that he shows us younger servants cheeking and abandoning the ageing Constance; not only that Dick Povey, with his gaiety and sense of the future, hints – along with Maggie and the others – at precisely that vitality or sense of renewal which Professor Kettle thinks leaks out of the novel. No, the point is that taken together such flickerings of unguessed-at consciousness and life make it clear that Bennett is by no means writing out of a sense of historical or social catastrophe. He simply isn't that kind of an author (though as we shall see in later chapters he came nearer to it after 1918). I do not find Bennett's historical sense at all bothersome in *The Old Wives' Tale*. He doesn't possess the kind of middle class consciousness that is masochistically attuned to its own feeling for defeat. What does worry me is his refusal to tell us enough about his own characters, and his occasional altering of them in the interests of a (perhaps) fixed disposition which he himself sees in metaphysical terms and which sounds out loud and clear when he

remarks of Sophia that 'the vast inherent melancholy of the universe did not exempt her' (Book 2, chapter 2, iii). At its truest, *The
Old Wives' Tale* combats such melancholy; at its falsest it endorses
it and does so through the deliberate interventions of its author. It
is as though he is saying that all we need to know about Miss Insull
is that she is unhappy, and will die; and that the rest is vanity.
Which it clearly isn't, as his presentation of Maggie shows.

And there is Sam. When we first meet him he is suffering from
toothache, and is too cowardly to go to the dentist. For Sophia and
Constance he is a figure of fun. And he is a shade ridiculous, a Mr
Polly. But like Mr Polly he has qualities which we come to admire
because Bennett makes us see that Sam amounts to much more than
his absurdities. He is certainly absurd when he asks Mrs Baines if
he may marry Constance. But not *merely* absurd.

> The aspirant wound up: 'I must leave if that's the case.'
> 'If what's the case?' she asked herself. 'What has come over him?'
> And aloud: 'you know you would place me in a very awkward position
> by leaving, and I hope you don't want to mix up two quite different
> things. I hope you aren't trying to threaten me.'
> 'Threaten you!' he cried. 'Do you suppose I should leave here for
> fun? If I leave here it will be because I can't *stand* it. That's all. I
> can't stand it. I want Constance, and if I can't have her, then I can't
> *stand* it. What do you think I'm made of?'
> 'I'm sure—' she began.
> 'That's all very well!' he almost shouted.
> 'But please let me speak,' she said quietly.
> 'All I say is I can't *stand* it. That's all. . . . Employers have no *right*.
> . . . We have our feelings like other men.'
> He was deeply moved. He might have appeared somewhat grotesque
> to the strictly impartial observer of human nature. Nevertheless he
> was deeply and genuinely moved, and possibly human nature could
> have shown nothing more human than Mr Povey at the moment
> when, unable any longer to restrain the paroxysm which had so
> surprisingly overtaken him, he fled from the parlour, passionately, to
> the retreat of his bedroom. (Book 1, chapter 7, ii)

Bennett's authorial comments are a little clumsy but they are in
no way offensive. They reveal how seriously he takes Sam, and
from now on everything he shows us of him increases our respect
and admiration. Sam, new-married, daring to smoke a cigar, Sam

designing a new signboard for Baines's, Sam chastising his son for stealing: the more we see of this entirely ordinary and unremarkable person the more impossible it becomes to take up a condescending attitude towards him. Sam is, quite simply, a good man. And his efforts to secure a reprieve for his cousin, condemned to death for the murder of a drunken wife, ennoble and kill him. Bennett comments:

> A casual death, scarce noticed in the reaction after the great febrile demonstration [a protest ceremony over Daniel Povey's execution]. Besides, Samuel Povey never could impose himself on the burgesses. He lacked individuality. He was little. I have often laughed at Samuel Povey. But I liked and respected him. He was a very honest man. I have always been glad to think that, at the end of his life, destiny took hold of him and displayed, to the observant, the vein of greatness which runs through every soul without exception. He embraced a cause, lost it, and died of it. (Book 2, chapter 5, vi)

I see no reason to complain about Bennett's use of the word 'destiny' in this passage. True, it would have been more accurate for him to have written that Sam took hold of destiny, not destiny of him, and Bennett's way of putting it hints at that pessimism which elsewhere can be so debilitating. But not here.

One is, however, troubled by the statement that Sam 'lacked individuality'. He didn't. I know Bennett is thinking of the unobservant burgesses on whom Sam could hope to make no impression, but it is surely proper to note that Sam is fully individualized, and that such individuality doesn't have to be traced to the 'vein of greatness which runs through every soul without exception'. Bother greatness, one wants to say, Sam is unique enough as it is. You have shown us as much. We don't need the rhetoric, it demeans everyone, you, Sam, and the reader. After all, there is nothing at all implausible about the moment when we are told that Constance has gradually 'constructed a chart of Sam's individuality, with the submerged rocks and perilous currents all carefully marked, so that she could now voyage unalarmed on those seas' (Book 2, chapter 2, ii).

Why, then, did Bennett feel impelled to say that Sam 'lacked individuality'? The answer to that question is that somewhere very deep inside him was an habitual melancholy, and indeed he admitted as much. 'Like most writers', he confessed in *The Truth About An Author*, 'I was frequently the victim of an illogical, indefensible and causeless melancholy.' It is this melancholy whose presence can be so disturbing in *The Old Wives' Tale*, because so misplaced. Bennett shows us how remarkable the unremarkable can be, and then denies it, as who should say: there is nothing remarkable beneath the visiting moon, nothing can be said except that I am sick, I must die. Tragedy, Lawrence said, ought to be a great kick at misery. And the remark was directed against Bennett. As Bennett's treatment of Sam shows, there is much more than misery to *The Old Wives' Tale*. But it cannot be denied that running through the novel there is a streak of something which it is perhaps more accurate to call melancholy rather than misery, often submerged but sometimes rising to gleam blackly through its study of provincial lives. So Bennett writes of Mrs Baines and Sophia:

> They sat opposite to each other, on either side of the fire – the monumental matron whose black bodice heavily overhung the table, whose large rounded face was creased and wrinkled by what seemed countless years of joy and disillusion; and the young, slim girl, so fresh, so virginal, so ignorant, with all the pathos of an unsuspecting victim about to be sacrificed to the minotaur of Time! (Book 1, chapter 6, iv)

And there is no doubt that Sophia is a victim. Bennett sees to that.

Yet it would be quite wrong to conclude that he does no more than pursue her career along labyrinthine paths that lead her unerringly to defeat and death. He also convincingly gives her a toughness and resilience, an imaginative liveliness and vitality which don't really square with an account of her as victim. Nor do I think that in any serious sense Sophia is a blurred figure. It is rather that Bennett, as commentator, interferes with his own creation in order to haul us back, preacher-fashion, to that vanity of vanities which, as melancholic, he takes life to be. And though this doesn't radically damage his study of Sophia it can be irritating. It is also liable to produce some very odd moments, as when Sophia comes to the bedside of her paralysed, dying father.

> And, with his controllable right hand, he took her hand as she stood by the bed. She was so young and fresh, such an incarnation of the spirit of health, and he was so far gone in decay and corruption, that

> there seemed in this contact of body with body something unnatural
> and repulsive. But Sophia did not so feel it. (Book 1, chapter 3, iii)

But if Sophia didn't feel it, why bother to mention it? Why draw
attention to what 'seemed' unnatural and repulsive in the contact of
father and daughter? The answer is that here as elsewhere Bennett
is determined to suck melancholy out of a scene. He is unfairly
intruding into the novel. One remembers, and with a certain
uneasiness, that 'strictly impartial observer' to whom the im-
passioned Samuel Povey might have appeared 'somewhat grotesque'; and reflects that too often such an observer is supposed to
be one possessed of Bennett's own glum reading of life.

Yet read on a little further and you find him using the same contact between father and daughter to establish a perception of an
altogether different order. Sophia wants to train as a teacher. That
is why she has been sent to her father, for her father will refuse
permission and she will have to abandon the idea. Or so her
mother thinks. And indeed, he won't allow it. 'You understand
me!' he says, speaking as head of the household.

> It was her father who appeared tragically ridiculous; and, in turn, the
> whole movement against her grew grotesque in its absurdity. Here
> was this antique wreck, helpless, useless, powerless – merely pathetic –
> actually thinking that he had only to mumble in order to make her
> 'understand!' He knew nothing; he perceived nothing; he was a
> ferocious egoist, like most bedridden invalids, out of touch with life, –
> and he thought himself justified in making destinies, and capable of
> making them! Sophia could not, perhaps, define the feelings which
> overwhelmed her; but she was conscious of their tendency. They aged
> her, by years. They aged her so that, in a kind of momentary ecstasy of
> insight, she felt older than her father himself.
>   'You will be a good girl,' he said. 'I'm sure o' that.'
>   It was too painful. The grotesqueness of her father's complacency
> humiliated her past bearing. She was humiliated, not for herself, but
> for him. Singular creature! She ran out of the room.

Compared with the previous moment quoted, that seems to me
utterly authentic and really very moving. Bennett is so sensitive,
tactful and imaginative in his understanding of the young girl. And
although one regrets the rather lumpen facetiousness of 'singular

creature!' it doesn't take away from the rightness of the scene as a whole.

The whole of Book 3 is a triumph of Bennett's art. Whether he is writing about Sophia's elopement with Gerald Scales, his desertion of her in Paris, her struggle to survive, her eventual triumph as owner of Frensham's, the small Paris pension, or whether he is writing about her tangles with other women and her rejection of proffered love, Bennett writes and imagines flawlessly. And how convincing it is that, after so many years of exile, Sophia should suffer a partial crack-up when confronted by a young man from the Five Towns who has links with her family – the family from which she has cut herself off. She reflects:

> She was the most solitary person on earth. She had heard no word of Gerald, no word of anybody. Nobody whatever could truly be interested in her fate. This was what she had achieved after a quarter of a century of ceaseless labour and anxiety, during which she had not once been away from the Rue Lord Byron for more than thirty hours at a stretch. It was appalling – the passage of years; and the passage of years would grow more appalling. Ten years hence, where would she be? She pictured herself dying. Horrible. (Book 4, chapter 1, iv)

She gives up Frensham's, goes home to Bursley, and she and Constance live together once more. And still Bennett follows her career with such tact and discreet understanding that one marvels that he should ever go wrong. But then a telegram comes to inform her that Gerald, the long-lost husband, is dying in Manchester. The news shocks her. And Bennett comments:

> One might have pictured fate as a cowardly brute who had struck this ageing woman full in the face, a felling blow, which however had not felled her. It seemed a shame – one of those crude, spectacular shames which make the blood boil – that the gallant, defenceless creature should be so maltreated by the bully, destiny. (Book 4, chapter 4, ii)

One notices with what apparent inevitability the word 'seemed' has cropped up here, as it had in the scene between the young Sophia and her crippled father. And one also notices – how could one not? – the crudeness of Bennett's rhetoric when he writes of fate and destiny, and the sad sentimentalizing of Sophia as a helpless victim. *Sophia* defenceless? In view of what we have been so fully and sensitively shown throughout Book 3 the word is absurdly inappropriate. It can be there only because Bennett is determined to make his 'point'. What point? Well, it can be understood once we attend to the title of Book 4, 'What Life Is', and as soon as we realize the significance of that moment when Sophia turns from Gerald's dead body and thinks that 'Youth and vigour had come to that. Everything came to that.'

> It was the riddle of life that was puzzling and killing her. By the corner of her eye, reflected in the mirror of a wardrobe near the bed, she glimpsed a tall, forlorn woman, who had once been young and now was old; who had once exulted in abundant strength, and trodden proudly on the neck of circumstance. He and she had once loved and burned and quarrelled in the glittering and scornful pride of youth. But time had worn them out. 'Yet a little while,' she thought, 'and I shall be lying on a bed like that! And what shall I have lived for? What is the meaning of it?' The riddle of life itself was killing her, and she seemed to drown in a sea of inexpressible sorrow. (Book 4, chapter 4, iii)

And there the word is, once more – 'seemed'. It provides the clue to what I find truly unsatisfactory about this passage (leaving aside such vague and windy phrases as the 'neck of circumstance' and the 'glittering and scornful pride of youth'). The fact is, that in the last analysis you cannot tell when Bennett imagines that he is transcribing Sophia's thoughts and when he is interpolating his own. Of course, all the thoughts are really his own, since he has invented Sophia. But the Sophia he has invented and so finely put before us in Book 3 cannot be the one who 'seems' to be drowning in a sea of inexpressible sorrow. She is simply too tough a nut to do anything of the sort. And why 'seems'? Doesn't he know? Is it that she seems to herself or to him to be drowning? It isn't that I think Sophia is being imposed on. Faced with the fact of her dead husband it is obviously very possible that she would ask herself what she had lived for. At a pinch one might even concede that she felt inexpressibly sorrowful. But however that may be, one must surely object to Bennett's identification with her – 'the riddle of life itself was killing her' – since one comes to this moment with the magnificently impressive study of Sophia's life so fully and weightily in one's mind. To put it rather differently, 'What Life Is' ought to be the subtitle for *The Old Wives' Tale* as a whole, not just for the last book. If it had been, one wouldn't have needed to feel that Bennett was perilously close to Constance when, after Sophia's death, she reflects:

> What a career! A brief passion and then nearly thirty years in a boarding-house! And Sophia had never had a child; had never known either the joy or the pain of maternity. She had never even had a true house till, in all her sterile splendour, she came to Bursley. And she had ended – thus! This was the piteous, ignominious end of Sophia's wondrous gifts of body and soul. Hers had not been a life at all. And the reason? It is strange how fate persists in justifying the harsh generalisations of Puritan morals, of the morals in which Constance had been brought up by her stern parents! Sophia had sinned. It was therefore inevitable that she should suffer. (Book 4, chapter 4, iv)

A passage such as that is plainly clogged with the misery that Lawrence so despised and which he insisted should be kicked, hard. The point I think it important above all others to make is that *The Old Wives' Tale* itself provides the kick, which is why it is so considerable an achievement. It is there in Book 2, in the study of Samuel Povey, it is there in Book 3, where Sophia is neither a victim nor defenceless – indeed, it would be absurd to apply either word to her – and it makes itself equally felt in the account of Constance's life. It remains for me to say a little about her.

Bennett offers Constance's life as a kind of ironic counterpoint to Sophia's. Constance is the stay-at-home. She is thoroughly conventional and completely ordinary. But she is also shown to us as the sister who perhaps achieves more. Bennett very successfully employs a double perspective when he is writing about her. We both see her from the outside – through the eyes of Sophia, Cyril, her son, and Cyril's friend, Matthew Peele-Swynnerton, Dr Stirling, Dick Povey and Lily, all of whom condescend to her – and from Bennett's nearer point of view, which allows us access to her thoughts and feelings. I do not pretend that he always succeeds here. He claims more than he is able to show. As a young wife, Constance is, we are told, aware of death and sorrow, but she is also aware that any feeling of melancholy was 'factitious, was less than transient foam on the deep sea of her joy' (Book 2, chapter 1, ii). Which would be all very well if Bennett could make her joy seem convincing. But in fact he shows us next to nothing of Constance as a young wife enjoying her marriage. The result is that when, after Sam's death, she is made to reflect that 'she had had nearly twenty-one years of happy married life', one is bound to wish that we had seen something of its happiness. Constance goes on to think of 'their naïve ignorance of life, hers and his, when they were first married, [so that it] brought tears into her eyes. How wise and experienced she was now!' What is the point of that exclamation mark? Is Bennett being ironic? Should we assume that Constance isn't really wise and experienced, or are we meant to read into it her own firm sense of these gradually acquired possessions and knowledge? And either way, where in the novel itself can we find the necessary evidence of her wisdom and experience? To be honest, I am not sure that we can find it at all, and at best it is only thinly imagined for us. Constance's career isn't nearly so richly presented to us as Sophia's is, though I do not think Bennett intends us to see her life as in any way empty. It is simply that he does not give us any sustained insight into the way she can be redeemed from unexceptionable drabness. Hence, so I suspect, that exclamation mark. He approves of Constance right enough, but he can't 'see' her with the kind of intensity and verve that would allow him to do away with guarded qualifications about it.

This is not, however, to say that Constance is an imaginative failure of Bennett's. For in some respects he brings her very remarkably alive. And this is especially true in his writing about her feelings for Cyril. Here at least Bennett gives Constance a depth and reality which makes it impossible for us to speak about his 'external' treatment of character, and seems to me to provide the perfect rejoinder to Virginia Woolf's complaint that he couldn't imagine what went on in his characters' minds. Constance wanting to cling to Cyril but unable to throw off the habits of restraint, Constance pained and grieving over Cyril's careless indifference to her; or Constance in an ecstasy of self-pity when Cyril goes away to London, thinking to herself 'I'm a lonely old woman now. I've nothing to live for any more, and I'm no use to anybody.' Again and again Bennett pierces through to the very heart of the matter in his study of Constance as mother (and he is unwaveringly exact in his treatment of the spoilt, talented, ruthless son). There can be no complaints here. Nor can there be any about his study of the ageing Constance, her devotion to her home, her keen regret that it has to be altered, her flaring out at Sophia when she suggests they should leave it: ' "Now, what do you say?" Sophia gently entreated. "There's some of us like Bursley, black as it is!" said Constance. And Sophia was surprised to detect tears in her sister's voice' (Book 4, chapter 3, vi). This surprise, the access to a point of view of Constance which disturbs us by unsettling our fixed view of her, is one that Bennett repeatedly springs in Book 4. I think, for example, of that moment when Matthew Peel-Swynnerton has returned from Paris to Bursley, having discovered Sophia's whereabouts, and meets a 'short, fat, middle-aged lady dressed in black, with a black embroidered mantle, and a small bonnet tied with black ribbon and ornamented with jet fruit and crape leaves'. The lady is, of course, Constance, and the description of her comes as a considerable shock, since the last glimpse we had of her was taking leave of Cyril, and for all her mournful feelings that she was to be a 'lonely old woman', she was so intensely present to us that it would have been impossible to think of her as quaint and mildly ridiculous, which is how she now appears. But then we adjust to the shock because between that earlier view and this one has come the long Book 3, taken up with Sophia's career, so that we feel that a considerable passage of time has passed between the last close view we had of Constance and the one we are now given, through Peel-Swynnerton's eyes. And in addition, we have by now acquired Sophia's 'foreign' perspective. The positioning of Book 3 is crucial. Yes, we come to agree, in the eyes of the young and of those who can now see Bursley from the outside, Constance is bound to seem quaint. The young man tells her of his meeting with Sophia: 'She stopped and looked at him with a worried expression. Then he observed that the hand that carried her reticule was making strange purposeless curves in the air, and her rosy face went the colour of cream, as though it had been painted with one stroke of an unseen brush.' He takes her home:

> It seemed to him that gladness should have filled the absurd little parlour, but the spirit that presided had no name; it was certainly not joy. He himself felt very sad, desolated. . . . He knew simply that in the memory of the stout, comical, nice woman in the rocking-chair he

had stirred old, old things, wakened slumbers that might have been eternal. (Book 4, chapter 1, iii)

In its unobtrusive way this is surely masterly. It so finely catches Constance's position in a shifting social process – she is outmoded, has gone down a little, just as St Luke's Square has; and it also makes perfect use of that double perspective by means of which we see her through Peel-Swynnerton's eyes as 'comical' and at the same time see her as much more than that, because we know so much more about her than he does.

If Constance doesn't feel gladness, what is it that she does feel? We find out in the letter she writes to Sophia. This letter is, I think, one of the very highest achievements of Bennett's art, and a triumphant vindication of his realism. It is quite unremarkable and also very remarkable. For more than anything else in the novel it establishes how decent a person Constance is, how loving; and how being these things matters. The letter is too long to quote and if it were lifted out of context it would not seem so unerringly right and movingly true as it does when we come to it towards the end of the novel itself; but Sophia's reflections on it are perfectly accurate. 'Tact? No; it was something finer than tact. Tact was conscious, skilful. Sophia was certain that the notion of tactfulness had not entered Constance's head. Constance had simply written out of her heart' (Book 4, chapter 1, v). Anyone wanting to take the measure of Bennett's achievement would be well advised to start with Constance's letter to Sophia.

After Sophia's death, Dick Povey and his fiancée, Lily, help to solace Constance's loneliness. Bennett is again able to bring the double perspective into action, and to good effect. Constance gives Lily a fine cameo brooch.

'I should like to see you wearing it. It was mother's. I believe they're coming into fashion again. I don't see why you shouldn't wear it while you're in mourning. They aren't half so strict now about mourning as they used to be.'

'Truly!' murmured Lily ecstatically. They kissed. . . .

'What a magnificent old watch!' said Lily, as they delved together in the lower recesses of the box. '*And* the chain to it!'

'That was father's,' said Constance. 'He always used to swear by it. When it didn't agree with the Town Hall, he used to say: "Then th'

Town Hall's wrong." And it's curious, the Town Hall *was* wrong. You know the Town Hall clock has never been a good timekeeper. I've been thinking of giving that watch and chain to Dick.'

'*Have* you?' said Lily.

Later, Lily tells Dick of Constance's idea:

'Thank you for nothing!' said Dick. 'I don't want it.'

'Have you seen it?'

'Have I seen it? I should say I had seen it. She's mentioned it once or twice before'. . . .

'Poor old thing!' Lily murmured, compassionately.

Then Lily put her hand silently to her neck.

'What's that?'

'She's just given it to me.'

Dick approached very near to examine the cameo brooch. 'Hm!' he murmured. It was an adverse verdict. And Lily coincided with it by a lift of the eyebrows.

'And I suppose you'll have to wear that!' Dick said.

'She values it as much as anything she's got, poor old thing!' said Lily. (Book 4, chapter 5, i)

It seems as though Constance is now to be put firmly into perspective as a relic of the past, mocked at by the younger generation. But Bennett has not quite done. For a little later, when she is lying ill – it is to be her last illness – and musing over her life, she thinks of Dick and Lily:

Perhaps they would have been startled to know that Constance lovingly looked down on both of them. She had unbounded admiration for their hearts; but she thought that Dick was a little too brusque, a little too clownish, to be quite a gentleman. And though Lily was perfectly ladylike, in Constance's opinion she lacked backbone, or grit, or independence of spirit. (Book 4, chapter 5, v)

It is, I think, an important moment just because it prevents Constance from being merely a figure of pathos, of 'running down like a worn-out spring'. Given the drift towards melancholy resignation that shows itself in *The Old Wives' Tale*, Bennett must have been strongly tempted to let the last word on Constance be spoken by the necessarily impercipient young. And if we think back to the younger Bennett determinedly recording in his *Journal* in 1903 that the fat woman he had observed was 'repulsive; no one could like or sympathise with her', we are bound to recognize how far he has travelled in order to be able to say that Constance 'lovingly' looked down on Lily and Dick; and without a shade of irony.

I do not mean that my earlier criticisms of Bennett's failures with Constance can now be withdrawn. Just above those sentences on Dick and Lily, we read that when she 'surveyed her life, and life in general, she would think, with a sort of tart but not sour cheerfulness: *Well, that is what life is*'. The italics are Bennett's and they provide a ready-to-hand objection. Life in general isn't what Constance takes it to be, yet there is every indication that at this moment Bennett totally identifies himself with her. Bennett, that is, the disciple of de Maupassant, Bennett the man of causeless melancholy. But the truly important Bennett is the one who throughout the pages of his novel has shown us that life is much more various, bewildering and fulfilling than any one person can know, the Bennett who comes near to achieving that absolute realism which he found and cherished in Chekhov, and as a result of which he created one of the finest of twentieth-century novels.

Chapter 4
The Last of the Five Towns

I

Although *The Matador of the Five Towns* was published as late as 1912, most of the stories in it had been written some two or three years earlier. It is a much more even achievement than *The Grim Smile of the Five Towns*. There are fewer makeweight anecdotes, and taken together the stories help fill out our awareness of the Five Towns and of those people whom Bennett created to live there. The same characters crop up in novels and stories of two decades – from *A Man From the North* to *The Roll-Call* – now merely mentioned, now glimpsed in a scene or two, now playing a major part. A feeling of solidity, of a place that becomes more familiar the more we read, grows on us as we work our way through Bennett's fiction. Dr Stirling is Constance Baines's doctor. He is also the friend of Brindley, the architect, and as such appears in 'The Death of Simon Fuge'; and he is very important in the title story of *The Matador of the Five Towns*. In other stories from the same volume there is mention of Mrs Clayton-Vernon, whom Richard Larch had visited, and of the Countess of Chell, who is frequently mentioned in other stories and novels and of whom a good deal is made in *The Card*. We meet young Lawton, the solicitor (he has a key moment in *Hilda Lessways*), Duncalf, the town clerk (he also appears in *The Card*), Jos Curtenty (who had been the hero of 'His Worship, the Goose-Driver' in *Tales of the Five Towns*), Mrs Sutton (she had been important in *Anna of the Five Towns*); and so on. And there are the casual, regular references to the Tiger, Bursley Town Hall, Trafalgar Road, Toft End, Bleakridge, the *Staffordshire Signal*, Knype F.C.: to those places, landmarks and features of the Five Towns by means of which Bennett builds up a peopled townscape.

The football club is at the centre of the title story. Once again, Loring has come to stay with Brindley, and since Brindley has unexpectedly to go off for the day, he gives Stirling the task of entertaining the southern aesthete. Stirling decides to take Loring to see the second half of Knype's football match, a key one since its result will more or less decide whether Knype stay in Division One or are relegated. It is a brilliant dodge to show us something of what matters so hugely to the Five Towns' way of life, but I am not sure that Bennett brings off the very difficult task of getting us to see the match through Loring's 'innocent' eye. I put that word in quotation marks because there are moments when Loring is made altogether too knowing, and in fact uses the language of football reporters (it is astonishing how early that language had developed and hardened into banality). He refers to the players as 'a scattered handful of doll-like figures', he remarks of one doll that he 'overtook the ball and scudded along with it at his twinkling toes', and he offers a heavily facetious account of the cheer which greets a Knype goal:

> This massive cheer reverberated round the field like the echoes of a battleship's broadside in a fiord. . . . Simultaneously with the expulsion of the unique noise the expression of the faces changed. Eyes sparkled; teeth became prominent in enormous, uncontrolled smiles. Ferocious satisfaction had to find vent in ferocious gestures, wreaked either upon dead wood or upon the living tissues of fellow-creatures. . . . The host of fifteen thousand might have just had their lives saved, or their children snatched from destruction and their wives from dishonour; they might have been preserved from bankruptcy, starvation, prison, torture; they might have been rewarding with their impassioned worship a land of national heroes.

He is better when he notes the crowd going away after the final whistle, its taciturnity, 'the steady stare . . . and the heavy, muffled, multitudinous tramp shaking the cindery earth'. Even so, these descriptions aren't as impressive as one wants them to be. The truth is that Bennett rather botched his opportunity of capturing the feel of a football match. On the other hand, his comparative failure here doesn't affect what is most important about the story – the matador himself.

Jos Myatt, he is called. We are told that he is rising thirty-four, and hasn't many seasons left in him. But he is still a splendid performer at full-back and the one man – or so the locals argue – who stands between Knype and relegation. The match Loring watches ends in a draw, and this result is largely due to Myatt's toughness and skill. Loring has heard Jos's ability spoken of before he and Stirling decide to go to the game, for the town is full of talk about him and of Knype's future. In his imagination, Loring pictures Myatt as a 'matador, with a long ribbon of scarlet necktie down his breast, and embroidered trousers'. The reality is very different:

> His mouth and his left knee were red with blood, and he was piebald with thick patches of mud from his tousled crown to his enormous boot. His blue eyes had a heavy, stupid, honest glance; and of the three qualities stupidity predominated. He seemed to be all feet, knees, hands and elbows. His head was very small – the sole remainder of the doll in him.

Later, Loring learns that Myatt is paid 'about £4 a week', that he keeps 'The Foaming Quart up at Toft End', and that his wife is about to produce their first child.

The rest of the story is taken up with Stirling's being called out to Mrs Myatt late at night (Loring, of course, goes with him), and of her eventual death in childbirth. And as the night wears on and the moment of birth comes nearer, Loring studies Myatt as the ageing football hero slowly and clumsily does his accounts in the pub parlour, and shows off his cups and medals. And through Loring we come to understand the very real pathos of this hero of the Five Towns, near the end of his reign, grotesque, stupid, vulnerable:

> Jos [Loring muses] you ought in justice to have been José, with a thin red necktie down your breast (instead of a line of mud up your back), and an income of a quarter of a million pesetas, and the languishing

acquiescence of innumerable mantillas. Every moment you were getting older and stiffer; every moment was bringing nearer the moment
when young men would reply curtly to their doddering elders: 'Jos
Myatt – who was '*e*?'

When he hears of his wife's death, Myatt swears, 'As God is my
witness . . . I'll ne'er touch a footba' again!' And his friend and
hanger-on (Bennett is very good at noting the half-cringing, half-
familiar behaviour of the type) replies, 'It's goodbye to the First
League then, for Knype!' The remark, as Loring later reflects, is
understandable: 'It was not that he did not feel the tragedy in the
house. He had felt it, and because he had felt it he had uttered at
random, foolishly, the first clear idea that ran into his head.'

This part of the story is well done. I am glad that Bennett took
seriously the seriousness of football in the Five Towns community
and the sadness of Jos Myatt. But there is no doubt that he over-
inflates the experience, or rather allows the worst, rhetorical side
of himself to take over, with predictable results. 'Historical room,
surely!' Loring thinks to himself in the parlour of the Foaming
Quart. 'And yet not a house in the hundreds of houses past which
we slid but possessed rooms ennobled and made august by happen-
ings exactly as impressive in their tremendous inexplicableness.' It
would be nice to think that Bennett was being ironical at the
expense of the southerner-aesthete. Unfortunately that moment is
matched by others in the story where Bennett is plainly speaking
in his own voice. And such moments weaken what is otherwise an
impressive tale.

There is no other story as good in the collection. There are,
however, a number of very funny tales, among them 'The Heroism
of Thomas Chadwick', 'Three Episodes in the Life of Mr Cowli-
shaw Dentist', and 'Jock-at-a-Venture' (which has the added bonus
of being crammed with fascinating information about street theatre
and entertainments in the Five Towns during the 1850s). All these
are deftly told, they all use the comic method Bennett had first
employed in *A Great Man*, and if they slightly relax the grim smile
of the Five Towns they nevertheless tell us much of real interest
about the place. The same cannot be said for 'The Glimpse', a tale
which is neither deft nor amusing, and which certainly isn't interesting. It is a clumsy piece about a man who 'dies' and sees

God. The only reason for mentioning it is that Bennett expanded it into a novel of the same name, published in 1909. There is a footnote to the story version, explaining that the author withdrew it from its intended place of publication because the editor had said that he dared not offer it to his readers. I was glad to have withdrawn it, Bennett says, 'for I perceived that its theme could only be treated adequately in a novel'. Perhaps so, but my own view is that the novel is in no way an improvement on the story. If anything it is even more tedious. Bennett simply doesn't have a religious temperament or the kind of interest in metaphysical speculation which might have made it a worthwhile novel. And though he later noted in his *Journal* that 'the first and third part of *The Glimpse* contained a lot of essentially autobiographical stuff', Edwin Clayhanger is surely much closer to Bennett's own position when he bursts out with the remark that so impresses Hilda: ' "You can't make yourself believe anything. And I don't see why you should, either. There's no virtue in believing." ' (*Clayhanger*, Book 2, chapter 8, ii). With the exception of *Sacred and Profane Love*, *The Glimpse* is the most embarrassingly bad novel that Bennett wrote.

Helen With the High Hand is certainly not embarrassing. It is, however, very slight, scarcely more than an extended anecdote. Bennett himself called it an 'Idyllic Diversion', and since he wrote it during the early part of 1908 it probably isn't too much to suggest that like *Buried Alive* it was undertaken as a welcome diversion from the protracted labours of *The Old Wives' Tale*. He noted in his *Journals* that 'the reviews of *Helen With the High Hand* are exceedingly polite and kind, but they do not gloss over the slightness of the thing'.

The tale concerns a young girl, Helen Rathbone, who goes to live with her uncle, James Olleranshaw, and becomes involved with a young man called Emanuel Procktor. James ends up by marrying Procktor's mother while Helen herself marries another young man, Andrew Dean.

We are told that Olleranshaw is the richest man in Bursley after Ephraim Tellwright. He is also something of a miser. And a card. He 'kept the tea-leaves in a tea-caddy, locked, in his front room. . . . Every day Mrs Butt brought to him the tea-pot (warmed) and a teaspoon, and he unlocked the tea-caddy, dispensed the right quantity of tea, and re-locked the tea-caddy' (chapter 7). He plays the Hallelujah Chorus on his concertina, and he can be caustically funny. When Helen asks him why Emanuel has called to see him James replies: ' "Maybe he felt faintlike, and slipped in here, as there's no public nearer than the Queen Adelaide. Or maybe he thought as I was getting on in years, and he wanted to make my acquaintance afore I died. I didna' ask him" ' (chapter 11). He dresses in a style which is outrageously indifferent to fashion, but which is recognizably 'Five Towns':

> He carried his hands in the peculiar horizontal pockets of his trousers, and stuck out his figure, in a way to indicate that he gave permission to all to think of him exactly as they pleased. Those pockets . . . divide the garment by a fissure whose sides are kept together by many buttons, and a defection on the part of even a few buttons is apt to be inconvenient. . . . His suit was of a strange hot colour – like a brick which, having become very dirty, has been imperfectly cleaned and then powdered with sand – made in a hard, eternal, resistless cloth. . . . His low, flat-topped hat was faintly green, as though a delicate fungoid growth were just budding on its black. His small feet were cloistered in small, thick boots of glittering brilliance. (chapter 1)

We learn that James had argued with his stepniece, Susan, over her proposed marriage, 'and that each of them had sworn not to speak until the other spoke' – a vow of the kind which frequently occurs in Bennett's fiction. Finally, James's house is representative of the Five Towns: 'It is a point of honour, among the self-respecting and industrious classes, to prepare a room elaborately for a certain purpose, and then not to use it for that purpose. . . . If they have an income of six rooms they will live on five, or rather in five, and thereby take pride in themselves' (chapter 6). So James's kitchen is used as the scullery, the dining room as the study and the sitting room as the dining room.

I have made mention of these features of James Olleranshaw's life because he is the only figure to whom Bennett gives any real attention, and because that attention is all in the interest of saying things about the Five Towns. The study of James tells us much about Bennett's wry, affectionate, exasperated attitude towards his native district. It is packed with the exact observations and curious knowledge that make him so inimitable a novelist of provincial life;

and it is very enjoyable. There is nothing at all wrong with James except that there is hardly anything of a story for him to be in. For all her high-handed ways Helen is seen very much from the out-side, and with a kind of humorous condescension that inevitably makes her trivial. ' "Well," she said, "I like frocks. It just happens that I can't do without frocks. It's just frocks that I work for; I spend nearly all I earn on them" ' (chapter 4). If such conde-scension never becomes more than mildly irritating in the novel it is only because *Helen With the High Hand* doesn't take itself seriously enough to require of us any more than the undemanding pleasure we take in Bennett's presentation of James Olleranshaw.

II

The Card (1911) and *The Price of Love* (1914) are also comic novels about the Five Towns. But they are much more solid performances than *Helen With The High Hand* pretends to be. *The Card* is, of course, one of Bennett's best-known and most popular novels. Yet he himself was very uncertain of its worth. He noted in the *Journal*: 'Yesterday I finished three-quarters of *Denry the Audacious*. I think that in book form I shall call it *The Card*. Good honest work, vitiated by my constant thought of a magazine public.' And a few weeks later, on 2 March 1909, he wrote: 'I finished *Denry* or the *Card* yesterday at 11 a.m. Began it on January 1, I think. 64,000 words. Stodgy, no real distinction of any sort, but well invented, and done up to the knocker, technically, right enough.' When *The Card* was finally published in book form he noted laconically, 'Reviews of the *Card* much too kind on the whole.'

It may come as a surprise to find Bennett admitting to these doubts, even in the privacy of the *Journals*. Surprising, too, that he should consider having to think of his magazine public as vitiating. True, *The Card* is episodic in structure and therefore fits neatly enough into serial form. But then its tale of the rise and rise of Henry Machin is by nature episodic (it is a good example of Bennett's use of the technique which he had first mastered in *A Great Man*: the telling of a story in separate but neatly joined in-cidents – Scenes from the Life of). Yet perhaps his reference to the magazine public provides an important clue to something that rightly worried Bennett. For I think that *The Card* is vulgar and complacent, and its brand of humour is a long way from the bland, laconic acceptance of things as they are which had characterized the tone of *A Great Man*. *The Card* strikes a note that is new in Bennett's fiction, though it will sound increasingly in later work, especially *The Regent* and the execrable *Mr Prohack*. It is at once boorish and philistinic, and at this stage at least must have come as a troubling surprise to Bennett himself. After all, the hero of *The Card* was based on an old acquaintance, Harold Keates Hales (who was to publish his *Autobiography of the Card* in 1936), and Bennett obviously felt enough lively sympathy with the Card to share with him his own date of birth, 27 May 1867. Besides, he enjoyed the notion of the 'Card', the Five Towns type about whom he had already written on a number of occasions but who hadn't so far been put at the centre of a novel. Yet now that he has been, Bennett is not altogether pleased with the result. For on close inspection the Card turns out to be a kind of character who will inevitably appeal to a 'magazine public' – with all that that phrase implies of unthinking guffaws and uncritical acceptance. To put it rather differently, I think that when Bennett came to write *The Card* he discovered that he was writing about a kind of life which he could not admire, and that he used humour to fend off any really severe questioning about his hero, though in its complacency the humour itself indicates an uneasy conscience.

These are severe words and they must not stand on their own. For there is much to enjoy in *The Card*. The novel establishes a feeling of continuity with other Five Towns novels. We see Denry in conversation with Charles Fearns at the Sports Club, we hear rumours concerning Anna Tellwright and Henry Mynors, and we also hear of Sir Jehoshophat Dain (the villain of the piece in 'The Burglary', one of the tales in *The Grim Smile of the Five Towns*). There are marvellous moments of detail, as for example when Henry has to put his coat on in his mother's kitchen, because the passage isn't wide enough. And always, of course, there is the feel for the place, its energies, squalors, amusements and scandals, its generations moving rapidly up and down the social scale. Denry's mother is not happy with wealth. She is, we are told, 'too profoundly rooted in her habits'. Like Constance Baines she does not want to leave the house in which she has lived for so long and to which she has become so accustomed. Denry's visions of splendour fill her with distaste and anxiety.

Denry is on the rise. Others fall. Chief among them is Councillor Cotterill. He has built up a business to the point where it has made him a rich man. Now it crashes and he is forced to emigrate to Canada, aided, but very perfunctorily, by Denry, who refuses to help Cotterill shore up his tottering business affairs. And it is here that one's doubts about Denry swell into a real uneasiness. For the blunt truth is that at this point he is quite plainly a ruthless, cynical person. He dismisses Cotterill's plea for a loan, and Bennett writes: 'Denry does not appear to advantage in this interview. He failed in magnanimity. The only excuse that can be offered for him is that Mr Cotterill had called him "young man" once or twice too often in the course of ten years. It is subtle' (chapter 10, ii). Subtle? Crass seems nearer the mark. The same goes for Denry's reflection that it is a mistake to be a failure: 'You could do nothing with a failure.' Such a reflection is meant to be redeemed by the fact that Denry pursues the Cotterills to Liverpool, pays for them to be moved from steerage to second class, and then whisks their daughter, Nellie, off the ship because he intends to marry her – and does. All this comes of his being a Card and it no doubt anticipates the 'magazine public's' approval.

But what exactly is a Card? Denry has two visions. The first comes to him when he attends a grand ball: 'The thrill of being magnificent seized him, and he was drenched in a vast desire to be truly magnificent himself' (chapter 1, vi). The way to magnificence is paved by money. And this leads to Denry's second vision, which has to do with himself.

> He did not consider himself clever or brilliant. But he considered himself peculiarly gifted. He considered himself different from other men. . . .
> And he knew of a surety that he was that most admired type in the bustling, industrial provinces – a card. (chapter 2, iii)

He begins to make his way as a man of means and at Llandudno he has 'not only his first vision of the sea, but his first genuine vision of the possibilities of amassing wealth by honest ingenuity' (chapter 4, i). The rest of the novel is taken up with Denry's achievement of magnificence through amassing wealth. By honest ingenuity? If honest means lawful, yes. Denry never steps beyond what the law allows. But it is an impoverished definition, just as his vision is impoverished. The problem for the novel is that Bennett half knows as much. At Llandudno Denry is, we are told, 'much impressed by the beauty and grandeur of the sea. But what impressed him far more than the beauty and grandeur of the sea was the field for profitable commercial enterprise which a place like Llandudno presented.' The tone is unruffled, neutral. Yet without wanting to be unduly heavy-handed – for *The Card* is a comparatively unambitious comedy, whose success probably surprised Bennett himself – I think it proper to suggest that its characteristic tone is an attempt to deflect unsympathetic responses to Denry. True, the 'magazine public' might not respond to him unsympathetically, but he could well end up by being unpopular with a more discriminating, sensitive observer – Arnold Bennett, for instance. I simply do not believe that Bennett is telling the truth when, in a letter to the Duchess of Sutherland – who had clearly recognized herself in 'Interfering Iris', the novel's Countess of Chell – he says that 'the whole book is written in a fiercely sarcastic vein' (*Letters*, vol. II, p. 285). But I am quite ready to believe that an uneasy conscience forced him to recognize that it ought to have been so written, and that as it stands *The Card* amounts to little more than a strategic use of deflections. We are asked to admire without thought Denry the Audacious, the man of honest ingenuity; and when deflection becomes impossible – as in the treatment of Cotterill – the strategy nearly falls apart. It certainly isn't put together again by the plea made at the very end of the novel. Denry is now mayor and is being discussed by his fellow councillors. ' "And yet," demanded Councillor Barlow, "what's he done? Has he ever done a day's work in his life? What great cause is he identified with?" "He's identified," said the speaker, "with the great cause of cheering us all up." ' That is no more than a final deflection, though it does remind us that *The Card* shows us hardly anything of the inevitable ruthlessness that accompanies Denry's vision, so that we do not have to worry about the consequences – for others – of his honest ingenuity.

If the novel doesn't become entirely distasteful it is because Denry possesses qualities that really are attractive. He is audacious, he is funny, he is alive with energy and wit; he has, in short, qualities which Bennett brings out well enough to compel our affectionate liking for his hero. There is a particularly good scene where Denry, on his honeymoon – and being a provincial he would have thought it odd, so Bennett assures us, to go on his honeymoon in any month other than August – both puts down and is put down by an 'eye-glass johnny'. Such scenes abound in *The Card* and they give Denry a proper and valuable comic gusto. But what Bennett won't bring out are the dubious ways in which that gusto has so often to express itself. To have done so would, of course, have strained our sympathies with Denry, perhaps to breaking point. It would perhaps have made *The Card* what it most certainly isn't, fiercely sarcastic. And it would certainly have made it another and a better novel.

I am aware that I may seem to have been taking a steam-hammer to crack a nut. Why bother to be so severe about a modest comedy? There is a reason. For *The Card* stands as the first of a number of novels where Bennett settles for a formula of complacent acceptance, although here at least he seems to have been uneasy about his own attitude. In the later novels I have in mind such uneasiness is dispelled. The result is that they become irritating, vulgar and thoroughly distasteful. There will be more to say of them in a later chapter. My immediate task is to say something about *The Price of Love*.

Bennett's own comments on it are not promising. He called it 'a damned thing', and in a letter to a friend remarked that 'The best judges I know are of opinion that *The Price of Love* is A1. This rather surprises me, but it relieves me' (*Letters*, vol. II, p. 358). I find such doubts surprising because *The Price of Love* is, I think, a very attractive novel. It may be that Bennett worried about it simply because by his standards it took him an unusually long time to write – over a year – especially since it isn't a long novel. And perhaps he also feared for the consequences of having to consider that 'magazine public' which had, so he felt, hurt *The Card*. *The Price of Love* was serialized in *Harpers* prior to book publication, and it has the craftsman-like neatness which lends itself to serialization.

It is more than a deftly told tale, however. In the first place, it is packed with information about provincial life. Indeed one chapter, about a film show which the hero and heroine attend, is probably the first instance in English fiction where due attention is paid to the importance that the coming of the cinema had on provincial life (Lawrence was later to make much of it in his *Lost Girl*). *The Price of Love* also has a stupendously detailed, informative and telling description of a sitting room. The description takes up most of the first chapter and it tells us much that we need to know about the kind of person who furnishes and cares for such a room.

> Mrs Maldon had, it transpired, her 'ways'; for example, in the matter of blinds and in the matter of tapers. She would actually insist on the gas being lighted with a taper; a paper spill, which was just as good and better, seemed to ruffle her benign placidity: and she was funnily economical with matches. Rachel had never seen a taper before, and could not conceive where the old lady managed to buy the things. (chapter I, iii)

It is good that we should be made aware of Mrs Maldon's individuality here, her determination to do things her way, and her knowing things of which the young girl is ignorant. It gives her an implied roundedness, a hint of complexity which can't always be claimed for Bennett's characters but which he unfailingly achieves in *The Price of Love*. It comes out in the following moment, where we are told about the water-colour of Mrs Maldon's dead son, which hangs on the sitting room wall.

> Her pictures were admired.
> 'Your son painted this water-colour, did he not, Mrs Maldon?'
> 'Yes, my son Athelston.'
> 'How gifted he must have been!'
> 'Yes, the best judges say he showed remarkable promise. It's fading, I fear. I ought to cover it up, but somehow I can't fancy covering it up –'
> The hand that had so remarkably promised had lain mouldering for a quarter of a century. Mrs Maldon sometimes saw it, fleshless, on a cage-like skeleton in a dark grave. The next moment she would see herself tending its chilblains. (chapter I, iii)

Restraint and tenderness of regard are both finely in evidence there. Bennett, of course, disassociates himself from the empty, flattering voices and the mother's simple vanity. 'The hand that had so remarkably promised' has just the right sardonic edge. But the sudden, and very touching intrusion into Mrs Maldon's thoughts gives her a solidity and real presence that is both impressive in itself and another reminder of just how wide of the mark Virginia Woolf's criticism is when Bennett is at his best. And though there is something undeniably comic about Mrs Maldon seeing herself tending the hand's chilblains, it is worth remembering Goethe's remark that the clever man finds almost everything ridiculous, the wise man almost nothing. *The Price of Love* is a novel that only a wise man could have written.

It is also drenched with references to Five Towns characters – Mrs Sutton, Mrs Clayton Vernon, Mrs Hamps (the famous bullying aunt of the *Clayhanger* trilogy), Denry Machin; and to Bursley itself: Trafalgar Road, the Town Hall, the *Staffordshire Signal*. And because, added to that, there is a fleshing out of even of the most marginal characters, *The Price of Love* overwhelmingly persuades that it is about real people in a real place.

At its centre is the relationship between Rachel, Mrs Maldon's young companion, and Louis Fores, her grand-nephew, who marries Rachel. Louis is a no-good, a man without scruple who cannot help thinking well of himself. He spends money recklessly, cheats his successive employers and, on the evening on which the novel opens, thinks to steal some of his aunt's money. For on this same evening Mrs Maldon has received a large sum of cash, the settlement of one of her properties, from Councillor Batchgrew. Because of twists in the plotting of things which are too complicated to go into here Louis doesn't manage to steal the money, though it is lost, and he thinks himself partly responsible for the loss. But being Louis he also thinks himself partly justified and perhaps even innocent: 'He knew that with all his sins he possessed the virtues of good nature, kindness, and politeness. He was not wholly vile. In some ways he honestly considered himself a model to mankind' (chapter 13, i). Rachel suspects him of having taken the money, but is desperate that he shouldn't confess – above all, to her. So that when, after their marriage, he admits what he thinks is the truth, driven to it because he imagines that he is dying – he's been thrown by a horse and is in fact mildly hurt – she bursts out

'You've ruined everything now. Everything!' (chapter 12, v). The scene may, I realize, seem no more than trivially farcical when quoted out of context. And it is of course very funny. But it is more than merely comic, because Bennett succeeds so well in making credible Rachel's decency, her forbearance and generous love for her errant husband, mixed now with a real scorn for him. And Bennett equally succeeds in hitting off Louis's shallowness.

> One thing was absolutely sure – he could not and would not endure her contumely, nor even her indifferent scorn. For him to live with it would be ridiculous as well as impossible. He was weak, but two facts gave him enormous strength. First, he loved her less than she loved him, and hence she was at a disadvantage. But supposing her passion for him was destroyed? Then the second fact came into play. He had money. He had thousands of pounds, loose, available! To such a nature as his the control of money gives a sense of everlasting security. Already he dreamt of freedom, of roaming the wide world, subject to no yoke but a bachelor's whim. (chapter 13, iv)

Bennett does not always securely dovetail the narrator's voice into a character's musings, but he does so here, and very adroitly, too. Indeed, the very fact that we can't know for sure whether Louis is consciously thinking that he loves Rachel less than she loves him, so that she is 'at a disadvantage', prevents us from dismissing him as despicable. The same holds true for a later moment when, after Louis's sudden and absurd decision to run away, Bennett remarks of him:

> He could no longer stand, even for a single hour, her harshness, her air of moral superiority, her adamantine obstinacy [needless to say, this is Louis's hysterical interpretation of Rachel's perfectly reason-able behaviour, and one that allows him to justify his own actions]. He missed terribly her candid worship of him, to which he had grown accustomed and which had become nearly a necessity of his existence. He could not live with an eternal critic; the prospect was totally in-conceivable. He wanted love, and he wanted admiring love, and with-out it marriage was meaningless to him, a mere imprisonment. (chapter 17, i)

Why does Rachel love him? Well, she is an innocent, a Five Towns virgin who sees in Louis someone of above-average charm and gaiety. And who is quickly disillusioned. Candid love is what she may force herself to show Louis, but underneath she knows too much about him to dare to be truly candid. There is, for example, his sudden decision to go to church:

> she was disconcerted and even alarmed by Louis' manifest tendency to settle down into utter correctness. Louis had hitherto been a disciple of joy – never as a bachelor had he done aught to increase the labour of churchwardens – and it was somehow as a devotee of joy that Rachel had married him. Rachel had been settled down all her life, and naturally desired and expected that an unsettling process should now occur in her career. (chapter 10, iii)

Again, one notices the deft interlocking of narrator's voice with his character's own musings – for if Rachel were to think all that is here recorded we should regard her as priggish or plain silly. She is saved from becoming either because of Bennett's narrative intercessions.

Indeed, she is one of his most attractive creations. Rachel is a good person. Her love for Louis is, of course, nearly all giving, but she gives uncomplainingly even after she knows the worst about him. In fact she is more likely to accuse herself of having behaved badly and harshly to him: 'and as for herself, she, Rachel, was an over-righteous prig, an interfering person, a blundering fool of a woman, a cruel-hearted creature' (chapter 16, iii). We understand why she says that to herself. If she were to withhold such self-accusations, the accusations against Louis would become too terrible for either of them – and especially Louis – to cope with. For she knows as much about Louis as he knows about himself. That is why at the end she apologizes to him. And he sincerely forgives her.

This wryly humorous acceptance of things as they are isn't mechanically neat, nor is it cynical. On the contrary, Bennett's affectionate regard for Rachel and the assured way with which he establishes her worth make *The Price of Love*, though it is by no means one of the major novels, a warm, considerate and humane work.

III

It is, of course, the *Clayhanger* trilogy which stands out as the major work of the period under present review. *Clayhanger* (1910) comes first, and is followed by *Hilda Lessways* (1911), and finally by *These Twain* (1916). A fourth novel, *The Roll-Call*, is connected to the trilogy but only loosely, and it will be discussed in the next chapter.

Bennett was intensely ambitious for *Clayhanger* and he agonized over it in a way which, while not necessarily unique for him, is recorded in the *Journals* with an unusual fullness. 'I am trying to lift the whole thing up to a great height,' he noted soon after beginning it, 'but I feel sure that up to now it is nothing more than interesting in a nice quiet way.' A little later he rereads what he has so far written and to his great relief finds it 'more "coloured" and variegated than I had expected'. But doubts return: 'I am not very hopeful about the absolutely first-class quality of the whole book.' And the best that he can bring himself to say about the second section is that it is 'honest and conscientious'.

We need not be surprised at Bennett's doubts. Genuinely creative writers do worry about their work, become depressed by what they consider to be its failings. 'The reality so far short of the expectation', Wordsworth remarked gloomily, a fortnight after completing *The Prelude*. Depression is the other side of the coin of exultation in creativity. In Bennett's case, the doubts and uncertainties partly spring from what he knew he had achieved in *The Old Wives' Tale*. When he had all but finished the second section of *Clayhanger* he confided in the *Journal* that 'I was frightened by a lot of extraordinary praise of *The Old Wives' Tale* that I have recently had. I was afraid that Clayhanger was miles inferior to it. . . .' And though he bucked up when he read the novel in proof – 'A great deal of it is as good as anything I've done' – he agonized over the reviews, to the extent of recording the number of column inches given him by each reviewer. Such concern is clear evidence of Bennett's ambitions for the novel. *The Old Wives' Tale* had proved to him how much he was capable of; *Clayhanger*, which from the beginning was planned as a trilogy, is to build on the earlier achievement.

He did a considerable amount of research for it, and again the *Journals* allow us to chart his course of reading. On 14 September 1909 he begins to reread *When I was A Child*, an autobiography by 'an Old Potter' which had been published in 1903, and which Bennett needed in order to authenticate details of a 'grimmish detailed sketch of industrial child-life in 1840, about', which is to come at the beginning of the novel. By 21 October he has finished it and 'all I need of Shaw's *North Staffordshire Potteries*, and to-night I re-read the social and industrial section of the Victorian history, which contains a few juicy items I can use'. On 3 November he transcribes 'from the Victorian *History of Staffs* all the notes I want for my next novel'. On 1 December he comes home to Burslem, noting 'for third novel in trilogy, scene in train'. The next day he is digging information out of 'Dawson', Burslem shop-keeper and registrar; he calls twice again the following week and gets further essential information, and on 15 December he does 'part of the walk that Clayhanger must do as he comes finally home from school in the first chapter of *Clayhanger*'. And then he is ready to begin.

Wednesday, January 5th. [1910]
> This morning at 9.45 I began to write *Clayhanger*. I felt less nervous and self-conscious than usual in beginning a book. And never before have I made one-quarter so many preliminary notes and investigations. I went out for a little recess, and at 1.30 I had done 1,000 words, which was very good for a first day.

I have followed this through in some detail because I think it important that we grasp how deeply committed Bennett was to *Clayhanger*. Such commitment is by no means common with him; indeed he sometimes gives the impression of merely throwing novels off (an impression which some of the novels sadly reinforce). And the impression has often encouraged a dismissive attitude to all of Bennett's work. If he took so little care over his work, why should we bother? The attitude is familiar enough, but in the case of *Clayhanger* it cannot be justified. And though the pains Bennett took with his novel don't necessarily make it any good, they ought to encourage us to take it seriously. Equally, I think, they ought to alert us to what Bennett is doing. An old imitator, Lawrence called him, but there is nothing of imitation about *Clayhanger*. It is a genuinely original work, a novel which, for all that it seems ordinary, slowly and almost imperceptibly builds up a rich, detailed and dense study of provincial life. If one thinks of it in the context of those other works which I have discussed in this chapter, one feels that they are somehow spillings from the full vat of *Clayhanger*. Speaking of *The Lost Girl*, F. R. Leavis remarks that 'as a rendering of English provincial life, it strikes one as what Arnold Bennett would have wished to have done, though, being the work of a great creative genius, it is utterly beyond Bennett's achievement' (*D. H. Lawrence : Novelist*, Harmondsworth, p. 31). Certainly there are things in *The Lost Girl* that are beyond Bennett's achievement, but not the rendering of English provincial life. And this is not because Bennett puts that life before us in a series of massive set scenes, even though such scenes are not entirely absent from the novel. The section dealing with the Sunday school centenary celebrations, for example, is very fine, and is in the tradition which has for starting point in English fiction the Derby Day scene in George Moore's best novel, *Esther Waters*. Bennett's scene is better done than Moore's but it isn't by itself enough to make *Clayhanger* an outstanding novel. No, the real strength of Bennett's work depends on the extraordinary fidelity with which the ordinariness of provincial lives is placed before us and the close, loving scrutiny given to them so that we become deeply engaged with them and care about them. There is nothing in the Bennett of *Clayhanger* of that cool, remote manipulator of forms which he had earlier laid claim to being, nothing of distaste or keeping of distance in the way he writes about ordinary people. And yet without attempting to inflate the lives or experiences he studies and without wanting to lift the novel by improper rhetorical means, Bennett compels us to be interested in and moved by his characters and their lives. To take just one example. Darius Clayhanger, the semi-tyrant father of the novel's hero, Edwin Clayhanger, has slowly and painfully worked his way up from the abject poverty of the workhouse to reasonable prosperity as a printer. Edwin knows nothing of his father's early history – Darius has taken good care that he *shan't* know – and he sees in the old man only an awkward, boorish, tough, uncommunicative and perhaps hostile parent. There seems to be little love lost between father and son, and Darius ruthlessly stamps on Edwin's dream of becoming an architect. When his father becomes mortally ill, Edwin takes over the business and one of his first actions is to look into the safe which Darius has always jealously guarded. And in one of the safe-drawers he finds a map:

> It was coloured, and in shaky Roman characters underneath it ran the legend 'The County of Staffordshire.' He seemed to recognise the map. On the back he read, in his father's handwriting: 'Drawn and coloured without help by my son Edwin, aged nine.'
>
> He had utterly forgotten it. He could in no detail recall the circumstances in which he had produced the wonderful map. A childish, rude effort! . . . Still, rather remarkable that at the age of nine (perhaps even before he had begun to attend Oldcastle Middle School) he should have chosen to do a county map instead of a map of that country beloved by all juvenile map-drawers, Ireland! He must have copied it from the map in Lewis's Gazetteer of England and Wales. . . . Twenty-one years ago, nearly! He might, from the peculiar effect on him, have just discovered the mummy of the boy that had once been Edwin. . . . And his father had kept the map for over twenty years. The old cock must have been deuced proud of it once! Not that he ever said so . . . Edwin was sure of that. (Book 3, chapter 8, i)

It is one of the most moving moments in the whole of Bennett's fiction, and much of its strength stems from the way in which it hauls us back into the past, makes us aware of the slow, remorseless passage of years which the novel has slowly and remorselessly built up. How finely Bennett tracks Edwin's thoughts as they idle, quicken, catch hold of salient facts to do with the map, and lead him back into his own childhood. And how psychologically accurate that, kind and generous man though he is, he should first and unashamedly be absorbed with his own past and the details of his map-making, and only belatedly call to mind his father. And when he does, unconscious egoism yields to a tremor of genuine self-consciousness: 'The old cock.' The near-jauntiness of the phrase is meant to keep sentimentality at bay. Yet in its striking familiarity – Edwin has never before referred to his father in such a manner – we recognize that he is operating under the stress of considerable feelings, is genuinely moved by his father's pride in him. 'Not that he ever said so – Edwin was sure of that.' The son's fastidious mind rejects any possibility that Darius might openly have spoken his love. Of course not. For Darius cannot communicate with the son who has come to feel socially above him and with whom he feels hopelessly ill at ease. The passage of time, shifts in social allegiances, the strained and diffident love between father and son, and as always the sense of place and date – Oldcastle Middle School, Lewis's Gazetteer: they are all present in this marvellous and utterly representative passage.

The centre of interest in *Clayhanger* is, of course, Edwin himself. We follow him from awkward adolescence through to early middle age and his eventual marriage to Hilda. The novel covers a period of some twenty years and it does so at a slow, measured pace that gives us a real and weighty sense of time passing. This is assisted by the deftly casual introduction of events of national importance (at the house of his fashionable friends, the Orgreaves, Edwin discusses the Bradlaugh question; later he reads the *Manchester Guardian*'s 'long and vivid obituary of Charles Stewart Parnell'). Bennett also makes good use of minor characters to mark the passing of time. There is old Shushions, whom Edwin first meets talking with his father when he returns from his last afternoon at school:

> He balanced himself on his legs with conscious craft; he directed carefully his shaking and gnarled hand to his beard in order to stroke it. When he collected his thoughts into a sentence and uttered it in his weak, quavering voice, he did something wonderful, he listened closely, as though to an imperfectly acquired foreign language; and when he was not otherwise employed, he gave attention to the serious business of breathing. He wore a black silk stock, in a style even more antique than his remarkable headgear, and his trousers were very tight. He had survived into another and a more fortunate age than his own. (Book 1, chapter 3, iii)

Shushions links the novel to that world of the 1840s in which Darius – the man-child of seven – had had his miserable beginnings, and which is the subject of the superbly told chapter 4. That chapter no doubt owes much in the way of fact to *When I was A Child*, but the laconic toughness of the telling is Bennett's alone. And it shows us things about Darius that Edwin will never know. Indeed, Edwin has never before seen Shushions.

'Nay, nay, my boy,' trembled the old man, 'don't bare thy head to me . . . not to me! I'm one o' th' ould sort. Eh, I'm rare glad to see thee!' He kept Edwin's hand and stared long at him, with his withered face transfigured by solemn emotion. Slowly he turned towards Darius, and pulled himself together. 'Thou'st begotten a fine lad, Darius! . . . A fine, honest lad!'

'So – so!' said Darius gruffly, whom Edwin was amazed to see in a state of agitation similar to that of Mr Shushions.

Edwin knows nothing of his father's history, nor of Mr Shushions's honourable place in it. To him, they are merely old men behaving in a slightly absurd way. He forgets all about Shushions. But much later on the old man shows up at the Sunday school centenary celebrations, very aged, very ridiculous – Bennett manages heartrendingly to catch the pathos and absurd indignity of decrepitude; and later still we hear mention of his death and of Darius's attendance at his funeral (it will mark the onset of Darius's own steep decline).

Shushions, the Primitive Methodist, is part of the life of the Five Towns. And as with all other characters in the novel he is the victim of time, not just because he grows old but because he is rooted in a moment of history which becomes outmoded. Much of the success of *Clayhanger* has to do with Bennett's extraordinary feel for social change, the very texture of living in time in a particular place. This occasionally leads to the set piece – as for example, the description of the popular theatre, The Blood Tub (Book 1, chapter 9, iv), and the free-and-easy (chapter 10), a musical evening in the Dragon public-house to which Edwin is taken by Big James, his father's printer, who sings bass in the Bursley Male Glee Club, and where he is also entertained by the Bursley Prize Handbell Ringers, comic recitations, and Miss Florence Simcox, 'the champion female clog-dancer of the Midlands'. But though these are undoubtedly impressive, they would not of themselves give us that feel of provincial life which *Clayhanger* establishes – and, *pace* Dr Leavis, in an almost definitive manner. What makes for that are the ways in which the sights and sounds of Bursley become an inescapable element in the novel and also Bennett's attention to the kinds and quality of life that the town provides. And these are established through Edwin's various relationships: with his family, with his friends and with Hilda.

His most important relationship is with his father. There is every temptation to take sides here, to see Edwin as the outraged victim of his father's boorish ill-temper. And certainly there are occasions when Edwin himself takes that view. Darius prevents him from training to become an architect, makes him work long hours in the stationery shop, pays him a mere pittance, insults him over his proposed marriage. But we are forbidden from thinking of Darius as a kind of Tellwright writ large because we know about his dreadful beginnings, and can therefore understand his glowering, taciturn pride in the business he has so painfully built up and by means of which he has achieved respectability. Edwin knows nothing of this – for Darius to have confessed his origins would have been impossibly lowering to his hard-won self-esteem – and he therefore sees his father as a hopelessly unimaginative and crude domestic tyrant:

> He looked at his father and saw an old man, a man who for him had always been old, generally harsh, often truculent, and seldom indulgent. He saw an ugly, undistinguished and somewhat vulgar man . . . a man who had his way by force and scarcely ever by argument; a man whose arguments for or against a given course were simply pitiable, if not despicable. (Book 1, chapter 11, iii)

As the controlled tone of that suggests, Edwin has something of the aesthete's temperament, and in fact Bennett refers to the 'impartial and unmoved spectator that sat somewhere in Edwin'. He is shocked by and disdainful of his father's involvement with his business. There can be no understanding between them. But there are at least moments when Edwin is startled into an awareness that his uncouth father may feel real love for him. I think not only of his discovery of the map, but of the sad and absurd episode where the stricken Darius tries to make Edwin take his watch:

> 'I want ye—' the old man began, and then burst into violent sobs; and the watch dangled dangerously.
> 'Come now!' Edwin tried to soothe him, forcing himself to be kindly. 'What is it? I tell you I've wound it up all right. And it's correct time to a tick.' He consulted his own silver watch.
> With a tremendous effort Darius mastered his sobs, and began once more, 'I want ye—'

He tried several times, but his emotion overcame him each time before he could force the message out. It was always too quick for him. Silent, he could control it, but he could not control it and speak. (Book 3, chapter 13, iii)

This passage comes at the end of a very remarkable chapter, 'The Journey Upstairs', describing how Edwin and his sister's husband, Albert, have to half-carry, half-drag Darius up to his bed, from which they know he will never descend; and Bennett doesn't attempt to hide Edwin's irritation with the helpless old tyrant as Darius falls first in one direction, then another: 'Edwin restrained his exasperation; but though he said nothing, his sharp, half-vicious pull on that arm seemed to say, "Confound you. Come on up – will you!" ' No softening there, and none at all in Bennett's study of Darius's slow, utterly humiliating death. Nor in the relationship between father and son. To the last, they keep their distance from each other. Yet we never lose sympathy with Edwin. Indeed, this is perhaps the point at which to say that Edwin is an extraordinarily attractive character: his diffidence, sensitivity, concealed toughness, wry good humour, occasional bursts of anger – are all seen with such radiant intensity that they make this seemingly ordinary man the very opposite of dull or insipid. And in his bitter, unyielding relationship with his father Bennett has, I think, created a great study of mutual misunderstanding, of thwarted and misused love. One cannot lift chunks out and offer them for critical inspection. One has to experience the relationship as it unfolds in the pages of the novel. But it is masterly.

Just as masterly, to my way of thinking, is the treatment of Edwin's relationships with the rest of his family. There is a very fine and delicate tact about the handling of Maggie, the elder sister, and her gradual decline into spinsterhood, her acceptance of her role as dependable family drudge and Edwin's loving but untroubled acceptance of her. And Bennett is especially good on Clara, the younger sister: her bright adolescence, the contented, unambitious marriage to Albert Benbow, the birth of their several children, and her imperceptible progress towards incurious philistinism. As with Edwin and Darius, so with Edwin and his relationships with his sisters. They gradually unfold, develop, settle, and one simply can't quote in order to do Bennett justice. But perhaps the following moment may indicate something of the quality of his achievement. Clara has arrived at the shop – it is the morning of the centenary celebrations – hot, heavily pregnant, and with orders from Albert that she is to rest:

> Albert said! Albert said! Clara's intonation of this frequent phrase always jarred on Edwin. It implied that Albert was the supreme fount of wisdom and authority in Bursley. Whereas to Edwin, Albert was in fact a mere tedious, self-important manufacturer in a small way, with whom he had no ideas in common. 'A decent fellow at bottom,' the fastidious Edwin was bound to admit to himself by reason of slight glimpses which he had had of Albert's uncouth good-nature; but pietistic, overbearing, and without humour.
>
> 'Where's Maggie?' Clara demanded.
> 'I think she's putting her things on,' said Edwin.
> 'But didn't she understand I was coming early?' Clara's voice was now querulous, and she frowned.
> 'I don't know,' said Edwin.
> He felt that if they remained together for hours, he and Clara would never rise above this plane of conversation – personal, factual, perfectly devoid of wide interest. They would never reach an exchange of general ideas; they never had done. He did not think that Clara had any general ideas.
> 'I hear you're getting frightfully thick with the Orgreaves,' Clara observed, with a malicious accent and smile, as if to imply that he was getting frightfully above himself, and – simultaneously – that the Orgreaves were after all no better than other people.
> 'Who told you that?' He walked towards the doorway uneasily. The worst was that he could not successfully pretend that these sisterly attacks were lost on him.
> 'Never mind who told me,' said Clara.
> Her voice took on a sudden charming roguish quality, and he could hear again the girl of fourteen. His heart at once softened towards her.
> (Book 2, chapter 10, iii)

I do not know whether, torn from its context, that passage seems particularly impressive. Yet it is. For by the time we come to it we have seen something of Edwin's growing dissatisfaction with his family, of his slightly self-conscious hunger for knowledge, ideas, literature and his equally self-conscious awareness that his family's life is 'devoid of wide interest'. And we have seen him chafing at the limits of Bursley life, typified by the Wesleyan Methodist Young Men's Debating Society of which he is a member and at which he delivers a paper, 'Is Bishop Colenso, considered as a Biblical commentator, a force for good?' Yes, according to Edwin. No, according to all the others:

> Young man after young man arose to snub Bishop Colenso, to hope charitably that Bishop Colenso was sincere, and to insist that no Bishop Colenso should lead *him* to the awful abyss of polygamy, and that no Bishop Colenso should deprive *him* of that unique incentive to righteousness – the doctrine of an everlasting burning hell. Moses was put on his legs again as a serious historian, and the subject of the resolution utterly lost to view.

It is after that meeting that Edwin realizes that 'the chasm between himself and the others was a real chasm' (Book 1, chapter 15, iv–vi). For he is comparatively indifferent to religion, whereas most of his acquaintances and family are soaked in the uneasy, often hypocritical but intense and unquestioning pietism that has its most memorable exponent in Auntie Hamps.

Even the most determined opponent of Bennett would be hard put to it to deny his success with Clara Hamps. She is the central force of the Clayhanger family, and in her sentimental, ruthlessly hypocritical, egotistic and magnificently insincere way she actually cares about it. As a family tyrant she outdoes even Darius, but her tyranny lies in the manner in which she uses her superb and despicable arts to put all adversaries in the wrong. Inevitably, Edwin is the leading adversary. Planning his first revolt, he makes up his mind to tell his father that he won't enter the family business, but in the face of his aunt's enthusiastic remark that it does her good to think what a help he'll be to his father, 'with that clever head of yours', all Edwin can say is, 'Well, that remains to be seen.' ' "Remains to be *seen*?" Auntie Clara repeated, with a hint of startled pain, due to this levity.' She subdues him just as she subdues Maggie. Maggie is an easy victim. She has been making jam and offers her aunt some:

> 'Beautiful' she murmured [tasting it].
> 'Don't you think it's a bit tart?' Maggie asked.
> 'Oh no!' protestingly.

'*Don't* you?' asked Clara, with an air of delighted deferential astonishment.

'Oh *no*!' Mrs Hamps repeated. 'It's beautiful!' She did not smack her lips over it, because she would have considered it unladylike to smack her lips, but by less offensive gestures she sought to convey her unbounded pleasure in the jam. 'How much sugar did you put in?' she asked after a while. 'Half and half?'

'Yes,' said Maggie.

'They do say gooseberries were a tiny bit sour this year, owing to the weather,' said Mrs Hamps reflectively. (Book 1, chapter 7, ii)

Through Auntie Hamps Bennett gives us the very stuff of the family's flesh-creeping pieties and emotions. When she hears of the death of the vicar with whom Maggie has had some sort of an 'understanding', Auntie Hamps eyes are 'swimming in the satisfaction of several simultaneous woes'; when she discovers that Darius is seriously ill she tells Edwin: ' "Of course Maggie's the eldest and we think a great deal of her, but you're the son – the only son!" '; and Edwin must fume impotently as she responds to the domestic crisis with 'positive sensuality'. She is obviously the guiding spirit behind Albert and Clara's wish that Darius should make his will; and throughout she maintains an imperturbable certainty in the rightness of her opinions, responses, poses:

'I don't know what's coming over things!' Auntie Hamps murmured sadly, staring out of the window at the street gay with October sunshine. 'What with [Home Rule]. And what with those terrible baccarat scandals. And now there's this free education, that we ratepayers have to pay for. They'll be giving the children of the working-classes free meals next!' . . .

'Oh well! Never mind!' Edwin soothed her.

She gazed at him in loving reproach. And he felt guilty because he only went to chapel about once in two months, and even then from sheer moral cowardice. (Book 4, chapter 1, vii)

She is impossible and irreproachable, and she conveys the essence of that stultifying provincial life which surrounds Edwin.

Why, then, doesn't he leave? The answer lies partly in his nature. He lacks the adventurousness of Richard Larch or Cyril Povey. But he also cares about his family, maddening though it is.

And there are compensations in staying put. To some extent this derives from a deep-rooted inertia. Edwin finds it easier to let life come to him than to go in search of life. He has his work, his study-bedroom, his books, his accepted position in local society. They don't add up to a great deal, but they count for something. 'How we live measures our own nature', Philip Larkin remarks of Mr Bleaney, and it is true of Edwin. But then in his domestic circumstances he has more to show than Bleaney's 'hired box'. And he also has the Orgreaves.

Compared with the Clayhanger household, the Orgreave family is all sweetness and light. It is one of the 'best' families in Bursley. Osmond Orgreaves is a clever, hardworking architect and within his house Edwin finds music, poetry, discussions of general ideas, a civility and grace of living that Bennett shows and Edwin finds to be truly attractive. Small wonder that he should become 'frightfully thick' with the Orgreaves, or that his friendship with them should widen the gap between himself and the rest of his own family. Bennett establishes the connections between the two families with a practised and professional ease. Osmond Orgreave does business with the firm of Clayhanger, and when Darius wants to move up in the world he builds himself a new house at Bleakridge, the 'best end' of Bursley, beside the Orgreave house. Edwin is soon accepted into the Orgreave family, and though his initial diffidence never entirely leaves him – Bennett finely catches his shy sense of wonderment at a family so unlike his own – he becomes friendly with them and especially with Janet Orgreave: 'Janet had everything: a kind disposition, some brains, some beauty, considerable elegance and luxury for her station, fine shoulders at a ball, universal love and esteem' (Book 2, chapter 1, i). She is also in love with Edwin, and one of the most moving elements in the novel (and in *These Twain*) is the tact with which Bennett shows Edwin's total unawareness of her feelings for him and her gradual, sad acceptance of this fact. More or less our last view of her in *Clayhanger* is this one:

> She was the kindliest, the most dignified, the most capable creature; but she was now an old maid. You saw it even in the way she poured tea and dropped pieces of sugar into the cups. Her youth was gone; her complexion was nearly gone. And though in one aspect she

seemed indispensable, in another the chief characteristic of her existence seemed to be a tragic futility. (Book 4, chapter 9, iii)

By the end of the novel the Orgreave household itself is more or
less broken. The various sons have left home, Osmond is ageing
and no longer has the fascination for Edwin that he once held (this
is underlined by Edwin's discovery of Osmond's sharp business
dealings with the firm of Clayhanger, a typical Bennett touch).
'His voice had changed on the last sentence. He had meant to be a
little facetious about the Greek words; but it was the slowly prepared and rather exasperating facetiousness of an ageing man, and
he had dropped it listlessly, as though he had perceived this'
(Book 4, chapter 9, ii). All human things are subject to decay, including the Orgreave household. This aspect of the novel is most
beautifully and naturally done. Indeed it is so natural that it hardly
seems done at all. (' "It is life itself" we murmur as we read, "and
not this or that or the other story-teller's more or less 'clever
arrangement' of life." ')

At the Orgreaves' house Edwin meets Hilda Lessways. She is
staying there as a friend of Janet's, and her unusual, awkward and
fierce intensity alarms and fascinates him. After their first meeting and his famous remark at the Orgreave dinner table about there
being no virtue in believing, she follows him into the night to ask
him if he meant what he said:

'I dare say you think it's very queer of me,' she continued.

'Not at all,' he said quickly.

'Yes you do,' she bitterly insisted. 'But I want to know. Did you
mean it when you said – you know, at supper – that there's no virtue
in believing?'

'Did I say there was no virtue in believing?' he stammeringly demanded.

'Of course you did!' she remonstrated. 'Do you mean to say that
you can say a thing like that and then forget about it? If it's true, it's
one of the most wonderful things that were ever said. And that's why
I wanted to know if you meant it or whether you were only saying it
because it sounded clever. That's what they're always doing in that
house, you know – being clever!' Her tone was invariably harsh.

'Yes,' he said simply, 'I meant it. Why?'

'You did?' Her voice seemed to search for insincerity. 'Well, thank you. That's all. It may mean a new life to me. I'm always trying to believe; always! Aren't you?'

'I don't know,' he mumbled. 'How do you mean?'

'Well – you know!' she said, as if impatiently smashing his pretence of not understanding her. 'But perhaps you do believe?'

He thought he detected scorn for a facile believer. 'No,' he said, 'I don't.'

'And it doesn't worry you? Honestly? Don't be clever! I hate that!'

'No,' he said. (Book 2, chapter 9, iv)

Hilda's disconcerting abruptness shakes Edwin and also forces him into the kind of truth-telling that is exhilarating to him. So that although she isn't conventionally attractive it is no surprise that he should fall in love with her. It is her very unconventionality that appeals to his sensitive nature. That, and her unique vitality, finely touched on by Bennett as she and Edwin watch together the centenary celebrations and he thinks that 'Every curve of her features seemed to express a fine arrogant acrimony and harsh truculence. At any rate she was not half alive; she was alive in every particle of herself. She gave off antipathies as a liquid gives off vapour' (Book 2, chapter 11, iii). Bennett's images do not often have the accuracy and suggestiveness of that one, nor does he often manage to present women without at some stage or another sliding into condescension towards them. But his presentation of Hilda never falters. To the last she is quick, intensely and nervously alive, enigmatic and vitally attractive to Edwin. His relationship with her blooms, is broken, recovers and is shattered. They become engaged and she goes away. Soon, he hears she is married to another man. Years later her son comes to stay with the Orgreaves. Finally Edwin traces her to the impoverished squalor of her Brighton boarding house and learns about her marriage to the bigamous George Cannon. *Clayhanger* ends with the pair planning to marry. It is a perfectly satisfactory ending to a stunningly rich novel of provincial family life, perhaps the finest novel of its kind that any English writer has produced.

Unfortunately, however, Bennett was not content to leave well alone. He wants to explain Hilda, to tell her side of the story. So he writes *Hilda Lessways*. But whereas the Hilda of *Clayhanger* seems to me entirely satisfactory, the heroine of *Hilda Lessways* is an altogether inferior creation. What went wrong?

The clue may lie in an anxious *Journal* entry:

> I didn't seem to be getting near the personality of Hilda in my novel. You scarcely ever do get near a personality. There is a tremendous lot in fiction that no one has yet done. When M. comes downstairs from the attic, in the midst of some house arrangements, and asks me if such and such a thing will do and runs up again excited – why? And the mood of the servant as, first thing in the morning, she goes placidly round the house opening the shutters! The fact is, the novelist seldom really *penetrates*.

It is very odd that Bennett should make the transition from the fictional to the factual without apparently noticing that he has done so. Granted that a novelist may often be puzzled by people he meets, he surely ought to know a good deal about the characters he himself creates? Yet to ask that question is to become aware of the fact that Hilda is the most unconventional female character Bennett was ever to invent and that she therefore causes him all sorts of difficulties simply because he is most at home with more conventional women, such as Alma Fearns and Constance Baines, or women whom he can conventionalize, as for example Leonora. These difficulties don't matter as long as Hilda is seen from the outside, as she is in *Clayhanger*. For in that novel we see her through Edwin's eyes and Bennett's bewilderment at the kind of person he has created can be properly indistinguishable from Edwin's own bewilderment. But Hilda can hardly appear bewilderingly mysterious in the novel which seeks to tell her side of the story. Nor is she. Unfortunately, however, she becomes thoroughly conventional. In writing her story Bennett comes nowhere near accounting for the personality of Hilda as it had gleamed out in *Clayhanger*. What he does provide is a trivialized study of a provincial girl. We can see how if we compare a moment from *Clayhanger* with one from its sequel. In both, our attention is directed to Hilda's sensitivity to poetry.

Clayhanger first. Hilda and Edwin are watching the Sunday school centenary celebrations. The massed choirs and brass bands are singing Watt's famous 'When I survey the wondrous cross'.

Hilda shook her head.

'What's the matter?' he asked, leaning towards her. . . .

'That's the most splendid religious verse ever written!' she said passionately. 'You can say what you like. It's worth while believing anything, if you can sing words like that and mean them!'

She had an air of restrained fury.

But fancy exciting herself over a hymn!

'Yes, it is fine, that is!' he agreed.

'Do you know who wrote it?' she demanded menacingly.

'I'm afraid I don't remember,' he said. The hymn was one of his earliest recollections, but it had never occurred to him to be curious as to its authorship.

Her lips sneered. 'Dr Watts, of course!' she snapped.

He could hear her, beneath the tremendous chanting from the Square, repeating the words to herself with her precise and impressive articulation. (Book 2, chapter 12, iii)

Now *Hilda Lessways*. Hilda is in George Cannon's office, alone. She sees a volume of Victor Hugo's poems on the shelf, takes it down and opens it at *Les Rayons et les ombres*, a poem which, years earlier, she had learnt by heart at school.

> . . . she shook as though a miracle had been enacted. . . . Hilda had apparently forgotten most of her French, but as she now read the poem (for the first time in print), it re-established itself in her memory as the most lovely verse that she had ever known, and the recitations of it in Miss Miranda's small class-room came back to her with an effect beautiful and tragic. And also there was the name of Victor Hugo, which Miss Miranda's insistent enthusiasm had rendered sublime and legendary to a sensitive child! (Book 1, chapter 6, ii)

The differences are obvious enough. Hilda's gauche intensity at the celebrations is both credible and attractive. It is only shortly before this that she has had her night-time meeting with Edwin and questioned him about belief. Now she is emotionally swung away from his cool agnosticism and is understandably furious with his diffidence, which can look like indifference. After this she will go to Brighton and marry George Cannon, who is masterful where Edwin is submissive. And the fact that he does not understand her passion – 'fancy exciting herself over a hymn' – is a comment on them both. Edwin is startled by Hilda's intensity and he tries to play it down. But the clumsy jokiness of his thought makes it plain how intrigued he is by this girl's nervous vitality.

But in the second episode there is no nervous vitality at all. Instead, Bennett produces his stock of clichés – miracle, beautiful, tragic, sublime – in an attempt to flog into life what is itself a cliché. For the Hilda of this scene is the clubman's eternal school-girl, 'all feeling'. And this is what she remains throughout the novel. Bennett's desperate attempts to convince us of her sensitivity become merely embarrassing. The novel is littered with passages such as the following. Hilda has just arrived at Brighton with Sarah Gailey, to run George Cannon's boarding-house:

> And as she heard the ceaseless, cruel play of the water amid the dark jungle of ironwork under the pier, and the soft creeping of the foam-waves behind, and the vague stirrings of the night-wind round about – these phenomena combined mysteriously with the immensity of the dome above and with the baffling strangeness of the town, and with the grandeur of the beaten woman by her side; and communicated to Hilda a thrill that was divine in its unexampled poignancy. (Book 3, chapter 4, iii)

Worst of all, perhaps, is the scene in Bursley where Hilda sees some ragged children and 'Pain and joy ran together in her, burning exquisitely; and she had a glimpse, obscure, of the mystical beauty of the children's suffering'. This kind of thing is spread over some 400 pages and by the time one comes to the end one feels like applying to Hilda the unhappy phrase which Gissing had pinned on to the Westgates, those dreamy idealists of *Demos*. Like them, Hilda is 'a poetry-fed soul at issue with fate'. In her case fate is the stifling provincial life which she suffers with her fussy, inefficient, pious mother. The parallels with Edwin are obvious. But in *Hilda Lessways* Bennett treats the provinciality of Hilda's life perfunctorily and quite without the care and density that help to make *Clayhanger* so remarkable.

But then everything about Hilda's life is treated perfunctorily. I utterly reject F. R. Leavis's claim that Bennett cannot render provincial life as Lawrence can, but it has to be admitted that a comparison between Alvina Houghton, the Lost Girl, and Hilda, does Bennett no good at all. For quite apart from the fact that he stumbles into cliché when he tries to write of Hilda's 'poetry-fed soul', he is hardly better when he comes to write of her sexuality. And this matters. He needs to establish the fact that Hilda impulsively agrees to marry Cannon because she is sexually excited by him (her last contact with Edwin had been at the celebrations, when he had been at his most diffident, and least sexually aggressive). The idea is good, but not the attempt to put it into words:

> And the fact was that she overwhelmingly wanted George Cannon, and, as she now recognised, had wanted him ever since she first saw him. The recognition afforded her intense pleasure. She abandoned herself candidly to the luxury of an unknown desire. It was incomparably the most splendid and dangerous experience she had ever had. (Book 4, chapter 2, iii)

I do not object to that. It is a perfectly reasonable and sympathetic attempt to track the ways of Hilda's consciousness, to discover her sexuality ('luxury' is a discreetly planted clue). But I do object to the fact that we never get beyond such passages. How can we be expected to believe that Hilda 'had passed through painful, shattering ecstasies of bliss, hours unforgettable, hours which she knew would never recur. And yet she was left sated and unsatisfied' (Book 5, chapter 1, ii). Or that 'Already she was disappointed with her marriage. Amid the fevers of bodily appetite she could clearly distinguish the beginnings of lassitude; she no longer saw her husband as a romantic and baffling figure; she had explored and charted his soul, and not all his excellencies could atone for his earthliness' (Book 5, chapter 1, iv). How can we believe these things when we are denied the slightest indication as to how the ecstasies of bliss or fevers of appetite modify Hilda's personality, or are real to her? It is not that I want Bennett to take us into Cannon and Hilda's bed, but I think that at the very least he ought to show them together. Yet we hardly ever see them in anything like intimate conversation, let alone close to each other in different ways. The result is that Hilda's sudden disillusionment with her husband is strictly meaningless. 'His charm was coarse and crude,' we are told, 'but he was very skilful, and there was something about his experienced, weather-beaten, slightly depraved air, which excited her. She liked to feel young and girlish before him; she liked to feel that with him, alone of all men, her modesty availed nothing'

(Book 5, chapter i, ii). One cannot argue that Cannon is to Hilda in this novel as Hilda is to Edwin in *Clayhanger*. Because in Clayhanger we see Hilda with Edwin, are shown enough of her to understand why and how Edwin reacts to her as he does. But in *Hilda Lessways* we are constantly told how Cannon affects Hilda but shown hardly anything of him as her lover and husband. So that his charm and her gathering indifference to it are equally unreal. Of course, she has to change her mind, otherwise the scheme of the trilogy would never work. The sensitive Edwin must eventually triumph over the merely sensual Cannon. But that doesn't help to make Hilda any more credible.

I suspect that Bennett knew as much himself. There is a grim doggedness about *Hilda Lessways* that suggests he put into it little of the imaginative energy that fires the pages of *Clayhanger*. It is a tedious, repetitive novel – literally. In Book 1, chapter 4, there is a passage about servants which turns up again in Book 4, chapter 3. And in chapter 5 of the first book we are treated to a heavily ironic piece on Cannon's laundry that is repeated, almost word for word, in Book 2, chapter 2. Bennett's prose is tired and feeble, full of those squashy epithets he falls back on whenever he can't be bothered to invent. And in a late chapter, 'Some Secret History', there is a long, garbled and unfinished sentence – sure evidence that he nodded not only over the composition of the novel but over his proof-reading (on the accuracy of which he prided himself). And the stony silence in the *Journals* over the novel's progress makes clear Bennett's dislike of the chore he had set himself.

Hilda Lessways is not a complete failure. George Cannon is an interesting creation, though Bennett hardly gives us enough of what is most interesting about the man: his shady financial dealings, and determination to succeed whatever the cost to himself or to others. It is annoying. Also annoying is the fact that although he lets us into Cannon's mind on one or two occasions, as when he thinks of how he has succeeded in Brighton – 'the rapid progress, he felt, was characteristic of him' – he keeps us at bay when we want to know Cannon's thoughts about Hilda or his business methods. But Cannon is obviously the invention of a good novelist. And Bennett handles very smoothly the retelling from Hilda's point of view of her encounters with Edwin. Yet even here we become aware of how far *Hilda Lessways* goes wrong. For Bennett does not tell us anything about these encounters that we could not guess from *Clayhanger*. Hilda's view of Edwin at the celebrations is as we had known it would be. And here lies the nub of the matter. In so far as it covers the same ground as *Clayhanger*, *Hilda Lessways* is simply unnecessary. In so far as it tries to break new ground, by studying Hilda in some depth, it is a near disaster. The important question to consider is what effect all this has on *These Twain*.

The answer is that *These Twain* is not as damaged by *Hilda Lessways* as we might fear. This is partly because the third novel picks up much of the material of *Clayhanger* and carries it to a conclusion. At the very least we have the simple pleasure of following the histories of various characters through to their end. In the course of *These Twain* Auntie Hamps and the Orgreave parents die, the Orgreave family is finally broken up, Edwin and Hilda are increasingly separated from the rest of the Clayhangers; and the novel ends with the couple about to move to a large house some miles from Bursley. The end of an era is in sight for Clayhanger and, I think, for Bennett also. He will never again write at length about the Five Towns. Perhaps he had nothing left to say. Perhaps the death of his mother, in November 1914, which broke the last important family link with Burslem, had something to do with it. And perhaps the war shook him far more than he is prepared to give away in his *Journals* and letters. Much of *These Twain* was written after the outbreak of war and there is a moment, late on in the novel, which stands out oddly and suggestively from the rest, and which may hint at how deeply shaken Bennett was by the course events had taken. Edwin and Hilda have gone to eat Christmas dinner with their friend, Tertius Ingpen, who lives in the country village of Stockbrook:

> More suave than a Dutch village, incomparably neater and cleaner and more delicately finished than a French village, it presented, in the still, complacent atmosphere of long tradition, a picturesque medley of tiny architectures nearly every aspect of which was beautiful. And if seven people of different ages and sexes lived in a two-roomed cottage under a thatched roof hollowed by the weight of years, without drains and without water, and also without freedom, the beholder was yet bound to conclude that by some mysterious virtue their existence

must be gracious, happy and in fact ideal . . . after all the illusion of
Arcadia was not entirely an illusion. In this calm, rime-decked,
Christmas-imbued village, with its motionless trees enchanted beneath
a vast grey impenetrable cloud, a sort of relative finality had indeed
been reached – the end of an epoch that was awaiting dissolution.
(Book 3, chapter 20, ii)

'The end of an epoch.' It does not refer directly to the Five Towns,
but it well might. Bennett seems anxious to complete his dealings
with the place. The plotting of *These Twain* is frequently perfunctory and awkward. People are introduced, dismissed, forgotten
about. The Orgreaves are packed off to their deaths with what feels
to be an almost indecent haste. An episode in Devon is curiously
unreal. And in addition some of the characters themselves are
poorly done, Ingpen in particular.

More than that, however, there is an undertow of feeling against
the Five Towns that pulls more strongly and steadily through this
novel than has ever before been the case. Mostly it is channelled
through Hilda's loathing of the Clayhanger family: 'Their narrow
ignorance, their narrow self-conceit, their detestation of beauty,
their pietism, their bigotry – revolted her' (Book 1, chapter 8, iv).
But by the end of the novel Edwin has also come to accept his
separation from the 'mass' of Five Towns life:

Now the whole mass seemed to be rising, under the action of some
strange leaven, and those few who by intelligence, by manners, or by
money counted themselves select were fleeing as from an inundation.
Edwin had not meant to join in the exodus. But he too would join it.
Destiny had seized him. Let him be as democratic in spirit as he
would, his fate was to be cut off from the democracy, with which, for
the rest, he had very little of speech or thought or emotion in common,
but in which, from an implacable sense of justice, he was religiously
and unchangeably determined to put his trust. (Book 3, chapter
20, v)

There is some decidedly shaky language in that passage, and indeed
the whole treatment of Edwin's political and social conscience is a
matter that I shall take up a little later. For the moment I merely
want to observe that Edwin's move away from the Five Towns is,
like his creator's, final. And Edwin's sense of separateness is so

complete, so much a way of insisting that he might as well be moving to France as to the mansion Hilda has chosen for him and which is no more than ten miles from Bursley, and is so emphasized by Bennett's own stance in the novel, that it soon becomes clear that *These Twain* must be the last extended study of Five Towns life.

This is not to imply that Bennett is merely dismissive in his treatment of the Five Towns. He isn't. But he nevertheless ruthlessly cuts through the tissue of provincial family life to lay bare the defects of which Hilda so bitterly complains. And he does it in some of the finest chapters he ever wrote: the novel's first four, in which Hilda and Edwin, newly married, are 'At Home'; and chapter 8 of Book 1, called 'The Family at Home', in which Clara and Albert organize a birthday party for one of their numerous children. This chapter in particular has the unique strengths of Bennett's best work. Once again I find myself having to say that it is impossible to quote from any of the chapter's forty-four pages and hope to indicate its worth. Even so, I offer the following snippet, on the offchance that it may convey something of Bennett's achievement. At this point the birthday tea is nearing its end. It is seen through Hilda's eyes, who has very inconveniently called on the Benbows (they hadn't wanted her to know of the party's existence since her son George hasn't been invited, it being Albert's opinion that George exerts a bad influence over his own children), and the Benbows are inevitably behaving with awkward, hypocritical goodnature. Flossie, a neighbouring child who has arrived late, finishes eating:

> 'I've had quite enough, thank you,' said she, in answer to expostulations.
> 'No jam, even? And you've not finished your tea!'
> 'I've had quite enough, thank you,' said she, and folded up her napkin.
> 'Please, father, can we go out and play in the garden now?' Bert asked.
> Albert looked at his wife.
> 'Yes, I think they might,' said Clara. 'Go and play nicely.' They all rose.
> 'Now quietly, quietly!' Albert warned them.

How much of the absurd pathos of attempted gentility and of joy-less respectability are contained in Flossie's well-mannered, auto-matic responses, in the folding of her napkin, in Clara's 'go and play nicely' – *nicely*, for goodness sake – and in Albert's 'Now quietly, quietly'. It is Bennett's unobtrusive accuracy that is so telling here, his extraordinary gift for knowing how to use the trivia of customs and habits and speech in order to catch the quality of provincial lives. When it comes to the family, *These Twain* is on a par with *Clayhanger*.

But of course its main subject is the relationship between Edwin and Hilda. How well does Bennett manage here? In some ways, very well indeed. He is, for example, scrupulous in giving us both Edwin's and Hilda's points of view, and as a result he builds up a taut and convincing sense of their numerous frictions, misunder-standings and sexual tensions. In a lecture on the scope of the novel which he gave to The Times Book Club in 1910, Wells asked:

> What is the good of pretending to write about love, and the loyalties and treacheries and quarrels of men and women if one must not glance at those varieties of physical temperament and organic quality, those deeply passionate moods and distresses from which half the storms of life are brewed? (quoted in Lovat Dickson, *H. G. Wells*, Harmonds-worth, p. 241)

Bennett had been present at Wells's lecture, and although several years would go by before he began the writing of *These Twain* his own novel does 'glance' as Wells had asked that the novelist be allowed to do. Glance and no more. There is no explicit sex in *These Twain*. But Bennett subtly and delicately establishes its atmosphere. To take just one example. After their triumphant 'At Home', Edwin and Hilda are upstairs, preparing for bed. Hilda puts on a shawl and stands there 'smiling, posing, bold, provoca-tive'. Then she asks him what he has been talking about with Johnnie Orgreave. Edwin has other things on his mind – her, in particular – and, wanting to dismiss her question, answers care-lessly:

> 'Talking a long time to Johnnie Orgreave? Oh, d'you mean at the front-door? Why, it wasn't half a minute! He happened to mention a piece of land down at Shawport that I had a sort of notion of buying.'

'Buying? What for?' Her tone hardened.
'Well, supposing I had to buy a new works?'
'You never told me anything about it.'

And they slip into an intensifying argument and sudden but un-
preventable emotional bitterness that shatters their mood of warm
sensual accord. Then Hilda leaves the room:

> She was away some time. When she returned, he was in bed, with
> his face averted. He heard her moving about.
> 'Will she, or won't she come and kiss me?' he thought.
> She came and kissed him, but it was a meaningless kiss.
> 'Good-night,' she said aloofly. (Book 1, chapter 6, ii)

Bennett brings off this kind of scene more than once in the novel
and in doing so he captures exactly that 'intimate conveyance of the
atmosphere of married life' which he had claimed in a letter he most
wanted to do (vol. II, p. 310). Whenever we see Hilda through
Edwin's eyes in *These Twain* she is credible as she never is in *Hilda
Lessways*, and the same is true of Edwin, when he is seen through
Hilda's eyes. And we understand now why she should use her
sexual attractiveness so aggressively. For Edwin quite lacks the
courage to try to dominate her. That is what makes him so
attractive to her and also at times so infuriating. It is always Hilda
who plays the part of aggressor in their (implied) sexual encounters,
never he. In a particularly keen-edged phrase, Bennett refers to
Edwin keeping resentment against Hilda hidden 'neatly in a little
drawer in his mind, and glanc[ing] at it now and then' (Book 1,
chapter 9, vii). Edwin enjoys surrendering to Hilda, and enjoys the
self-consciousness with which he does it.

So far, so good. Very good, in fact. But there is more to Edwin
and Hilda than their sexual feelings for each other, and more to
their marriage. And it is here that doubts about the novel inevitably begin to loom up. I think it important to try to pin these
doubts down, and I think it very important to note that Bennett
almost certainly wrote *These Twain* with Wells's novel, *Marriage*,
in mind. *Marriage* was published in 1912, it was dedicated to
Bennett 'fraternally', and Bennett corrected the proofs. It was
Marriage that Bennett was thinking of when he said that he hoped
to capture the '*atmosphere* of married life', because he judged

Wells to have managed it better than any previous novelist. I think myself that as far as capturing atmosphere goes *These Twain* emerges as a comfortable winner. Wells cannot write as accurately or as evocatively and discreetly as Bennett can, and he has none of Bennett's sensitivity to nuance of word, gesture, look. On the other hand, Wells aims with an uncomfortable directness at some questions which Bennett, although he glances at them, can't cope with. Here, for example, the hero of *Marriage*, a scientist called Trafford, ruminates on the position of married men and women in the modern world:

> The serious and responsible life of an ordinary prosperous man ful-filling the requirements of our social organisation fatigues and neither completely satisfies nor completely occupies. Still less does the respon-sible part of the life of a woman of the prosperous classes engage all her energies or hold her imagination. And there has grown up a great informal organization of employments, games, ceremonies, social routines, travel, to consume these surplus powers and excessive crav-ings, which might otherwise change or shatter the whole order of human living. (Book 3, chapter 1, vi)

In *These Twain* Hilda comes close to just such thoughts. That is, she expresses a real dissatisfaction with the life which she is forced to lead as a married woman. This has something to do with the fact that she and Edwin live in the Five Towns, where 'you might walk from one end . . . to the other, and not see one object that gave a thrill'. But there is more to her chafing at the restrictions of mar-riage than just that:

> She had nothing against [Edwin]. Yet she had everything against him, because apart from his grave abiding love for her, he possessed an object and interest in life, and because she was a mere complement and he was not. She had asked herself the most dreadful of questions: 'Why have I lived? Why do I go on living?' and had answered: 'Be-cause of *them*,' meaning Edwin and her son. But it was not enough for her, who had once been violently enterprising, pugnacious, en-dangered, and independent. For after she had watched over them she had energy to spare, and such energy was not being employed and could not be employed. Reading – a diversion! Fancy work – a detest-able device for killing time and energy! Social duties – ditto! Charity –

hateful! She had slowly descended into marriage as into a lotus valley. And more than half her life was gone.

It is an impressive and moving passage, in which Hilda's own thoughts are skilfully interwoven with Bennett's guiding narrative – '[she] who had once been violently enterprising, pugnacious, endangered, and independent' – and in which one really does get the sense of Hilda's frustration with a marriage which is effortlessly comfortable and harmful to her own sense of herself. For where is the passionate, awkward but intensely alive girl of *Clayhanger*? She shows through in glimmers: as when she shocks Auntie Hamps by telling her that she and Edwin aren't great chapel-goers, or when she herself is shaken by Whitman's great lines in *Song of Myself*; or when she becomes impulsively contemptuous of the Benbow family; or when, very importantly, she finds herself resenting being a 'kept' woman: 'the fact that he earned and she didn't was ever mysteriously present in his relatively admirable attitude. . . . And Hilda resented, not so much his attitude, as the whole social convention upon which it was unassailably based' (Book 2, chapter 13, ii). There are other moments but, significant though they are when taken on their own, they do not allow her to feel that she still has an identity with which she can be confident or at ease: nothing can outweigh the fact that she is now Hilda Clayhanger and not Hilda Lessways. Bennett and Wells seem at one in this. They both know, so it feels, how radical a sacrifice the married woman must make for the sake of her marriage, how deeply she must resent social organizations calculated to confirm her in her sense of being complementary, existing for someone else's purpose. And because Bennett is far better at an imaginative level than Wells, he makes the case for Hilda's sense of dissatisfaction much better than his contemporary and friend could do. But then see what happens to Hilda's thoughts:

Edwin needed to be inspired; she must inspire him. . . . Moreover, the household machine had been getting slack. A general tonic was required; she would administer it – and to herself also. . . . She would organise social distractions; on behalf of the home she would reclaim from the works those odd hours and half-hours of Edwin's which it had imperceptibly filched. She would have some new clothes, and she would send Edwin to the tailor's. She would make him buy a dog-cart and a horse. Oh! she could do it. She had the mastery of him in many things when she chose to be aroused. In a word she would 'branch out.' (Book 3, chapter 17, i)

I am not suggesting that we should object to Hilda's thinking as she does here. It may well be all that is possible to her. But surely Bennett himself ought not to be so neutral, so bland? Surely there ought to be some way of registering what has gone wrong with the process of Hilda's thoughts, of her swift decline into precisely that complementariness which had been the cause of her initial protest? For don't her plans amount to precisely what Wells had had in mind when he had spoken of the 'great informal organization of employments, games, ceremonies, social routines, travel'? Is *this* what the question 'Why have I lived?' comes down to?

Yet the sad truth is that Bennett does not appear to have noticed that something has gone badly awry with his presentation of Hilda's thoughts. After all, he does not dissociate himself from her plan to make Edwin move to Ladderedge Hall (itself a mark of her conventionalization and her move away from the truculent, unconventional Hilda Lessways). In *Marriage*, Trafford's wife, Marjorie, is keen to move to a bigger house, especially after she and her husband have returned from some months' leisurely holiday spent at a vast, well-organized house of friends in Switzerland. And at this point Trafford decides that they must cry halt, must examine themselves and their marriage. Before, he has wavered between wanting a woman as 'comrade', and regarding her as 'lifted a little off the cold ground of responsibility'. The friends in Switzerland think of women in the light of what he privately calls 'orientalism' or 'chivalry'. They feel that women should live 'in a magic security and abundance, far above the mire and adventure of the world' (Book 2, chapter 3, xiii). Or as Ingpen, more brutally but more realistically, puts it in *These Twain*: 'women are for the Harem'. Ingpen represents, though poorly, a version of the chivalric, sentimental attitude to women that is canvassed in *Marriage* and fiercely rejected. Trafford tells Marjorie that they have reached a crisis: ' "If we do not seize this opportunity – Then our lives will go on as they have gone on, will become more and more a matter of small excitements and elaborate comforts and distractions . . ." '

(Book 3, chapter 2, vii). It is clumsily done, and their attempt to cope with their crisis is even more clumsy. Yet what Trafford says does point us towards the very awkward question of what happens to Hilda and Edwin. For by the end of *These Twain* their life together is more and more a matter of small excitements and elaborate comforts and distractions. What does the move to Ladderedge Hall mean if not that? And what concerns me is not that Hilda and Edwin should fail to see the move in those terms, but that Bennett, having opened up the insufficiencies of Hilda's life, shouldn't see it either. One need not necessarily complain that their acceptance of their world amounts to compromise. It may, after all, be the anodyne for Edwin's fitful fear that 'his life seemed to be a life of half-measures, a continual falling-short' (Book 2, chapter 1, i). But Bennett's endorsement of their move is a very different matter.

To be blunt, there is a real hollowness at the heart of Edwin and Hilda's marriage, and I do not think that Bennett, who allows Edwin's sense of a life of half-measures to slip away from the novel, was prepared to see it as such (even though, deep down, he knew that that was what it amounted to). To take a trivial but betraying example. At the beginning of *These Twain* we are told of the pride that Edwin takes in his house:

> The nice fitting of a perpendicular spout into a horizontal one, and the curve of the joint from the eave to the wall of the house, and the elaborate staples that firmly held the spout to the wall, and the final curve of the spout that brought its orifice accurately over a spotless grid in the ground – the perfection of all these ridiculous details, each beneath the notice of a truly celestial mind, would put the householder Edwin into a sort of contemplative ecstasy. Perhaps he was comical. But such inner experiences were part of his great interest in life, part of his large general passion. (Book 1, chapter 1, ii)

It is hardly necessary to point out what is badly amiss here, from the silliness of pretending that Edwin's interest in drainpipes has anything to do with a 'great interest in life', to the blustering defensive irony – 'a truly celestial mind' – which is used to ward off criticism. Indeed, the tone may feel so insensitive as to prompt the impatient reader to wonder whether the whole marriage relationship shouldn't simply be written off. But that would be wrong. For

Bennett does make plausible various important decencies about Hilda and Edwin: he does quite enough to convince us of their kindness, generosity, good feeling, tact, their sexual battles and tendernesses. But what then? It is a large and unanswerable question. But then, I am afraid, nothing. Or rather much that turns out to be nothing. For there is about the novel a dominant or determined complacency that severely damages its worth. I want to believe that Bennett did not intend it, and that he only reluctantly turned away from Hilda's dissatisfactions and Edwin's sense of living a life of half-measures. But however that may be, the unavoidable fact is that in the last analysis *These Twain* must be reckoned a complacent novel. It shows itself not only in Edwin's contentedness at being a householder (and how that echoes what Veblen had been saying not many years before in the *Theory of the Leisure Class*). It is there in the deflection of Hilda's discontent into a desire to inspire Edwin and to 'branch out' (the 'duties of vicarious leisure and consumption devolve upon the wife alone', Veblen said); it is there in the move to Ladderedge Hall ('the motive is emulation – the stimulus of an invidious comparison which prompts us to outdo those with whom we are in the habit of classing ourselves' – Veblen again). And most of all it is present in the token salutes to Edwin and Hilda's social and political conscience. We are told of Edwin that

> he desired to be splendidly generous, to environ [Hilda] with all luxuries, to lift her clear above other women; he desired the means to be senselessly extravagant for her. To clasp on her arm a bracelet whose cost would keep a working man's family for three years would have delighted him. And though he was interested in social schemes, and had a social conscience, he would sooner have bought that bracelet, and so purchased the momentary thrill of putting it on her capricious arm, than have helped to ameliorate the lot of thousands of victimised human beings. He had Hilda in his bones and he knew it, and he knew that it was a grand and painful thing. (Book 1, chapter 6, xi)

It would be wrong merely to object to Edwin's desire to buy his wife the bracelet. What really matters is that without qualification Bennett should refer to Edwin's love as a 'grand and painful thing'. Surely those words ought to be reserved for something more than the buying of expensive bracelets for your wife? And equally, it is surely regrettable that he so complacently opposes love and social conscience? We are referred more than once to Edwin's conscience. He thinks of his employees: 'A question obscure and lancinating struck upwards through his industrial triumph and through his importance in the world, a question scarcely articulate, but which seemed to form itself into the words: Is it right?' (Book 2, chapter 11, i). And much later we are told that Hilda admires in Edwin 'the fact that success had not modified his politics, which were as downright as they had ever been' (Book 3, chapter 20, i). Downright what? one wants to ask. The answer is meant to be, downright radical. Edwin is to be opposed to those privileged Devonians whom Hilda and he visit, 'an ideal world, full of ideal beings', who speak of a strike among miners and agree that 'the leaders ought to be shot, and the men who won't go down the pits ought to be *forced* to go down and *made* to work' (Book 2, chapter 15, iv). And no doubt we are also meant to recall that scene – it occurs in both *Clayhanger* and *Hilda Lessways* – in which Hilda and Edwin attend a meeting of striking potters and feel intense sympathy for them. Perhaps so. But as the poet Arnold Rattenbury puts it, 'we are not what we are but what we do', and the brute fact is that Edwin's conscience and his politics, be they ever so radical, cost him nothing at all. He may wonder 'Is it right?' but the only answer he comes up with is that the whole justification of his business and his money is in what it can do for Hilda:

> He did a little here and a little there, and he voted democratically and in his heart was most destructively sarcastic about toryism; and for the rest he relished the adventure of existence, and took the best he conscientiously could, and thought pretty well of himself as a lover of his fellow men. . . . And, fundamentally, she was the cause of the business; it was all for her; it existed with its dirt, noise, crudity, strain and eternal effort so that she might exist in her elegance, her disturbing femininity, her restricted and deep affections, her irrational capriciousness, and her strange, brusque commonsense.

It is no use hoping that Bennett's irony – 'he thought pretty well of himself as a lover of his fellow men' – will be sustained. The passage ends:

There was no economic justice in the arrangement. She would come in veiled, her face mysterious behind the veil, and after a few minutes she would delicately lift her veil, and raise it, and her dark, pale, vivacious face would be disclosed. 'Here I am!' And the balance was even, her debt paid. That was how it was. (Book 2, chapter 16, i)

That was how it was. It is a yielding up of moral, social and political questions in complacency. And the complacency is as much Bennett's as Edwin's, because Edwin's conscience is never put to any kind of a test (or when it is, he buys a bracelet). The result is that the essential sterility of his life passes unnoticed. Or unremarked. For I can't believe that Bennett didn't know, deep down, how sterile it was (that is why Hilda's bitterness at Five Towns life can seem so piercing). But something equally deep within him prevented him blowing the gaff on it. In a sense, of course, that is part of his fineness as a novelist. Without the patient study and exploration he offers of provincial life we wouldn't have *Clayhanger*, which is a masterpiece. And there is much to admire in *These Twain*. But the patience and neutral tone of exploration become a liability. Let me quote Masterman:

Many writers with an intimate knowledge of suburban and English Middle-Class provincial life have attempted a sympathetic and truthful description: the sincere representation of a civilization. But in all their efforts the effect is of something lacking; not so much in individual happiness, or even in bodily and mental development, as of a certain communal poverty of interest and ideal. (*The Condition of England*, p. 76)

It fits the case of *These Twain* perfectly. And I think that Bennett knew, darkly and imperfectly, what was wrong with the Clayhanger life. It comes out in Hilda's momentary flashes of rebellion, in Edwin's sense of the essentially aimless pursuit of more money and bigger houses, and in Bennett's own sharp detestation of the narrowness of the Five Towns. But to have admitted this sense of wrongness at all adequately, to have tested it, explored it, would have meant inquiring deeply and at length into the adequacy of Edwin's conscience and the basis of his married life with Hilda. And Bennett would not do it.

I shall perhaps be told that I am really asking for a different kind of novel and that in doing so I have reached the frontiers of criticism. If so, I can see no alternative but to risk crossing over. I do not think it wrong to regret that Bennett failed to write the novel for which his experience and particular talents uniquely prepared him. For *These Twain* does not seriously discompose; it does not attack its subject with the kind of sustained ferocity that would make it a great work. Compassion – yes, it has compassion. But that counts for less than it should, simply because there is too little to forgive, too much merely to accept. 'Why have I lived?' Hilda's question hangs over the novel, as potentially threatening as George Emerson's mark of interrogation which hangs in Miss Bartlett's room at the Pension Bertolini. There is no reason why Bennett, any more than Forster, should attempt to answer the question. But there is reason why he should not settle for the empty evasiveness of the move to Ladderedge Hall, because such a move dissolves what is properly threatening in Hilda's question and unintentionally parallels the 'miserable failure' that the hero of *Marriage* realizes he has made of his life with Marjorie.

When Bennett touches on the issue of failure in *These Twain* he immediately shrouds it in the language of enervate melancholy. So Edwin walks out at night, deliberating whether he should buy Ladderedge Hall:

> Melancholy, familiar, inexplicable, and piteous – the melancholy of existence itself – rose like a vapour out of the sodden ground, ennobling all the scene. The lofty disc of the Town Hall clock solitary in the sky was somehow so heartrending, and the lives of the people both within and without the houses seemed to be so woven of futility and sorrow, that the menace of eternity grew intolerable. (Book 3, chapter 20, v)

No, one wants to protest, this isn't the menace of eternity, or the melancholy of existence itself; it is the melancholy of Edwin's existence and of the incomplete lives with which he is brought into contact. Bennett's confusion is crucial and damaging, because for Edwin's moment of near despair to have become a significant feature would have required a less complacent novel than *These Twain* finally is. Instead, Bennett settles for the ambiguous and sometimes troubled recording of incomplete lives which he either will not properly show to be incomplete or which he suggests would be complete if they were lived elsewhere. At Ladderedge Hall, for example, or in Devon. But then, faced with the Devonians, he is forced to admit that no amount of moving to a world next door will make up for what is wrong. The result is something that approaches muddle. I think we can explain why.

'Keep apart', Gissing had admonished himself at the outset of his career. One has the feeling throughout *These Twain* that Bennett has decided to act on Gissing's words. And of course wanting to keep apart may have had much to do with his desire to get away from the Five Towns. And not merely from *them*. In October 1908 Bennett and his wife returned to Paris from an Italian holiday, and Bennett noted in his *Journal*:

> I was more than ever convinced of the unhappiness of the vast majority of the inhabitants of a large town – owing to overwork, too long work, and too little pay and leisure. I had more than ever the notion of a vast mass of stupidity and incompetence being exploited by a very small mass of cleverness, unjustly exploited. The glimpses of the advanced and mad luxury floating on that uneasy sea of dissatisfied labour grew more and more significant to me. I could have become obsessed by the essential wrongness of everything, had I not determined not to be so. These phenomena must be regarded in a scientific spirit, they must be regarded comparatively, or a complete dislocation of the mind might ensue.

For all the unconscious comedy of that last sentence, I think we have to take the entry very seriously indeed. Wanting to keep apart was, for Bennett, a need prompted not by complacency but by his sense of 'the essential wrongness of everything'; a sense which he felt would be harmful to his fiction if he allowed it to get the whip hand. And he may well have been right. Certainly, *Anna of the Five Towns*, *The Old Wives' Tale* and *Clayhanger* owe their especial distinction to his controlled, deeply knowledgeable and on the whole balanced awareness of Five Towns life. But in *These Twain* the balance is lost. For that novel asks questions, offers us a glimpse of wrongness – and then turns away. Bennett keeps apart here at the expense of his own subject. He shows himself aware of what, if it isn't 'the essential wrongness of everything', is certainly troubling. And he copes with the trouble only by evading it (as he had more easily done in *The Card*).

That is why, I think, he ceases to write about the Five Towns. For Bennett is too sensitive, intelligent and perceptive a writer not to know that he can continue to study Five Towns life realistically only if he is prepared *not* to keep apart. Really keeping apart means turning to less interesting fiction. Which is what, in effect, he does. I don't suggest that the decision was a conscious one, but I am convinced that Bennett sensed its inevitability. As a result we find ourselves confronted with a series of entertainments which hardly pretend to the kind of realism that characterize the best of his pre-war work, and which are marked by a bland acceptance of 'life' in a way that becomes both irritating and offensive.

Except that Bennett discovers that he cannot keep apart. He finds himself forced after all into contemplating 'wrongness'. *The Pretty Lady*, *Riceyman Steps*, *Lord Raingo*, *Accident* – none of these novels manages to keep apart, though it may also be that none fully avoids the consequences of Bennett's attempts to do so. But this is to anticipate.

Chapter 5
Keeping Apart ?

I

So it was we recognised our new needs as fresh invaders of the upper levels of the social system, and set ourselves quite consciously to the acquisition of Style and *Savoir Faire*. We became part of what is nowadays quite an important element in the confusion of our world, that multitude of economically ascendant people who are learning how to spend money. It is made up of financial people, the owners of the businesses that are eating up their competitors, inventors of new sources of wealth such as ourselves. . . . It is a various multitude having only this in common; they are all moving, and particularly their womenkind are moving, from conditions in which means were insistently finite, things were few and customs simple, towards a limitless expenditure and the sphere of attraction of Bond Street, Fifth Avenue, and Paris. Their general effect is one of progressive revelation, of limitless rope.

They discover suddenly indulgences their moral code never foresaw and has no provision for, elaborations, ornaments, possessions beyond their wildest dreams. With an immense astonished zest they begin *shopping*, begin a systematic adaptation to a new life crowded and brilliant with things shopped, with jewels, maids, butlers, coachmen, electric broughams, hired town and country houses. They plunge into it as one plunges into a career; as a class, they talk, think, and dream possessions. Their literature, their Press, turns all on that; immense illustrated weeklies of unsurpassed magnificence guide them in domestic architecture, in the art of owning a garden, in the achievement of the sumptuous in motor-cars, in an elaborate sporting equipment, in the purchase and control of their estates, in travel and stupendous hotels. Once they begin to move they go far and fast. (Book 3, chapter 2, v)

No, not Bennett, but George Ponderevo of Wells's *Tono-Bungay* (1909), reflecting on the world into which his uncle's sudden commercial success has catapulted them both. But the description of that world comes uncomfortably close to the one into which Edwin and Hilda are moving at the end of *These Twain*. And it is even closer to the one set out in the novels that Bennett began to write once he had shifted his fictional territory from the Five Towns to London.

The Regent (1912) is the first of these novels. It was planned as a sequel to *The Card*, was completed in a little less than two months and is awful. Bennett himself called it a 'piece of facetiousness', but in a letter to John Squire he defended it in a half-truculent, half-rueful manner:

> The fact is that the economic pressure upon me to write what I like at fantastic prices for periodicals with large circulations makes it very difficult to write for small circulations at no price, even though I don't want the money. Is there any reason why I should, unless I owned the paper I wrote in? *Brainy* people are always assuming that I write for money; whereas I only write what I want to write. It seems impossible for brainy people to conceive that I like writing *The Regent*. (*Letters*, vol. II, p. 338)

The Regent was serialized before it appeared in novel form and, though Bennett won't admit it, is obviously written with an eye fixed firmly on its audience. The story, thin and unconvincing, concerns Denry's successful ambition to conquer the London theatre world. It opens in the Five Towns with Bennett's Card suffering what amounts to a bad dose of accidie: 'He loathed and despised Trafalgar Road. What was the use of making three hundred and forty-one pounds by shrewd speculation? None. He could not employ three hundred and forty-one pounds to increase his happiness. Money had become futile to him. Astounding thought! He desired no more of it!' (Part 1, chapter 1, v). But as the tone of that makes plain, we are not meant to take Denry's mood seriously. What he really wants, or thinks he wants (Bennett doesn't bother to distinguish) is a new way of spending money and therefore of making it.

The action soon switches to London. Denry plays up to his role of Card by daring to book in at an exclusive hotel, and then finds that he has to dress for the part:

> In less than a quarter of an hour he appreciated with painful clearness that his entire conception of existence had been wrong, and that he must begin again at the beginning. Nothing in his luggage . . . would do. His socks would not do, nor his shoes, nor the braid on his trousers, nor his cuff-links, nor his ready-made white bow, nor the number of studs in his shirt-front, nor the collar of his coat. Nothing! Nothing! To-morrow would be a full day. (Part 1, chapter 3, iii)

But Denry survives such early humiliations as the problem of learning how to eat an artichoke, and quickly proves himself as good as the next man, especially if the next man, or woman, belongs to 'society'. *The Regent* provides scope for a good deal of satire on social pretensions and on those 'acquisitions of Style and *Savoir Faire*' to which George Ponderevo refers. But Bennett will have none of it. Such satire as there is in the novel is aimed not at Denry but at the theatre world itself. There is nothing necessarily wrong with that. But unfortunately we are asked to adopt Denry's point of view of that world; and it is an appallingly vulgar one. In the first place, it is dictated by money. Installed in his hotel, Denry receives a deputation of theatre people who want him to back their play, and looking at the supplicants he comes to the 'justifiable conclusion that money [is] a marvellous thing, and the workings of commerce mysterious and beautiful'. The play is a poetic drama in hexameters and Denry is not best pleased by the fact: ' "I've never even tried to be an intellectual" ', he says, ' "and I'm a bit frightened of poetry-plays." ' He attends a private performance of the play, at the Azure Society: 'He understood little more of the play than at the historic breakfast-party of Sir John Pilgrim; he was well confirmed in his belief that the play was exactly as preposterous as a play in verse must necessarily be; his manly contempt for verse was more firmly established than ever . . .' The audience, however, applauds: 'And the dreadful thought crossed his mind, traversing it like the shudder of a distant earthquake that presages complete destruction – "Are the ideas of the Five Towns all wrong? Am I a provincial after all?" ' (Part 2, chapter 8, ii). But his question is to be taken no more seriously than his momentary fit of melancholia. That 'manly contempt for verse' is not, as it might appear, a thrust at Denry's provincial ideas. On the contrary, Bennett makes it clear that the play itself is awful and the people who applaud it phonies (I take it that he has in mind the verse plays of Yeats and his circle and that the Azure Society is a reference to the Order of the Golden Dawn). Denry buys the play and presents it at his theatre – it is advertised as combining 'in the highest degree the poetry of Mr W. B. Yeats with the critical intellectuality of Mr Bernard Shaw', a certain recipe for disaster – and, after its first-night success he thinks that 'he had been wrong about "The Orient Pearl" ', and that 'all his advisers had been splendidly right. He had failed to catch its charm and feel its power.' But we are not to take this seriously, either. The audience is wrong, as the cool reviews of the following morning make plain and as later audiences testify by not turning up. In other words, Denry's hostility to the play is justified because it is a commercial failure. We are meant to approve his action in going to New York in order to persuade a famous suffragette actress, Isabel Joy, to take over the lead, because she will pack the theatre. And she does. The play's author, ill in bed, hears what has happened and sends a telegram:

'I absolutely forbid this monstrous outrage on a work of art – TRENT.'
'Bit late in the day, isn't he?' said Edward Henry, showing the telegram to [the house-manager].
'Besides,' [the manager] observed, 'He'll come round when he knows what his royalties are.' (Part 2, chapter 10, vii)

At the end of the novel Denry, having proved to the theatre world that in him it has met its match, sells up and returns to Bursley. But in case we should think ill of him for his financial dealings Bennett has him tell Dr Stirling about *The Orient Pearl*: ' "No modern poetry play ever did run as long in London, and no other ever will. I've given the intellectual theatre the biggest ad. it ever had" ' (Part 2, chapter 10, viii). In view of what we are supposed to think of *The Orient Pearl* it is difficult to forgive the casual vulgarity of that remark. But then the whole of *The Regent* has about it an almost cynical complacency that is a far remove from the rare good-natured comedy of *A Great Man*. It may not have been with this particular novel in mind that Pound had Mr Nixon advise the young writer to 'give up verse, my boy/There's nothing in it', but *The Regent* looks uncommonly like the work of a man who has come close to giving up art. One can only hope that Bennett was being disingenuous when he told Squire that he liked writing it. And to be fair, the novel doesn't mark the beginning of that steep, un-interrupted decline which, according to several critical accounts, is what happened to Bennett after *Clayhanger*. Both *The Price of Love* and *These Twain* were written later. Perhaps *The Regent* is no more than an isolated blemish, regrettable but not significant.

Perhaps. Yet the other novels of the period do little to ease our doubts. *The Lion's Share* (1916) is admittedly a much better novel, but it is by no means a satisfactory one. It was written in 1915, the year in which Bennett visited the fronts at Ypres and elsewhere in France. The visit caused him great distress. Frank Swinnerton, who was in a position to know, said that Bennett 'visited the front as a duty, and was horrified at what he saw' (quoted in *Letters*, vol. II, p. 364). It may be that the spottiness of *The Lion's Share* is partly due to the unnerving effect of his French trip.

Bennett was also upset by the fact that *Strand*, in which *The Lion's Share* was to have been serialized, suddenly backed down before the novel was even completed, because they would not tolerate its 'suffragette scenes'. Just before leaving for France, Bennett notes in the *Journal* that *Strand* held a meeting of directors 'and solemnly decided that the *Strand* could not print a suffragette serial. However, I think that I have reassured them.' But he hadn't, because when he returned to London he discovered that 'The *Strand* people are obstinate in their objection to "The Lion's Share".' There was also the aggravation of war work which, he told a correspondent, 'takes me 3 days a week'. All in all, therefore, one perhaps shouldn't be too surprised by the fact that *The Lion's Share* isn't among Bennett's best work.

Its heroine is a young girl, Audrey Moze, who inherits a fortune

and immediately takes off for Paris and 'life', and the novel is about
the ways in which she 'intensely lives'. That phrase is, of course,
characteristic of Bennett and frequently applied to the characters of
his later fiction, though it is much less frequently justified by what
we are actually shown. For in spite of the obvious Jamesian echoes
Bennett is not really interested in the dramas of inner consciousness. Certainly Audrey cannot be considered an exception to this
rule, though at the very end of the novel two women discuss her
and one says:

> 'One is forced to conclude that she has an appetite for life.'
> 'Yes,' said Miss Ingate, 'she wants the lion's share of it, that's what
> she wants. No mistake. But of course she's young.'
> 'I was never young like that.'
> 'Neither was I! Neither was I!' Miss Ingate asseverated. 'But
> something vehy, vehy strange has come over the world, if you ask me.'

The strangeness has nothing to do with war, however. True, there
are faint hints of its approach, but *The Lion's Share* is set in pre-
war Paris and London, and the rather desperate hilarity which
hangs over it probably owes much more to Bennett's own troubled
state of mind in 1915 than it does to anything in the novel itself.
This is not to say that *The Lion's Share* isn't genuinely comic. It has
some of the funniest scenes in the whole of Bennett. But the
amount of to-ing and fro-ing that the characters go in for is often
forced, a mildly frenzied pursuit of the lion's share of life which
always seems to be round the next corner. Perhaps this reveals
Bennett's own loss of purpose and is a further indication of that
hollowness which I detect in *These Twain*. But I don't think it
proper to push the argument very hard, because *The Lion's Share*
simply isn't so considered a work as *These Twain*. It is altogether
more random, more loose-jointed. And as Bennett himself remarked in his *Journal*, 'the novel is light, and of intent not deeply
imagined'.

Such coherence as it has builds round Audrey, her life in Paris as
a woman of means – she becomes the patroness of a violinist, Musa
– and her involvement with the suffragette movement. But the
novel is essentially a sequence of comic episodes, loosely stitched
together, and for the most part well enough done. There is, for
example, a good knockabout scene in Paris where Audrey plays

tennis with Musa and another pair, and the man bangs against Musa's arm, injuring it. But one cannot take seriously Audrey's discovery of 'life' in Paris, for all that Bennett makes mention of modern artists whose work she sees or is said to discuss (Vuillard, Signac, Bonnard, Matisse, among others), and for all that he tells us of her delight in the things that money can buy – such as the huge car with a liveried chauffeur, and a whole flat in the Hôtel de Danube, complete with maid.

Nor can I take seriously Audrey's involvement with the suffragette movement. She is led to this through the commitment of her companion, Miss Ingate, and her own admiration for Jane Foley, a leading suffragette whom they meet on their return to London and who, as a result of police brutality, walks with a permanent limp:

> What most impressed Audrey in Jane was Jane's happiness. Jane was happy, as Audrey had not imagined that anyone could be happy. She had within her a supply of happiness that was constantly bubbling up. The ridiculousness and the total futility of such matters as motor cars, fine raiment, beautiful boudoirs and correctness smote Audrey severely. She saw that there was only one thing worth having and that was the mysterious thing that Jane Foley had. This mysterious thing rendered innocuous cruelty, stupidity and injustice, and reduced them to rather pathetic trifles. (chapter 21)

We are not, I think, to accept this point of view. Audrey is being naïve. And her suffragette activities amount to little more than high jinks. Very funny ones. There is a splendid scene where she and Jane humiliate the detective who has been spying on them by dousing him with fire-extinguishers. And there is a much longer episode in which they plan to disrupt a Liberal Party rally in Birmingham by shouting 'Votes for women' and dodging arrest (women were, of course, justifiably furious with Asquith for reneging on his half promise of universal suffrage). All this is 'life' for Audrey: 'She had stepped into the most vivid romance of the modern age, into a world of disguises, flights, pursuits, chicane, inconceivable adventures, ideals, martyrs and conquerors, which only the renaissance or the twenty-first century could appreciate' (chapter 23). Again, it is Audrey whom we are to regard as naïve, not Bennett.

He does manage one very telling moment in this episode. A

stallholder helps Audrey and Jane to escape from the police, because he is a Tory and enjoys seeing a Liberal minister humiliated. A little later, when the girls have disguised themselves as waitresses, the stallholder fails to recognize them and shouts to them for drinks: 'The sharp tone, so sure of obedience, gave Audrey a queer sensation of being in reality a waitress doomed to tolerate the rough bullying of gentlemen urgently desiring alcohol.' But it is an isolated moment. Before long we are back to broad comedy. Audrey and Jane flee to the house of the Spatts, social snobs and vague sympathizers with the movement:

> Mrs Spatt was very tall and very thin, and the simplicity of her pale green dress . . . was calculated to draw attention to these attributes. She had an important reddish nose, and a mysterious look of secret confidence, which never left her even in the most trying crises. Mr Spatt was also very tall and very thin. His head was several sizes too small, and part of his insignificant face, which one was apt to miss altogether in contemplating his body, was hidden under a short grey beard. Siegfried Spatt, the sole child of the union, though but seventeen, was as tall and as thin as his father and his mother; he had a pale face and red hands. (chapter 24)

The episode becomes pure farce when Musa turns up and plays for the Spatts, Audrey and Jane, and a pompous German, a Mr Ziegler, who is also staying with the Spatts. Musa says he will play some good French music. Mr Ziegler announces that there is no such thing and begins to hum the 'Watch on the Rhine'. Musa's fury grows uncontrollable and he eventually takes the mute off his violin, rams it into the German's mouth, spills expensive Pilsener beer over him and rushes out into the night. Audrey and Mr Spatt go in pursuit:

> She thought:
> 'If this walking lamp-post does not say something soon I shall scream.'
> Mr Spatt said:
> 'It seems to be blowing up for rain.'
> She screamed in the silent solitude of Frinton.
> 'I'm so sorry,' she apologised quickly. 'I thought I saw something move.'
> 'One does,' faltered Mr Spatt. (chapter 26)

They do not find Musa, but they do discover Siegfried, down on the beach with village girls.

It is a marvellously rumbustious piece of comedy, perhaps the best broad comedy that Bennett ever wrote. And if 'life' means gusto then there is much life to Audrey's adventures among the suffragettes.

But for obvious reasons such an equation will not do. Besides, Audrey is soon back among the fleshpots, discovering that this, too, is 'life'. She finds herself on board a yacht:

> True, as she had heard, a crew of nineteen human beings was necessary to the existence of Mr Gilman and his guests on board the yacht. Well, what then? The nineteen were undoubtedly well treated and in clover. And the world was the world; you had to take it as you found it. . . . And then in her mind she had a glimpse of the blissful face of Jane Foley – blissful in a different way from any other face she had met in all her life. Disconcerting, this glimpse, for an instant, but only for an instant! She, Audrey, was blissful, too. The intense desire for joy and pleasure welled up inside her. (chapter 30)

I do not know whether Bennett intends to make anything of a possible tug between the worlds of private pleasures and social and political conscience and activity. If so, he fails. True, we are told that on the yacht Audrey goes in for 'profound reflections upon life and the universe' (chapter 31), but since we are not told what the substance or upshot of the reflections are we have to be content with the mere fact that she is as 'blissful' as Jane. And later we hear that Jane is to marry, which is no doubt meant to put her suffragettism in its place (at the bottom of the heap).

As for the other suffragettes, the only one of any importance to the novel is a rich megalomaniac, Rosamund, who announces that she has sacrificed everything for the cause:

> 'Pardon me,' said Audrey. 'I don't think you've sacrificed anything to it. You just enjoy bossing other people above everything, and it gives you every chance to boss. And you enjoy plots too, and look at the chances you get for that! Mind you, I like you for it. I think you're splendid. Only *I* don't want to be a monomaniac, and I won't be.' Her conviction seemed to have become suddenly clear and absolutely decided. (chapter 42)

Without much doubt she speaks with Bennett's approval here, and her words make plain the condescending manner in which he treats the suffragette movement throughout *The Lion's Share*. For even Jane is shown to have no real political awareness. Or perhaps one should say that she isn't shown to be politically aware. She's simply enjoying herself soaking policemen and evading capture. In so far as the novel is comic and 'not deeply imagined', I don't think this much matters. But to some extent it must if only because Bennett occasionally suggests that the movement deserves serious and sympathetic study. Besides, we are left with the problem that Audrey's search after the lion's share of 'life' never takes her anywhere important and yet that we are asked to see her as decidedly successful in finding it. 'The world was the world; you had to take it as you found it.' Yes, but which world? The late Edwardian world of money and privilege, of 'the acquisition of Style and *Savoir Faire*', or the world of 1915, of war and appalling devastation? And if the answer is, as it must be, the former, then one wants to ask, no matter how cautiously, why Bennett was not prepared at least to consider that that world composed what Henry James famously called 'the treacherous years'? And the answer to that question must surely be that Bennett could not bring himself to believe that they had been treacherous, because to have admitted as much would be to admit that they were well lost. So even suffragettism which, goodness knows, is hardly the most important token of social malaise has to be treated as a joke. The suffragettes are enjoying themselves; they are part of a happy, sunlit world. And at the centre of that world is Audrey, bursting with an insatiable appetite for life and grabbing every opportunity to glut herself on its infinite riches.

Hence the desperate hilarity that hangs over *The Lion's Share*. The novel is a last, forlorn attempt to create a world of presumed innocence and timeless appeal which is now, suddenly and irretrievably, lost.

> Never such innocence,
> Never before or since,
> As changed itself to past
> Without a word – the men
> Leaving the gardens tidy,

The thousands of marriages
Lasting a little while longer:
Never such innocence again.

The concluding stanza of Philip Larkin's *MCMXIV* says it all. Of course, Bennett *shouldn't* have been so wilfully innocent and of course both *The Lion's Share* and *These Twain* may in one sense be read as symptoms of the treacherous years, as betraying of their author as is the cry of Helen with which Forster had a few years earlier brought *Howards End* to its optimistic conclusion: 'it'll be such a crop of hay as never.' But granted that much, I do not find it surprising that Bennett should have been inventing comic episodes for his near-idyllic novel while inspecting the trenches at Rheims and noting in his *Journal* that at Ypres 'St Martin's stands, but irreparable. Only walls left, and tower skeleton'. The trauma of 1914 is not something about which we can afford to be glibly knowing. More surprising, perhaps, is Bennett's comparative inability to get into later fiction what, in so sensitive and intelligent a man, must have seemed at least questionable about taking the world as you found it. Which leads us to the 'war-novels'.

II

The phrase is Bennett's own. He used it in a prefatorial note to *The Roll-Call* (1918). 'This novel was written before *The Pretty Lady* and is the first of the author's war-novels.' It is difficult to see why Bennett should have used the phrase at all. We know that as early as 1910 he had been thinking of a possible fourth novel to complete the *Clayhanger* sequence, for in that year he wrote to E. A. Rickards telling him that 'you will appear in the following two novels of the "trilogy" (as the publishers and critics love to call it) and then you will be the hero of the fourth book, about London' (*Letters*, vol. II, p. 266). The novel was begun in late 1916, and not until it was nearly complete did Bennett decide on its title. Before that it is simply referred to in the *Journal* and letters as the 'London novel', which suggests that Bennett was still thinking along lines he had laid down six years earlier and that the later description of it as a 'war-novel' is something of an afterthought.

The Roll-Call covers a period from about 1900 to the outbreak of war. It follows George Cannon, Hilda's son, from his early years in London, struggling to succeed as an architect, and in love, to marriage and modest success. And it ends with his joining the army. In other words the substance of the novel isn't about war at all, though it is true that the last pages indulge some mild propaganda about the glory of fighting. Once he is in uniform, George discovers that 'the illusion of home was very faint. His wife and family seemed to be slipping away from him' (Part 2, chapter 3, iv). He also finds that

> he was astoundingly happy. He thought, amazed, that he had never been so happy, or at any rate so uplifted, in all his life. He simply could not comprehend his state of bliss, which had begun that morning at 6.30 when the grey-headed, simple-minded servant allotted to him had wakened him, according to instructions, with a mug of tea. Perhaps it was the far, thin sound of bugles that produced the rapturous effect, or the fresh air blowing in through the broken pane of the hut, or the slanting sunlight, or the feeling that he had no responsibility and nothing to do but blindly obey orders. (Part 2, chapter 3, v)

And as the novel ends we are told of George that 'The vast ambitions of the civilian had sunk away. He thought, exalted as though by a wonderful discovery: "*There is something in this Army business.*" ' The something is not merely a matter of blindly obeying orders. More important, or so Bennett wants us to believe, the call to arms comes when George hears that 'Namur has fallen'. The message is on a piece of paper which a butler carries out into the sunlit garden of an MP with whom George and some others are playing tennis. The scene has an obvious symbolic resonance:

> George missed his strokes. . . . He saw the Germans inevitably in Paris, blowing up Paris quarter by quarter, arrondissement by arrondissement, imposing peace, forcing upon Europe unspeakable humiliations. He saw Great Britain compelled to bow; and he saw worse than that. . . . The solid houses of Elm Park Gardens, with their rich sun-blinds, the perfect sward, the white-frocked girls, the respectful gardeners, the red motor-buses, flitting past behind the screen of bushes in the distance, even the butler in his majestic and invulnerable self-conceit – the whole systematised scene of correctness and tradition trembled as if perceived through the quivering of hot air. (Part 2, chapter 2, iii)

It is not unlike the hockey match in Wells's *Mr Britling Sees it Through* (1916), where one has that sense of distant apocalypse: of correctness and tradition waiting to be consumed in vast and terrible fires. But there is one very important difference. The scene in *Mr Britling Sees it Through* comes very early on, and the rest of the novel is devoted to endless and, it must be said, boring talk about the cause of the international catastrophe and what can be done about it. But the scene in *The Roll-Call* is very near the end. One would be justified, therefore, in thinking that the entire novel has been leading up to this moment. Yet the fact is that the moment is more or less isolated, its resonance limited. *The Roll-Call* is never more than incidentally or accidentally concerned with the 'whole systematised scene of correctness and tradition'; it does not question, attempt to diagnose or sharply focus the scene's possible significance. One could, it is true, go some way towards making a patchwork of the 'whole systematised scene' from what *The Roll-Call* offers, but to do so would not be of much value. For Bennett is not really interested in George as a representative human being leading us through various components of the scene so that we can build up a sense of what it is and what underlies and perhaps threatens its continuation. It is George himself who takes Bennett's attention. Not London, even. The setting of the novel is London, but Bennett does not establish its presence as he had established the presence and feel of the Five Towns.

The Roll-Call is really two quite separate novels. The first and longer part is about George the talented egoist, a rather less ruthless Cyril Povey. And it tracks his career from fighting beginnings to his making good. The second part is about the outbreak of war and its effect on him. As a whole the novel is, I am afraid, almost unbearably dull. Bennett seems to have suspected as much. He told one correspondent that 'I am two-thirds through my novel. My secretary is delighted with it; but I don't think I am' (*Letters*, vol. II, p. 27). And on 1 May 1917 he informed Hugh Walpole that 'I finished my damned novel yesterday'. True, he perked up when he came to check the proofs: 'Now when I was writing this I didn't think much of it. . . . But at the present moment it seems to me quite all right, & very interesting' (*Letters*, vol. II, p. 55). But it is impossible to share Bennett's more cheerful estimate. One of the problems one has in reading the novel is in coping with its desperately tired language, full of the worst Bennett and more or less empty of the best. Another is that although we are told much about George's career we are shown hardly anything. The two faults come together in the account we are given of George's first love, Marguerite Haim.

Marguerite is the daughter of the man with whom George lodges. She is an artist who has a woman friend, Agg, also an artist and (so it is hinted) a lesbian. Agg finally throws up art to join the suffragette movement. Both she and Marguerite are potentially interesting characters, but virtually nothing is made of them. There is, however, a superabundance of cliché surrounding all descriptions of them: 'He looked at [Marguerite] in the twilight and she was inimitable, unparalleled. And yet by virtue of the wet glistening of her eyes in the cathedral she had somehow become mystically his' (Part 1, chapter 2, iii). One feels that 'mystically', 'somehow', and their stablemates 'sublime' and 'unique' ought to have been pensioned off years before Bennett came to write *The Roll-Call*. But they stagger across its pages with a quite exasperating frequency. Neither Marguerite nor Agg is given much of a chance to escape from the withering clutch of the novel's prose. Whenever they do actually get a chance to say something Bennett immediately steps in to tell you how miraculous or mystical or somehow inexplicable the female mind and/or temperament is. And yet there is one touching and utterly authentic scene for which one can forgive him a good deal.

It occurs in chapter 7 of Part 1. George and Marguerite are engaged but Marguerite won't marry yet because her father is deeply offended by her engagement. That he should be so is very improbable and Bennett doesn't do much to convince us otherwise. But his opposition to George is essential to the plotting, since George needs an excuse to break off his engagement. He is after an altogether richer and more presentable girl, Lois Ingram, whom he eventually marries. It is Marguerite who makes the actual break. They are on a Thames steamer, George truculent, egotistically indifferent to the girl's emotional vulnerability, bullying her into agreeing they must marry soon while knowing full well that she feels she can't, trying to manoeuvre himself the perfect let-out from their engagement. Eventually, she can stand it no longer. She takes off her engagement ring and hands it to George. And he throws it into the river. For once in the novel Bennett lets his characters talk and reveal themselves through their talk; and he catches their conversational manners with the practised ease of a master. George, full of cold bluster and guilty defensiveness, trying to excuse his inexcusable hardness; Marguerite, bewildered, hurt and, finally, sad and beaten. It is a very fine scene indeed. But it stands almost alone.

There is another character in the novel who looks potentially very interesting. Her name is Irene Wheeler and she is Lois's friend and incredibly rich (it turns out that she is kept by an American millionaire). But long before she commits suicide our hopes that Bennett will make something of her have evaporated. Once again, he tells us much, shows us nothing.

It is the same with Lois: 'She cried: "Oh! I do love pleasure! And success! And money! Don't you?" Her eyes had softened; they were liquid with yearning; but there was something frankly sensual in them' (Part 1, chapter 8, iv). One could say that Lois's voice, like that of a much more famous fictional heroine, is full of money. But Bennett does not explore the possible connection between Lois's love of money and success and her sensuality. Indeed, he explores nothing of interest about her. She is merely a cypher for George's dream of attainment.

And very little is made of George's connections with the Five Towns. This, in spite of the fact that he is in partnership with Johnnie Orgreave. Janet appears, even more time's victim than she had been when last glimpsed in *These Twain*: 'Janet was a prim, emaciated creature, very straight and dignified, whose glance always seemed to hesitate between benevolence and fastidiousness' (Part 1, chapter 4, iii). But her appearance is no more than a token gesture – typically, she isn't allowed to speak – and the same is true of Edwin and Hilda when they visit George and Lois. All in all, *The Roll-Call* is a depressingly drab affair.

The Pretty Lady, which was also published in 1918, is a much better novel. Writing to André Gide, Bennett reported that 'the younger men here are inclined to think it my best novel'. He added, 'It is not' (*Letters*, vol. III, p. 135). Indeed, he told a friend, Mrs

Herzog, that '*The Roll-Call* is a much better book than *The Pretty Lady*. . . . The latter is too brilliant. No really first-class book is ever glittering' (*Letters*, vol. III, p. 68). I do not know that brilliant is quite the word, but *The Pretty Lady* is certainly far livelier than *The Roll-Call* and Bennett plainly enjoyed the ripples of displeasure its publication caused. 'This book is getting me into a hades of a row with the Catholics,' he wrote to Geoffrey Madan:

> Various attempts have been made to suppress it. Smiths, after doing exceedingly well out of it, have decided to ban it. Boots of course won't touch it. I doubt whether the attempts to suppress it are yet over. However, I have influences in high places which ought to be able to counteract such moves. The book sells like hot cakes. (*Letters*, vol. III, pp. 60–1)

The row was over the Pretty Lady herself, a high class French prostitute who works in London and is a practising and devout Catholic. From this distance it is difficult to see why the novel should have upset anyone – except, perhaps, French prostitutes. For the lady is treated in a fairly trivial, condescending way (the way of de Maupassant, whose comic story, 'Madame Tellier's Establishment', about sentimental and good-hearted whores, seems to be behind Bennett's own Pretty Lady). Christine, to give the lady her name, is nothing if not warm-hearted. She is also utterly sentimental, sincerely devout, unreflective, indolent, careless with money and fond of trashy novels. She is easily the least interesting of the novel's major characters and the plot which involves her in trying to give herself to an English soldier because she thinks it required of her by the Virgin is no more than a tiresome joke. I say this even though I suspect Bennett wants us to take it seriously. The soldier is a war casualty: drunk, pitiful, soon to return to the front and be killed. Christine's dutiful devotion to him is meant to reveal in her a depth of commitment that the other characters lack. But though we can sketch in these intentions so as to make them look decidedly impressive, the fact is that they suffer a fatal hurt because of Bennett's inability to convince us of Christine herself. As a result, her affair with the soldier comes out as mere sentimentality. It can hardly be said to make *The Pretty Lady* a 'war-novel'.

Yet the term is appropriate enough. For *The Pretty Lady* is the
darkest of all Bennett's novels, and its pages are shot through
with a sense of destruction, brutality, evil: of a civilization about
to plunge into the abyss of chaos. I do not mean that Bennett
deliberately sets himself to write finis. It is more that he uses disturbing and even horrific images and incidents to suggest a possible breakdown, an ultimate dislocation of civilization and order.
Much of the novel is set at night time: blackness is punctuated by
the lurid light of searchlight and fires, of zeppelin raids and the
thud of exploding bombs. On one of these raids the novel's central
character, G. J. Hoape, drops his stick in the road, searches for it
by torchlight and finds 'a child's severed arm, with a fragment of
brown frock on it and a tinsel ring on one of the fingers of the dirty
little hand' (chapter 30).

Hoape is a wealthy bachelor and Christine's part-time lover.
More important for the novel, he serves on war committees, and
through his eyes we see something of the goings on of these committees, their mismanagement and frequent nastiness, and the
jingoistic nonsense of those who run them. As a hardworking
committee man himself, Bennett was of course in a good position
to know how such committees functioned, and *The Pretty Lady* has
some sharply effective vignettes of civilians at war. I think for
example of the scene where the chairman of the hospitals committee
on which G.J. serves receives a vote of condolence for the loss of
his son:

> The proposer, with his gaze still steadily fixed on the table, said:
> 'I beg to put the resolution to the meeting.'
> 'Yes,' said the chairman with calm self-control in the course of his
> acknowledgement. 'And if I had ten sons I would willingly give them
> all – for the cause.' And his firm, hard glance appeared to challenge
> any member of the committee to assert that this profession of parental
> and patriotic generosity of heart was not utterly sincere. However,
> nobody had the air of doubting that if the chairman had had ten sons,
> or as many sons as Solomon, he would have sacrificed them all with
> the most admirable and eager heroism. (chapter 13)

'But the old man would not so, but slew his son, – /And half the
seed of Europe one by one.' That scene in *The Pretty Lady* helps
one to understand the intense bitterness of Owen's lines or of

Sassoon's 'Blighters'. And there is an equally effective scene later on, about an exhibition of portrait paintings to raise money for the Letchford hospitals, and of the society world that attends it, to see and to be seen. The chapter is called 'Getting on With the War'. And finally one might note the viciously cutting chapter in which a Nurse Smaith startles and upsets the committee by a first-hand report of war conditions in Serbia:

'All the bridle-paths were littered with dead horses and oxen. And when we came up with the Serbian Army we saw soldiers just drop down and die in the snow. I read in the papers there were no children in the retreat, but I saw lots of children, strapped to their mothers' backs. Yes; and they fell down together and froze to death. Then we got to Scutari, and glad I was.'

She glanced round defiantly, but not otherwise moved, at the committee, the hitherto invisible gods of hospitals and medical units. The nipping wind of reality had blown into the back drawing-room. (chapter 36)

These scenes and intimations of the reality of war are fine, but limited in their total effect. What makes *The Pretty Lady* a war novel in a more profound sense is Bennett's tactful probing at the causes of war, his ability to suggest that mere anarchy is loosed upon the world, that the war itself is an expression of a deep-rooted ill within civilization. The driving force behind the Letchford committee is G.J.'s acquaintance, Lady Queenie Paulle, a ruthless egotist, heiress and leader of society. G.J. thinks of her 'with sardonic pity. There she was, unalterable by any war, instinctively and ruthlessly working out her soul and her destiny' (chapter 18). Her role is that of Salome, the destructive beauty whose dance she intends to perform at a special charity concert 'for soldiers disabled by deafness'. Queenie, all lacquered egotism and aristocratic hauteur, is something new for Bennett; and he handles her extra-ordinarily well. There is no hint of deference or uncertainty in his writing about her. On the contrary, he brings out her nastiness, her ice-cold disdain, her beauty – and her spectacular indifference to fear and pain. She is killed watching a zeppelin attack from the roof of her London house. She is both a victim of war and, so it feels, one of its explanations. For her, war is a matter of rejoicing. She loves the excitement, and is herself part of its energy and violence.

Her friend, Concepcion Iquist, is also a victim of war. Early on in the novel we discover that her husband has been killed at the front and she narrowly avoids a nervous breakdown, steeling herself to dismiss the fact of his death (Bennett is very good on her scarcely contained hysteria at this point). She works with manic energy on various war jobs, especially at a munitions factory in Scotland, and, finally and terrifyingly, does break down. The cause of her collapse is partly due to her experiences in the factory – she tells G.J. of a ghastly accident which killed one of the girl workers – and partly because of the slow festering of horrors that finally break in her when she witnesses Nurse Smaith being cross-questioned by the Hospitals Committee about her expenses. She decides to commit suicide, tells G.J. about it, and although he tries to persuade her to change her mind, it is by no means certain that he will succeed. Concepcion is a highly disturbing study of a person at the end of her tether.

I do not find Hoape nearly as interesting as either Queenie or Concepcion. Indeed, the novel's worst moments usually occur when we are given his thoughts. They represent a concession to the vague and embarrassing rhetoric that Bennett indulges whenever he isn't writing at full imaginative stretch. At General Roberts' funeral in Westminster Abbey, G.J. is 'overwhelmed and lost in the grandeur and terror of existence' (chapter 10). And when he is out in an air raid he thinks of the German airmen in their zeppelins, wanting to kill him: 'it was a marvellous sensation, terrible but exquisite' (chapter 29). But these moments are few and far between, and they do not detract from Hoape's importance to the novel as a whole. Like Queenie, Hoape is something new for Bennett, a character who is at the centre of events without himself being their centre. *The Pretty Lady* is much more about Lady Queenie, Concepcion and Christine than it is about Hoape; and through them it hints at a wide and deep sense of destruction or breakdown. But Hoape fits into this because, initially aloof and detached, he becomes gradually involved with a range of people and emotions he cannot control. Against his own wishes he finds himself having to take responsibility for other human beings: for the soldiers whom he ineffectually serves on his hospital committee; for Concepcion, whose threatened suicide he may not be able to prevent; for Christine, whom he smuggles into his flat – her permit has just been revoked – and whom he then sees running out into the night, wrecking her own safety and G.J.'s trust in her (he does not know that she is looking for her soldier and concludes merely that she is a common whore). All his belated acts of responsibility turn out to be futile gestures. Perhaps because they come too late. For too long he has lived without love, and now, in time of war, love itself is a victim, its action no stronger than a flower (Christine's selfless devotion to her soldier is meant to be the tragic love's futility symbol of).

It may indeed be that Bennett wants us to see in Hoape's late awakening the tragedy of war itself. We must love one another or die. Hoape has been nurtured by the 'treacherous years' in self-sufficiency and has been taught to despise emotion – we are told that all his sexual experiences have been with prostitutes. Now he begins dimly to see what the war is an expression of. Consider this moment, for instance. It comes at the end of the novel. G.J. is alone, for Queenie is dead, Concepcion is away from London and threatening suicide and Christine has left his flat:

> He was in solitude, and surrounded by London. He stood still, and the vast sea of war seemed to be closing over him. The war was growing, or the sense of its measureless scope was growing. It had sprung, not out of this crime or that, but out of the secret invisible roots of humanity, and it was widening to the limits of evolution itself.

And he goes on to reflect that

> the supreme lesson of the war was its revelation of what human nature actually was. And the solace of the lesson, the hope for triumph lay in the fact that human nature must be substantially the same throughout the world. If we were humanly imperfect, so at least was the enemy.

But such a hope for triumph hardly amounts to a triumph of hope (or, just possibly, Hoape, though I do not seriously think we are meant to take his name as a symbolic irony). For as G.J. gloomily wonders: 'Perhaps the frame of society was about to collapse. Perhaps Queen, deliberately courting destruction, and being destroyed, was the symbol of society' (chapter 41). Perhaps. Those words return us to the phrase in *The Roll-Call* where George

Cannon had envisaged the whole systematized scene of correctness and tradition trembling 'as if perceived through the quivering of hot air'. And because, through the three women and Hoape, Bennett raises the possibility of collapse, *The Pretty Lady* can be called a war novel as *The Roll-Call* hardly can.

It also quickens our interest in his next fictions. May it be that the writer who in *The Lion's Share* had (desperately?) recommended taking the world as it was, has now discovered that such a recommendation for such a world is impossibly horrific, since what pulses through the secret invisible roots of humanity is a deadly poison? The deadliness is plainly enough hinted at in *The Pretty Lady*, with its perhaps deliberately flippant title glaringly at odds with its real concern.

Yet having said this much it would be dishonest not to admit that I am far from sure just how seriously Bennett took this concern, or was even aware of it. His published comments on *The Pretty Lady* are entirely taken up with commenting on its alleged indecency. He says nothing of any interest in 'the secret invisible roots of humanity'. And I would not want to argue that the novel is solidly built round the idea of destruction. The treatment is casual, intermittent. Yet maybe this is the point. It may well be a part of Bennett's tact and honest dealing with fiction that he should not proclaim apocalypse so much as allow for a possible dark reading of contemporary history. 'Perhaps Queen, deliberately courting destruction, and being destroyed, was the symbol of society.' Perhaps. If we are to pursue the speculation further we shall have to look at what happens next.

III

Mr Prohack and *Lilian* happen next. Both of them were published in 1922. *Mr Prohack* was started in October 1920 and finished in June 1921. In December of that year Bennett began *Lilian* and finished it two months later, in January 1922. In other words *Lilian* was written very quickly and this much is obvious from a cursory glance. It is a very slight book and at least one reviewer called it a potboiler. Bennett would not accept this. He wrote to the editor of the *Daily Express*:

Literary critics seem to have fallen into quite a habit of describing as a pot-boiler any novel which they do not like. They have not the least right to do so, and in doing so they presume upon the indifference of authors. Such a description is undoubtedly libellous. . . .

If [your reviewer] knew the literary world as he should, he would know that the writing of a novel like *Lilian* involves a considerable financial sacrifice to its author, in the matter of serial rights alone. It would have been easy for me to write a novel twice as remunerative as *Lilian*. Only I wanted to write *Lilian*. (*Letters*, vol. III, p. 174)

If Bennett is telling the truth here then one can only wish that he wasn't. It would be altogether better to assume that he hadn't wanted to write so silly a novel, that he did it for the money, and that E. V. Lucas was correct when he said that at this time in his career Bennett was too liable to boil the pot (*Reading, Writing and Remembering*, 1932, p. 199).

The novel is almost another *Woman Who Did*. Lilian Share works as secretary to a rich business man. She is, we are told, beautiful. And we are told it in language that is, quite simply, embarrassing. We are also told that she desires marriage and that she has read about the 'emancipation of girls', an experience which appears to have done her little good since she regards herself as 'the divine embodiment of the human and specially feminine desire to please, to please charmingly, to please completely, to please with the whole force and beauty of her personality' (Part 1, chapter 4). Given such a view of herself it is hardly surprising that she should become her boss's mistress. They go to France together, live the good life – very sedately – on his yacht and in Monte Carlo. She becomes pregnant, he marries her and promptly dies of double pneumonia. She returns to London triumphant, sole owner and manager of the business which she had left as a mere secretary.

If the point of *Lilian* was not to make its author some money, then I confess that I have no idea what the point might be, or might be intended to be. As a rags-to-riches tale it is ludicrous, as a love story it is absurd, as an attempt to create another idyllic diversion in the mode of *Helen With the High Hand* it is crippled by the hopelessly inept writing and by the central character herself. Helen is at least believable and lives in a real place. Lilian is and does neither. Certainly, one can't pretend that the novel is

Bennett's testimony to the sexual cynicism of the 1920s. In short, if we want to ask whether the sense of foreboding which is present in *The Pretty Lady* can be found in Bennett's later work it is no use going to *Lilian*.

What then of *Mr Prohack*? This is a much more skilful piece of work. To an admirer of Bennett's work it is also, so I find, the most upsetting of all his novels. For there is something deeply offensive about its smugness, its chortling complacency over the facts of money and material success. And there is also something decidedly odd about the book. It is set in post-war England. But one would hardly think so. On the contrary, the England of *Mr Prohack* feels precisely like pre-war England. This might not matter if the characters whose tediously smug lives fill the novel weren't held up for our admiration, were instead shown to inhabit a cloud-cuckoo land. But reading *Mr Prohack* one has the truly weird sensation that the war never actually happened, and that England is still a garden of 'correctness and tradition', where the sunlight will never harden and grow cold, and whose worthiest inhabitants are those who make and pursue further means of making money.

There is a passage in Orwell's wonderful essay, 'Inside the Whale', which recaptures the world in which *Mr Prohack* is at home. Orwell is recalling the literary scene of the 1920s, and he notes that

> even more than at most times the big shots of literary journalism were busy pretending that the age-before-last had not come to an end. Squire ruled the *London Mercury*, Gibbs and Walpole were the gods of the lending libraries, there was a cult of cheeriness and manliness, beer and cricket, briar pipes and monogamy, and it was at all times possible to earn a few guineas by writing an article denouncing 'high-brows.'

Those words fit *Mr Prohack* with uncomfortable exactness. I do not mean that Bennett makes no mention of war. It is *how* he mentions it that is so upsetting. Mr Prohack has a son called Charlie, and we are told that Charlie fought in the war. We are further told that he is something of a mystery to his father, who cannot understand why a son of his should be so 'unresponsive to the attractions of things of the mind, and so interested in mere machinery'. It seems fair to point out that the only things of the

mind which appear to have any attraction for Mr Prohack himself
are the possibilities of making money and spending it (chiefly on
clothes, cars and jewellery: the world of Ponderevo is the world of
Mr Prohack).

> Charlie had gone to war from Cambridge at the age of nineteen. He
> went a boy, and returned a grave man. He went thoughtless and
> light-hearted, and returned full of magnificent and austere ideals. Six
> months of England had destroyed those ideals in him. He had
> expected to help in the common task of making heaven in about a
> fortnight. In the war he had learnt much about the possibilities of
> human nature, but scarcely anything about its limitations. His father
> tried to warn him, but of course failed. Charlie grew resentful, then
> cynical. He saw in England nothing but futility, injustice and in-
> gratitude. He refused to resume Cambridge, and was bitterly sar-
> castic about the generosity of a nation which, through its War Office,
> was ready to pay to studious warriors anxious to make up University
> terms lost in a holy war decidedly less than it paid to its street-
> sweepers. Having escaped from death, the aforesaid warriors were
> granted the right to starve their bodies while improving their minds.
> He might have had sure situations in vast corporations. He declined
> them. He spat on them. He called them 'graves.' What he wanted was
> an opportunity to fulfil himself. He could not get it, and his father
> could not get it for him. While searching for it, he frequently met
> warriors covered with ribbons but lacking food and shelter not only
> for themselves but for their women and children. All this, human
> nature being what it is, was inevitable, but his father could not con-
> vincingly tell him so. All that Mr Prohack could effectively do Mr
> Prohack did, – namely, provide the saviour of Britain with food and
> shelter. (chapter 5, ii)

That passage is a fair indication of what can be found on any page
of *Mr Prohack*. I do not think it worthwhile to spend much time on
it, but it is at least necessary to note how clumsily insensitive the
semi-jocular tone is, and to ask why Charlie's 'magnificent and
austere ideals' shouldn't find room for the condition of street-
sweepers, and to wonder whether those same ideals oughtn't to
have been at odds with the 'holy war' which his father thinks he
and other 'warriors' fought, and to inquire whether he might not
turn to them as a means of disputing that apparently indisputable
knowledge of his father's about 'human nature being what it is'.

It would of course be better if one didn't have to take the passage at all seriously, or if one could forgive it as an uncharacteristic lapse. But its equivalents turn up all over the novel. Indeed, they more or less are the novel. For example. Mr and Mrs Prohack are out in their gleaming new car, driven by a chauffeur in gleaming new livery, when

> the car was held up by a procession of unemployed, with guardian policemen, a band consisting chiefly of drums, and a number of collarless powerful young men who shook white boxes of coppers menacingly in the faces of passers-by.
>
> 'Instead of encouraging them, the police ought to forbid these processions of unemployed,' said [Mrs Prohack] gravely. 'They're becoming a perfect nuisance.'
>
> 'Why!' said Mr Prohack, 'this car of yours is a procession of unemployed.'
>
> This sardonic pleasantry pleased Mr Prohack as much as it displeased Mrs Prohack. (chapter 13, ii)

Or as Henry Gowan might have said, 'What a capital world it is.' There is nothing at all wrong with such a world, once you have acquired Mr Prohack's 'ironic realisation of the humanity of human nature'. To be sure, not all is as it might be. But then Mr Prohack sees 'with the most sane and steady insight that the final duty of a Government was to keep order. Change there must be, but let change come gradually. Injustices must be remedied, naturally, but without any upheaval!' (chapter 3, iii). And in the meanwhile let Mr Prohack, whose 'characteristic expression denoted benevolence', go on making money and carrying with him that 'emotional reserve which is one of the leading and sublimest characteristics of the British governing-class' (chapter 10, i). And living a life of 'idleness', concentrating on the attractions of the things of the mind. Except that for all the idleness money can bring him he doesn't like it. There is nothing to *do*. By the end of the novel he has returned to the making of money.

At which point it seems worthwhile quoting Masterman again. He is speaking of the struggle to live which must engage most people, and he remarks that it often produces what is best in them:

> But where this 'struggle to live' has passed into a 'struggle to attain,' the verdict is less enthusiastic. For that struggle to attain too often

means absorption in ignoble standards, and an existence coming more and more to occupy a world of 'make believe.' When the family is in a position of assured comfort or of affluence, the houses ample stuccoed or pseudo-Georgian edifices, and the breadwinners in posts of established security in the commercial or financial houses of the city, the atmosphere often becomes stifling and difficult. . . . Liberated from the devils of poverty, the soul is still empty, swept and garnished; waiting for other occupants. This is the explanation of the so-called 'snobbery' of the suburbs. Here is curiosity, but curiosity about lesser occupations; energies – for the suburbs in their healthy human life, the swarms of happy, physically efficient children, are a storehouse of the nation's energy – but energies which tend to scatter and degrade themselves in aimless activities; 'random and meaningless sociabilities' which neither hearten, stimulate, nor inspire. (*The Condition of England*, pp. 79–80)

Masterman is of course writing about pre-war England, the England of *These Twain* and *The Lion's Share*; and one might think that such a world had been utterly destroyed by what happened in 1914. Yet as *Mr Prohack* makes clear, Bennett clearly believes that such a world has survived more or less unscathed. Everything that Masterman says against 'the struggle to attain' can be said against Bennett's novel. Even Charlie belongs to those whose energies are degraded into aimless activities. By the end of the novel he has, so he claims, got his own back on the country which has ignored him. How? By spending money in an entirely wasteful manner. It is, of course, utterly ludicrous; but it demonstrates that the world of *Mr Prohack* is a seamless continuation of Edwardian England. It is not wrong of Bennett to take this for fact. To a quite extraordinary extent the values of Edwardian England survived the war. Business was as usual. Or rather, people were determined that it should be. And Bennett is by no means alone in saying as much. There is, to take an example almost at random, Robert Graves's play, *But It Still Goes On*. Like Bennett, Graves shows us a post-war society which bears a startling resemblance to pre-war England. But whereas Graves, one of those 'warriors' whom Charlie is meant to represent and very plainly doesn't, hates what he sees about this society, Bennett seems perfectly content with it. There is no question but that he thoroughly approves of Mr

Prohack. Yet Mr Prohack is a man without any real ideas, who in his acceptance of the 'humanity of human nature' harks back to *The Lion's Share* and Audrey's blank acceptance of the world as it is, and beyond that to Edwin Clayhanger's acceptance of the suffering that business inevitably occasions.

There is, however, an important difference. Edwin does, after all, possess something of a conscience, even if Bennett too easily assumes that that is his salvation. In his mild, decent way Edwin cares – or tries to. But Mr Prohack, for all his characteristic expression of benevolence, cares for nothing and nobody not connected with money or social prestige. He is 'veritably a rich man – one who could look down on mediocre fortunes of a hundred thousand pounds or so. Civilization was not so bad after all' (chapter 15, iii). When his wife gives a reception for the League of all the Arts, 'What especially pleased Mr Prohack about the whole affair . . . was the perfect futility of the affair, save as it affected Eve's reputation. He perceived the beauty of costly futility . . .' (chapter 19, ii). And when he buys a necklace for his wife, what especially delights him is the fact that it costs £16,500. Mr Prohack is a perfectly contemptible, hollow man. And Bennett expects us to like him. It is a mystery.

For why couldn't Bennett himself see that he had created a monster of self-righteous complacency rather than someone who could be held up for our delighted approval? Several answers suggest themselves. Perhaps Bennett, like so many others of his generation, and in spite of *The Pretty Lady*, simply couldn't bring himself to believe that the war called into question the rightness of the Prohack universe. Perhaps Orwell was right when he said of the Edwardian novelists, Bennett included, that 'they have a background of ordinary, respectable, middle-class life, and a half-conscious belief that this kind of life will go on for ever, getting more humane and more enlightened all the time' (*Collected Essays*, vol. II, p. 232). Or perhaps Bennett could not bring himself to continue with the dark reading of history at which *The Pretty Lady* had glanced, and even, it may be, more than glanced. Or perhaps he was simply idling, trying to write a sophisticated urbane comedy. Above all, he was perhaps keeping apart.

Whatever the reason, there can be no justification for *Mr*

Prohack. It is not that one wants or expects Bennett to sound a note of doom in his post-war writing. But one is entitled to ask for a much more sensitive reading of the contemporary situation than *Mr Prohack* is prepared to offer. And one is equally entitled to protest against the jarring insensitivity of tone which controls Bennett's attempt at urbane social comedy. Or does this itself contain the real explanation for the novel? Is it that Bennett is somehow doing his best to divert attention – ours and his – from a fearful or at least troubled sense that after all something is rotten in the state of England? But even if this should be so – and I am inclined to think it the likeliest explanation for the novel – one can well understand why many younger writers and critics felt that with *Mr Prohack* Bennett had forfeited the right to any further consideration as a serious artist.

Chapter 6
Recovery

I

At the beginning of 1923 Bennett wrote to his friend, André Gide, to tell him that 'I am half-way through a long novel – genre "shop keeper" – which I hope will be fairly good'. Nine months later the novel was ready for publication. 'I will send you a copy', Bennett promised Gide. 'Scene – London. Type: réaliste. Old-fashioned, of course. C'est plus fort que moi' (*Letters*, vol. III, p. 201). Another seven months, and Bennett wrote once more to Gide, this time telling him that the novel had had a great success:

> I was undoubtedly, with H. G. Wells, falling under the whips of les jeunes. In fact every book was the signal for a general attack (Wells suffered more than me). Also my bourgeois public was considerably disgusted by those very innocent works *The Pretty Lady* and *Lilian*. . . . [But now] I am suddenly the darling of the public. (*Letters*, vol. III, p. 213)

The novel which Bennett thankfully saw as re-establishing his reputation was, of course, *Riceyman Steps*, and its critical success must have done much to restore his confidence in himself. Had he not discovered in the novel that he was still capable of writing good realistic fiction I doubt whether we should have had *Lord Raingo* or *Imperial Palace*, those substantial works of his last years.

But just how good is *Riceyman Steps*? And how close does it come to Bennett's own description of it as 'réaliste. Old-fashioned, of course'? Well, it is a realistic fiction, of that there can be no doubt. It has that extraordinary grainy feel for place and detail which is the hallmark of Bennett's best work. The area round Kings Cross Road, with its frowsty shops, tenement buildings and dingy pubs like the Percy selling imaginably awful beer – it is as palpably there as the Bursley of earlier work. Indeed, Orwell put *Riceyman Steps* beside *Bleak House* and *The Secret Agent* as novels which convincingly present different but recognizable aspects of London. To which list one might add Gissing's *The Nether World*. For *Riceyman Steps* is a novel about a shabby, scarcely genteel world of stunted, withering lives. It is very nearly an extremely depressing novel.

The main character, Henry Earlforward, is a bookseller. He is also a miser. Not that he is presented to us as a simple villain. Bennett shows him to be a man of some delicacy and tact. But his passion for hoarding money overrules all other considerations in his life. A middle-aged bachelor, he falls mildly in love with a widow, Violet Arb, who keeps an unprofitable shop opposite his, and the novel follows the progress of their courtship, their eventual marriage and their deaths. If we allow for one or two passages of clumsy rhetoric – the damnable trinity of miraculous, mystical and mysterious make their inevitable but very occasional appearance – *Riceyman Steps* is extremely well written. And this isn't simple praise. For quite clearly the problem of writing about a character like Henry Earlforward is to avoid making him appear merely farcical or villainous. On the whole Bennett triumphantly avoids either pitfall. Henry 'borrowing' a newspaper from someone else's front door step, Henry selling Violet's previous wedding ring so that he can buy her a cheaper one (he gives her the change), Henry buying bargain lots of clothes, putting them away and not wearing them, scrimping and saving on light, on fuel, on food (the details of household management are particularly fascinating – and nasty): all this is finely done.

Admittedly, there are false moments. On their marriage day the Earlforwards visit Madame Tussaud's. Violet wants to go into the Chamber of Horrors. But it costs extra money:

'Oh!' exclaimed Violet, dashed also. She was in a difficult position. She wanted as much as Henry to keep down costs, but at the same time she wanted her admired mate to behave in a grand and reckless manner suitable to the occasion.

Meeting her glance, Henry hesitated. Was there to be no end to disbursements? His secret passion fought against his love. He turned pale; he could not speak; he was himself amazed at the power of his passion. Full of fine intentions, he dared not affront the monster. Then, his throat dry and constricted, he said blandly, with an invisible gesture of the most magnificent and extravagant heroism:

'I hardly think we ought to consider expense on a day like this.'

And the monster recoiled, and Henry wiped his brow. (Part 2, chapter 3)

Taken out of context this perhaps looks worse than it is. Yet I do not pretend that Bennett entirely masters the problem of tone that such a passage raises. And it crops up again when we are told that Henry's wedding present to his wife is a safe, and that she 'was touched. Yes, she was touched; because she understood his motives; saw the fineness, the chivalry of his motives' (Part 2, chapter 5).

It would be wrong to make too much of these lapses, however. They are, after all, momentary, and they do not seriously damage what is an otherwise entirely impressive achievement. Nor is this achievement threatened by Bennett's referring to Henry's passion as a 'monster'. That word is not mere rhetoric. For although *Riceyman Steps* is a novel which in its detailed observation of the domestic scene looks back to *Anna of the Five Towns* it also makes discreet but important use of symbols in a manner which I think is new to Bennett and of which he may well have been partly unconscious (for how otherwise should he insist on the novel's being 'old-fashioned'?). Certainly, I can think of no other example of his fiction where the total meaning is so obviously conveyed by symbolic means.

Henry Earlforward dies of stomach cancer. And Bennett undoubtedly sees the cancer as an expression of his miserliness, indeed as caused by it. When Henry first walks out with Violet his lame leg hurts him but he refuses to take either a taxi or a bus home:

The grand passion which had rendered all his career magnificent, and every hour of all his days interesting and beautiful, demanded and received an intense, devotional loyalty; it recompensed him for every ordeal, mortification, martyrdom. He proudly passed the taxi-cab with death in his very stomach. (Part 1, chapter 13)

I do not know whether Bennett was acquainted with the teachings of Homer Lane, but it is very likely that he knew something about him. For Lane lived in London between 1918 and 1925, practising as a consultant psychologist and eking out his living with occasional lectures, and it is difficult to imagine that Bennett would have been unaware of his theory of the psychosomatic origins of all illness. Besides, these things were in the air. 'Cancer's a funny thing,' Auden was later to write:

> Childless women get it,
>   And men when they retire;
> It's as if there had to be some outlet
> For their foiled creative fire.

Henry Earlforward has retired from life. He is, as Bennett makes clear, incapable of sex. When he refuses to eat the steak that Violet has bought for him – he is in truth so ill that he can't eat – she bursts out, ' "Love? A lot you know about it! Cold by day and cold by night! And so now you know! I've often wanted to tell you, but I wouldn't, because I thought it was my duty to struggle on. Besides, I didn't want to upset you. Well, now I *do* want to upset you" ' (Part 3, chapter 5). And later, when Henry's illness has reached a more advanced stage, he lies in bed and asks Violet to come to him: ' "Why should I come back to bed?" she asked angrily, her voice thickened and obscured by sobs. "Why should I come back to bed? You're ill. You've got no strength, and haven't had for weeks. What do you want me to come back to bed for?" ' (Part 4, chapter 9). Even the description of Henry's looks has a symbolic feel about it. He has starved himself of life: 'Mr Earlforward was worse than shrunken – he was emaciated; his jaws were hollowed, his little eyes had receded, his complexion was greyish, his lips were pale and dry' (Part 4, chapter 3).

The bookshop and house are shrouded in dust. Violet's wedding present to Henry is to have the premises swept clean: 'One side of the place looked just as if it had been newly papered and painted, and all the books on that side shone like books that had been dusted and vaselined with extreme care daily for months; almost the whole of the ceiling was nearly white. . . . No grime, no dust anywhere!' (Part 2, chapter 4). But Violet's attempt to introduce some life and light into the place is doomed to failure. The dust settles back, thick and choking. Whenever a light bulb burns out it is left there, useless. The house slowly gutters down to darkness and death. The details by means of which Bennett establishes this encroaching sense of death are unobtrusive but when they are put together they establish the discreet symbolism by means of which *Riceyman Steps* declares its meaning. The house's windows are always closed: 'The atmosphere of the sealed house was infected by the strangeness of the master, who himself, in his turn, was influenced by it. Fresh air, new breath, a great wind, was needed to dispel the corruption. The house was suffocating its owners. An immense deterioration had occurred, unperceived till now' (Part 4, chapter 1). The Earl-forward servant does make an effort to cleanse the house. She opens windows, even cleans them. But the effect is no more than momentary. Fresh air and light give way to the habitual musty dankness and gloom.

Violet buys flower bulbs to try and establish some sense of growth in the house:

> The sight of the clean, symmetrically arranged pots on the sills might have given the idea that a new era had set in for T. T. Riceyman's, that the terror of the curse of its vice had been exorcised by the secret workings within those ruddy pots. Violet hoped that it was so. But it was not so. . . . The bulbs were not pushing upwards to happiness; they were pushing upwards to sinister consummations, the approach of which rendered them absurd. (Part 4, chapter 1)

And when the doctor comes to see Henry, pretending that he is merely interested in buying a book for his daughter's birthday, Henry offers him a 1768 edition of Gray's *Collected Poems*. The symbolism here is perhaps too easy:

> The doctor opened the book.
> 'Full many a flower is born to blush unseen
> And waste its sweetness on the desert air,'
> he read. (Part 4, chapter 3)

Henry refuses to believe that he is seriously ill. He announces that he is suffering from nothing more serious than indigestion, which he traces back to his wedding night:

A queer affair, that indigestion! He had never suffered from indigestion until the day after his wedding-night, when he had eaten so immoderately of Elsie's bride-cake. The bride-cake seemed to have been the determining cause, or perhaps it was merely the occasion, of some change in his system. (But naturally he had said nothing of it.) (Part 5, chapter 10)

If the planting of Gray is a trifle obvious, Bennett's use of Henry's guilty gorging is surely subtle and very clever. He has resisted all that marriage could have offered him. By feeling guilty at the 'change in his system', battening down his immoderate pleasures, he festers inwardly. His fight against the change in his system turns out to be a literally deadly one. Only at the end does he begin to realize that he is being destroyed because he has never truly lived. His thwarted energies are getting their own back: 'His splendid fortitude, his superhuman courage to recreate his existence over the ruins of it and to defy fate, were broken down. Life was bigger, more cruel, more awful than he had imagined' (Part 5, chapter 10). The language of that last sentence, so often the sign of a forced rhetorical grandiloquence in Bennett's work, has here a bleak and desolating ring of truth. Henry's breakthrough to something like self-knowledge of what he has done to himself and to Violet is intensely moving. So is the description of him in death. He dies making a last desperate attempt to work, to check his money:

The electric light descended in almost palpable rays on Mr Earlforward's grizzled head. The safe was open and there was a bag of money on the floor. . . . [Mr Belrose] bent down in order to look into Mr Earlforward's averted face. What a dreadful face! White, blotched, hairy skin drawn tightly over bones and muscles – very tightly. An expression of torment in the tiny, unseeing eyes! None of the proverbial repose of death in that face!' (Part 5, chapter 12)

Bennett makes hardly a false move in this relentless study of Earlforward's illness and death.

Nor does he in his handling of Violet. It may be that the conscientious sketch of her first husband is less than fully satisfying, but it at least establishes him as the necessary contrast to Henry Earlforward: lively, energetic, ebullient. And Bennett is very good on the pathos of Violet's buoyant affection for Henry, her desire to make her second marriage a living reality. Of course it turns into a ghastly parody of love. For all her resolve to make the marriage work, she is weighed down and finally destroyed by the monster of Henry's unselfconscious self-centredness, the will that masters and destroys him – and her. She becomes the inevitable victim of his corroding passion. The doctor sees in her 'a shrunken woman, subject to some kind of neurosis which he could not diagnose' (Part 4, chapter 3). She, too, suffers from a wasting illness whose psychosomatic nature is expressed in terms of thwarted energies. She grows thinner, is racked with dreadful gripping pains, and is finally carried away to hospital. What is wrong?

> 'Thought you might like to know something about your wife,' said Dr Raste, raising his voice. . . . 'They tell me at the hospital that a fibrous growth is her trouble. I suspected it.'
> 'Where?'
> 'Matrix.' The doctor glanced at Elsie as if to say: 'You don't know what the word means.' She didn't, but she divined well enough Mrs Earlforward's trouble. 'Change of life. No children,' the doctor went on tersely, and nodded several times. Mr Earlforward merely gazed at him with his little burning eyes. (Part 5, chapter 6)

Violet is operated on and dies. We are told that she hadn't the strength to rally after her operation, 'owing to – under-nourishment' (Part 5, chapter 8). The phrase is dreadfully eloquent of her married state. Undernourishment is what *Riceyman Steps* feels mostly to be about: Henry and Violet are reluctantly but finally quite starved of love and warmth by his monstrous passion. I think that this area of the novel is extraordinarily well managed, and in its narrow, unremitting intensity it is as impressive as anything Bennett did. It is also desolating.

Yet as a whole *Riceyman Steps* is not meant to depress. For against the death force of Henry's passion Bennett places the abundant energies and overflowing loving kindness of the Earlforwards' servant, Elsie. One is forced to describe her in slightly parodic language because there is something undeniably willed about Bennett's way with Elsie. I say this with absolutely no desire

to deride what he imagines for her. It is simply that try as he may
to make her a real person in a real place, he cannot always dispel the
haze of sentimentality which surrounds her. Elsie is, we are told,
'dominated and obsessed by a tremendous instinct to serve' (Part 1,
chapter 4), and we are given a good deal of convincing detail about
her home circumstances, including her first marriage, the death of
her soldier husband, and her romance with the shell-shocked
Joe.

> Elsie was a friend of the french-polisher's wife, and she slept in the
> infinitesimal back-room of the first floor with the elder child of the
> family. She paid three shillings a week for this accommodation, and
> also helped with the charing and the laundry work of the floor – in her
> spare time.
>
> Except Elsie, the adult inhabitants of the house were always un-
> happy save when drinking alcohol or making love. Although they had
> studied Holy Scripture in youth, and there were at least three Bibles
> in the house, they had failed to cultivate the virtue of Christian
> resignation. (Part 1, chapter 11)

And then follows a mordant catalogue of evils and wrongs that the
inhabitants have to suffer and against which in their different ways
they protest. The tone of the entire passage makes it clear that
Bennett sympathizes with them. But the book as a whole just as
clearly approves of Elsie because she is resigned, is dominated by
the tremendous instinct to serve: 'The expression on her mild face
and in her dark-blue eyes, denoted a sweet, unconscious resignation. No egotism in those features! No instinct to fight for her
rights and to get all she could out of the universe! No apprehension
of injustice! No resentment against injustice! No glimmer of
realization that she was the salt of the earth' (Part 2, chapter 2). But
would Bennett have approved of a resentful Elsie? I do not think
it irrelevant at this point to quote a couple of *Journal* entries, made
in May 1926, on the General Strike:

> I am still sticking to my point with everyone that the calling of the
> general strike is a political crime that must be paid for. Also that
> the general strike is revolutionary, that is, aimed at the authority of the
> Government. How this can be denied when the Unions Council has
> the infernal cheek to issue permits to goods and vehicles to use the
> roads and railways, I cannot understand. . . . The general strike now

seems pitiful, foolish, a pathetic attempt of the underdogs who hadn't a chance when the overdogs really set themselves to win. Everybody, nearly, among the overdogs, seems to have joined in with a grim enthusiasm to beat the strike.

So much for the salt of the earth.

The fact is, that Bennett can afford to be condescendingly in favour of Elsie because as an underdog she knows her place and keeps to it. And if one wants further evidence of this is can be found in a story he wrote after the success of *Riceyman Steps*. 'Elsie and the Child' is the title story of an otherwise undistinguished collection that Bennett published in 1924, and in it Elsie and Joe, now employed by the Dr Raste who had attended the Earlforwards, remember their place well enough to be shocked that the doctor's daughter should resist her parents' plans to send her away to school because of her affection for Elsie. It is an unsatisfactory tale. It is also odd that Bennett should have written it at all, for he claimed to have disliked the amount of attention Elsie received from critics and public alike. He told Gide that he was fed up with reviewers picking on her as the true centre of *Riceyman Steps*. The book is praised, he wrote, not for its excellence, but simply because 'the heroine thereof is a sympathetic, *good*, reliable, unselfish and chaste character' (*Letters*, vol. III, p. 213). And he confided to Frank Swinnerton that 'I am sick of the praise of Elsie. It is an acid-test (forgive the cliché) of critics. Jack Squire has fallen into it. As if the sympathetic quality of Elsie had anything whatever to do with the quality of the book' (*Letters*, vol. III, p. 210). Yet earlier Bennett had told George Doran that Elsie was the true heroine of the novel: 'She is a fine person, and I hope you will like her' (*Letters*, vol. III, p. 189).

Why the change of mind? I suspect that Bennett became embarrassed over the amount of praise lavished on Elsie because he knew in his bones that it was a sentimental response to what is, in part at least, a sentimental study. As he wryly and perceptively remarked to Gide: 'all London and New York is wishing that it could find devoted servants like her!' It is, of course, true to say that Elsie fits very neatly into the book's scheme, its symbolic method. She is large, buxom, brimming with vitality, she cannot prevent herself from eating (she swallows the steak which Mr Earlforward has rejected, gobbles down cold potatoes, cheese, raw bacon): she has indeed the appetite for life that her employers singularly lack. She likes warmth – she lights the fire which Mr Earlforward has laid but which he cannot bring himself to put a match to – and she also likes fresh air and cleanliness. It is Elsie who cleans the Earlforward windows, and who occasionally manages to open them in order to dispel the close, stifling atmosphere of the house.

Her lover, Joe, is a sick man. He has been badly shell-shocked in the war and is often violent. She does her best to love him out of his spasms of inarticulate rage and when, after a long absence, part of which has been spent in prison, he turns up suffering from malarial fever, she puts him in her own bed and watches over him until he is restored to health. Elsie's reckless loving kindness has life-giving properties which make her relationship with Joe the exact opposite of the Earlforward relationship.

Even from so brief an account it is probably apparent that Elsie fits a shade too neatly into the novel's patterning. There are moments when she seems not far from caricature. I do not suggest that Bennett meant to treat her in this way, but it seems clear that he approached her from the outside, as it were: her tremendous instinct to serve is a piece of sentimentality which constantly betrays itself in the language he uses to describe her, and whereas with the Earlforwards his accurate and unremitting control of realistic detail allows him to make unobtrusive use of his symbolic patterning, with Elsie there is too much of symbol, too little of flesh and blood.

We come back here to the question of just how good *Riceyman Steps* is. The answer must be that it is very good in its study of the Earlforward relationship, but not nearly so good in its study of Elsie. She doesn't really belong to the shabby world that Bennett so finely evokes in the best pages of the novel and I am inclined to suspect that she signals a rather desperate (mis)interpretation of the contemporary social situation. One has to tread cautiously here and it may well be that I am reading more into Elsie than is justifiable. But it does seem to me that Elsie reiterates the Prohackian view that all's right with the world. And I feel the more ready to claim this because it is a statement to which Bennett returns in his last novels. And since it is always accompanied by a forced or false note I think one is justified in arguing that deep inside himself Bennett was much troubled by what amounts to its stiff, no-nonsense complacency. Indeed, what makes the note of complacency so discordant is precisely the fact that it is out of tune with what else these late novels reveal. *Lord Raingo* alone narrowly avoids striking this particular note, and as a result is the most perfectly balanced of the late novels.

II

I realize that the preceding paragraphs may seem unacceptably tendentious. Why take an avowed realist to be working in a partly symbolic mode? The answer is, of course, that read without preconceptions *Riceyman Steps* undoubtedly shows itself to be in such a mode. And Bennett seems to have been aiming at something like it. Or so it would seem. In 1920 he wrote to Gide:

> As for my new manner, – well, it is not yet materialising! I have begun a new novel – true, it is only a light one – and I have not been able to get the new manner into it. After writing sixty books one cannot, I find, change one's manner merely by taking thought. However, I have hopes of my next novel after the present one. It will be entirely serious. There were, by the way, symptoms of the new manner in *The Pretty Lady*. (*Letters*, vol. III, p. 135)

At the time of that letter Bennett was writing *Mr Prohack*. 'My next novel' must therefore be a reference either to *Riceyman Steps* or the projected novel about Beaverbrook's father which was abandoned but which obviously is a partial source for *Lord Raingo*. We don't of course know what the 'new manner' is, because Bennett never tells us. But it is reasonable to assume that Gide knew (Bennett claimed to have had 'great book talks' with him). And if we take up the clue offered in the reference to *The Pretty Lady* it seems at least reasonable to assume that it had something to do with a way of treating contemporary lives so that they become, no matter how tentatively, representative. I myself would go further and suggest that what Bennett has in mind is a series of fictional readings of contemporary history in a way that allows him

– again tentatively – to throw out perspectives onto the past and the future. If we make an exception of *Mr Prohack* we can say that from *The Pretty Lady* onwards Bennett is consciously exercised about what is happening to England. He does not abandon realism but he adapts it to new concerns. Only in *Riceyman Steps* is there a symbolic patterning that strongly modifies the prevailing realistic slant of his writing; but in all the novels of this last period he uses a new manner to create reverberations and implications that give the individual lives about which he appears to be writing an added dimension, a larger significance.

I make these remarks as a way of introducing discussion of *Lord Raingo*. Yet at first sight this fine novel may not seem to be in the new manner at all. Bennett went to great pains to get all its details right, and when it was done he told Doran that 'politically and medically it is impervious to criticism. The political part was vetted by Beaverbrook, and the medical part was carefully vetted by my own doctor' (*Letters*, vol. III, p. 272). Bennett was right to be proud of his achievement. *Lord Raingo* is an extraordinarily impressive and interesting account of the in-fighting of ministers and their ministries in the War Cabinet, of the deviousness, backbiting, suspicions, false friendships, innuendo, sheer unscrupulousness – and intermittent decency – of public men. As a study of what goes on in the corridors of power it has few equals. It would be tedious to point this out in detail because, as always with Bennett, the novel's strengths are cumulative. Not this or that moment makes for what is fine about *Lord Raingo*, but all of them.

All of them, that is, which deal with Sam Raingo's public life. His private life is a rather different matter. We are shown his placid, unloving marriage – it ends when his wife crashes her car and kills herself in the process – and Bennett catches perfectly well the polite boredom and indifference which husband and wife feel for each other. But although their relationship is solidly realized it can hardly be very interesting for the important reason that in himself Sam is utterly without interest. Sam Raingo is a public man: a manipulator of men and money. As a private person he is remarkable only because he is so unremarkable. And this fact has damaging consequences for the second part of the novel, which traces, at considerable length, his illness and slow decline into death. Bennett takes us inside Sam's mind as he struggles against his approaching end but there is little in what we are shown that we can care about. The plain truth about Sam Raingo is that he is a boring person because there is nothing about him which at all redeems or qualifies his grey ordinariness. The last part of the novel is in a way a triumph of perversity. We follow Sam from the sudden onset of his illness to his very last breath and yet no real change takes place in that mundane, trivial mind of his: he goes on being placid, sentimental, mildly decent; not unlikeable, but dull, dull, dull. His indifference to death is not the expression of a noble stoicism but of a fatal unimaginativeness. The nearest he comes to recognizing that anything of importance could be happening to him is at the moment of death itself:

> he felt very lonely. Not pain and ceaseless labouring were his affliction but a terrible, desolating loneliness. It did not occur to him that he was dying. The idea of death troubled him not in the least. He thought that somehow it was a darker night than usual. (chapter 87)

But since that terrible, desolating loneliness is not something that has previously troubled him, it can mean very little now. This is not to suggest that the only way of writing about the subject is the one Tolstoy took in *The Death of Ivan Ilych*. But I do think it is very difficult to make major fiction out of the death of Sam Raingo.

And yet I can also see that Bennett would not have been true to his own fiction if he had failed to follow Sam remorselessly to the point of death. For as we shall see, Sam's particular kind of ordinariness is an important matter. Besides, the absolute severity of my remarks call for some qualification. We are, after all, told that Sam has a 'sorrow in his soul', and that this sorrow 'was his most precious possession, and jealously he would guard it' (chapter 82). It is caused by his knowledge of the fact that his mistress has drowned herself:

> As for her plunge, the occasion of it might be obscure, it might or might not be connected with her soldier – but the disposing cause of it was plain enough to him now: a war neurosis. She was yet another victim of the war. And how could he in decency accuse her of lack of imagination towards himself when he for his part had not had sufficient imagination to take her melancholia seriously? He had failed to appreciate that her melancholia was the symptom of some grave and

disconcerting disease, a disease which was just as much a disease as his own pneumonia. In his heart he had smiled superiorly at her melancholia, as something avoidable and unintelligent. Yes, he had resented her melancholia; he had permitted it to lower her in his esteem. Spiritual pride! Her tenderness had a deeper, a more comprehending wisdom than all his brains. . . . He thought all these thoughts over and over countless times. (chapter 72)

On the face of it, Sam's relationship with his mistress looks highly promising. It might suggest a major rethinking of G. J. Hoape's affair with Christine. But as with Christine, so with Delphine: she doesn't really emerge as a credible figure. We are told that it took Sam some time and trouble before she would become his mistress:

She fought illogically, and when according to all rules and precedents she ought to have yielded, she grew stiffer and stiffer. He won his victory only after a really terrible, ugly, messy, affray. But her surrender was complete. She adored him without reserve. She worshipped him. She was acquiescence incarnate. (chapter 5)

Delphine is a dream-mistress.

But she is clearly important to the novel, because her melancholia and eventual suicide fit into a pattern that Bennett seems consciously to have planned. By the end of *Lord Raingo* Delphine, Adela (Sam's wife) and Sam are all dead. It is as though a whole way of life is shown to carry death within it, and it may be that we should read this as Bennett's comment on the consequences of lovelessness, a reworking of the idea which had hovered about the pages of *The Pretty Lady*. There is no love between Sam and Adela. 'She was a cold woman', we are told, 'and the habit of life with her made Sam cold too' (chapter 39). And Sam's love for Delphine is corrupt, not because she is his mistress, but because he is ashamed of her and keeps her hidden. So that Delphine's own love becomes soured, diseased. I make this look a good deal more clearcut than it is in the novel and also inevitably give the impression that Bennett is in control of his material, whereas the truth is that Delphine in particular is an unrealized character. Her melancholia has to be taken on trust. 'She always had a general tendency to gloom: sometimes it came near to melancholia: a defect in her' (chapter 31).

It is, however, important that her melancholia should be linked to the war:

> 'I do wish this war was over,' she said unexpectedly, in a dissatis-fied, gloomy tone.
> He understood then the origin of the melancholy which he had noticed in her on his arrival. She was worrying again about the war. (chapter 31)

It is scarcely surprising that Bennett should wish to imply some connection between the appalling facts and nature of the war – just how appalling was becoming clearer as the 1920s wore on and produced a growing body of memoirs and statistics – and the love-lessness which characterizes Sam's generation. And it is with this in mind that we may find further justification for the close study of Sam in his approach to death. Sam's lack of imagination and his radical dullness are perhaps to be seen as indicative of his attitude to war and representative of the kind of mentality that caused it, or welcomed it, or rejoiced in its continuation. I do not mean that Bennett offers us anything so stark or tactless as a series of equa-tions based on the model 'Sam equals war'. It is rather that *Lord Raingo* broods over the kind of person Sam is – decent, obtuse, complacent, utterly incurious about other people's feelings and thoughts, his heart grown brutal from the fare of money and financial bargainings – and the ghastly holocaust which affects all the characters in the novel. Indeed, if Bennett hadn't been con-cerned with this larger question there would have been no point in his introducing Delphine at all. Unsatisfactory in herself, she never-theless opens up a perspective on those darker issues of *Lord Raingo*.

For the novel is not merely engaged with Sam's generation. His own son, Geoffrey, has been taken prisoner by the Germans. We learn that he has escaped and he unexpectedly turns up for his mother's funeral. He then furiously abuses the government which Sam serves:

> 'Good God! what a crew of circus-performers, liars, whoremongers, and millionaires! . . .'
> Sam could think of nothing to say. He was amazed at the force and crudity of his son's views on things. He had thought that young

soldiers were men who fought passionately for country, took orders, obeyed orders, and enjoyed themselves wildly when they could – and didn't argue or reflect. Now he stood like a tongue-tied criminal at the judgment-seat of his fierce and dangerous son – yesterday a boy, to-day an old, damaged, disillusioned man. (chapter 41)

Geoffrey is on the verge of a crack-up. He is acutely nervous and claustrophobic:

> 'Of course you will want a room,' said Sam firmly.
> Geoffrey turned on him:
> '*I can't sleep in a room.*'
> Sam was dashed, more alarmed and perplexed than ever.
> 'Then where shall you sleep?'
> 'Oh, anywhere. In the garden. Under the big cedar.'
> 'But look here, they'll think you have taken leave of your senses.'
> 'So I have.' (chapter 42)

It is an unnerving piece of dialogue and it hardly needs saying that Geoffrey is a much more convincing soldier son than Mr Prohack's Charlie. There is also Delphine's younger sister, Gwen, put to work on the buses, whom Sam first sees in exhausted sleep in Delphine's bedroom: 'She was wearing a common little chemise; one small hand lay on the eiderdown – and it was the worn, grimy hand of a bus-conductor that could not be restored in fifty washings to its rightful tints' (chapter 5).

And there is Mrs Blacklow. She works in Sam's office, is married to a soldier whom she hasn't seen since he was taken prisoner two years previously, and is pregnant by another soldier. A badly written but important passage helps show how Bennett's imagination shapes her to the novel's needs. She tells Sam of her pregnancy:

> He realised overwhelmingly the meaning of war, and felt that he was realising it for the first time. This was the meaning of war. The meaning of war was within her. . . . One man fast in the arid routine of a prison-camp; the other in a trench under fire. She had no home, only a lodging. The child ruthlessly, implacably growing, growing. And at the end of the war she would have to face the released prisoner, with the child. If the child did not die. Another woman, desperate, might kill the child or herself. But Mrs Blacklow would be incapable of any such deed. She must wish that the war would last for ever. And he,

Samuel Raingo, was making the war into politics and intrigue. He was not aghast at his conduct, for he perfectly understood that politics and intrigue are the inevitable accompaniment, as well as in part the cause, of war. But he was deeply affected by the contrast between the two aspects of war, as shown in himself and in her. (chapter 11)

I do not think that we need take very seriously the claim that Sam has suddenly seen the meaning of war. But I think we have to take very seriously indeed 'the two aspects of war, as shown in himself and in her'. 'Thou met'st with things dying, I with things new-born.' Mrs Blacklow's baby is the fruit of generous love, it symbolizes a principle of vitality that springs from the horror and deadliness of war; and it is obviously symbolic or suggestive of a regenerative force.

I need to step lightly at this point. Mrs Blacklow is in no sense a cypher figure, as Delphine, for example, is. She isn't merely a piece of symbolic machinery wheeled in every so often in order to provide us with Bennett's reassurance that the world has not become a waste land. At a purely realistic level he handles her with great assurance. She is acutely observed: a placid, good-natured, faintly silly woman, who dresses carefully but shabbily and who is almost embarrassingly grateful for Sam's kindness to her. For Sam not only keeps her in his employment as long as is possible, but gives her a considerable sum of money to help tide her over her confinement. But that kindness itself is a further sign that Sam recognizes in her a quality which he lacks. This is brought out when she goes to see him on his sickbed: 'Now he was dying with desire to bring the conversation to himself, so that she might pronounce words of hope, of assurance. . . . But she said nothing, and he dared not broach the topic, lest she might unwittingly condemn him to death by a single innocent phrase.' She says nothing because she is 'big with her happy child', and has the 'instinctive egotism of the mother'. (chapter 83). Her concern is with the new life, not the old. In short, although Mrs Blacklow may seem to be a victim of war, she is not destroyed by it, as Sam and Delphine are. On the contrary, she survives and ensures further survival.

The same is true of Geoffrey and Gwen. By the end of the novel it is clear that they are in love and that their love for each other is not hidden, is not the furtive secret that Sam's love for Delphine had been: 'Geoffrey took her by the arm. She resisted, yielded. She gave Geoffrey a long glance: her head fell on his shoulder, shamelessly' (chapter 86). Shamelessly here has a perfect rightness. It is a word of approbation, not reproach. And in the last chapter, as Sam sinks down into death, 'Gwen slipped into the room and stood close by Geoffrey, touching him; then she laid her light hand on his wrist and then she clasped his hand.' Out of context that may, I suppose, look clumsy. It isn't. Bennett manages the glimpses of their growing relationship with extreme tact; and of course it serves his larger design of giving the young people a certain representativeness.

This is even more true of Geoffrey than of Gwen. Apparently destroyed by the war, he slowly recovers, having 'put himself in the hands of a psycho-analyst from Cambridge' (a bow in the direction of Rivers?), and sets about refurbishing Sam's country house, Moze Hall. The Hall has brought Sam no pleasure:

> What a house! No comfort in it. What good was his house to him, his gardens, his cattle? He did not own them – they owned him. He recalled patting the flanks of the cattle – a purely mechanical gesture. They were not his; he had paid for them, but had failed to buy interest in them. His mouth was full of ashes. Ennui! Ennui! And the shadow of death! He always left London for [Moze Hall] as for an arctic and windy hell. (chapter 3)

But after Geoffrey has spent time and money working on the Hall, Sam is able to reflect that 'at last he had a home' (chapter 61). The house of death, house of a loveless marriage, is turned into something fine by Geoffrey's energy, taste and vitality.

These last remarks are by no means intended to imply that *Lord Raingo* is an affirmative rewriting of *Howards End*. Moze Hall is not of central importance in Bennett's novel and to have made it so would have been tactless simply because there could be justification in 1926 for echoing the optimism of 1910. The war had altered too much. But not perhaps everything. If Moze Hall does not endorse the notion of continuity that Howards End symbolizes, neither is it meant to be a Heartbreak House. Bennett's reading of contemporary history is altogether more discreet, more open-minded. Whatever there is in the novel of an old, deadly and loveless world is ranged against a younger one characterized by love and vitality which is yet linked to it and may, without undue friction, replace it. And in *Lord Raingo* both young and old are, so I would claim, given a kind of representative status, or are linked to or made indicative of large issues so that we can read the novel not merely as an admirable study of a public man but also as a tentative, allusive and questioning study of English society at a particular moment in time.

III

A month after he had completed *Lord Raingo* Bennett began another novel, *The Strange Vanguard*. It was to be the last of his 'fantasias', and was written at some speed, between February and July 1926. By August Bennett was able to offer it to Doran, to whom he described the book as 'in the vein of *The Grand Babylon Hotel* and *Hugo*' (*Letters*, vol. III, p. 272). He had earlier noted in his *Journal* that 'The *Vanguard* is better than *the Ghost* in truth to nature and in skill of handling material, but that it is fundamentally better in creativeness and verve, I doubt. Neither of them is more than a fantastic lark, nor pretends to be.' My own view is that *The Strange Vanguard* is by far the best of Bennett's 'larks'. I have never understood the success of *The Grand Babylon Hotel*, and Bennett's reputation being what it is I am not sorry that *Hugo* and *The Ghost* should be out of print. But *The Strange Vanguard* is a good piece of work. Bennett himself seems to have revised his own slight opinion of it, because although on the title page it is described as a 'Fantasia', in all later publications of Bennett's work it is listed under the novels, not put with the fantasias. Yet 'fantastic lark' is a perfectly good description of *The Strange Vanguard*. The difference between it and such works as *Hugo* or *The Grand Babylon Hotel* is that its farcically complicated plot is worked out with unfailing assurance (a result of Bennett's theatre work?), that it is very well written and that in its deadpan way it is often extremely funny. There is no need to say any more about it, except to suggest that Bennett used it as a holiday from more serious work, as he had used *Buried Alive* years earlier. In a little over three years he had written two full-length and demanding novels, he had produced one

volume of short stories and written others, he had been hard at
work on his journalism and various theatre activities; and he had
been pursuing a full social life. He even found time to learn some
of the arts of ballroom dancing. Extraordinary energy for a man in
his late fifties. Moreover, as the letters and *Journal* of the time
make clear, Bennett was very conscious of the fact that in *Riceyman
Steps* and *Lord Raingo* he had done really good work, and their
deserved success had given him new heart. He was now certain that
his 'new manner' had given him an extension of life as a novelist,
and that he could no longer be regarded as a 'back number', or be
thought like the other Edwardian novelists to have 'shot his bolt',
as Orwell was to put it later. With *The Strange Vanguard* one feels
Bennett to be pleasurably idling, saving his creative energies for
other and more important things.

One looks eagerly, then, to his next novel. *Accident* was written
between late 1926 and July 1927. Ominously, Bennett has very
little to say about it in either the *Journals* or letters. And reading it,
one can see why. *Accident* is a broken-backed affair. For something
like half its length it feels on the way to becoming a very fine, perhaps even great, novel. But then it abruptly changes course and
trails off into triviality.

It opens with Alan Frith-Walter catching the boat-train at
Victoria, and we follow him on the channel ferry, into a French
train, and watch as he changes trains at Paris, taking the Rome
express. This opening section is managed with the kind of easy
professional skill that one is so used to finding in Bennett one
takes it for granted. What really catches the attention is that from
the very outset a brooding, menacing sense of imminent disaster
hangs over Frith-Walter's journey. The possibility of an accident
never seems very far away. Some way out of Victoria the boat-
train stops suddenly, 'in the midst of a wide Kentish landscape'.
Chapter 4 is taken up with this unforeseen halt, with the passengers' chatter, their mounting irritation, the bland imperturb-
ability of the railway officials – no, they don't know why the train
has stopped, it could be some blockage on the line ahead – with the
general feeling of frustration at the delay. It is not a remarkable
occurrence, but a feeling of mystery and potential disaster clouds
the air.

The feeling gathers force. At Paris there is news of a major rail accident. 'The number of victims was variously stated – thirty, fifty, a hundred; very many deaths, some persons burned alive' (chapter 8). From the Rome express, hurtling through the French night, the passengers see what they take to be the aftermath of the accident:

> The train swerved violently, swaying human bodies. Everyone thought of the railway accident, and had qualms about the imminence of another accident. The train slowed down, approaching the suburbs of some city. Then a yellow illumination was seen, growing stronger. A shunting-yard. A flare. Many parallel lines of rail visible in the light of the flare. The flare, as it swam with strange deliberation past the train, was unusual in character, and the vision of its large, capriciously rising, smoke-emitting flame excited the whole car. Fragments of flame detached themselves from it, lived apart in the air for a fraction of a second, and expired. Another flare!
>
> An American in the restaurant-car cried:
> 'The accident! That's the accident, sure!' (chapter 10)

But they are told that it is only a minor accident, involving cattle, and that what they had seen lying beside the rails were not, in fact, the sheeted bodies which they had taken them to be. Has there been another accident, then, or was this it and were rumours about it grotesquely magnified by the time they reached Paris, or are they now being lied to? Fears and rumours increase. And then the Rome express crashes.

Soon after boarding his train in London Alan's attention is drawn to an ageing couple, who seem to be living 'in a state of acute emotion'. He discovers that the man, named Lucass, is an old business rival of his, now retired, and that the wife is an acute neurotic. The rumours of accidents exacerbate her condition, and after several frustrated attempts to leave the Rome express she finally manages her escape:

> Then the train had stopped. The hag-beauty had not cared where the stoppage was, nor for how long it would stop. She knew one thing – it had stopped and she might be able to escape from it. She was vic-timised by her nerves, obsessed utterly by the idea of the peril of the train doomed by the presage of her nerves to disaster. (chapter 15)

Before she gets away, companions on the train have reasoned with her. Alan and her husband, solid, reliable men, have reassured her that her fears are groundless. But she will have none of it. She leaves the express. And then it crashes.

The Lucasses are not the only people whom Alan meets on the train. At Victoria he thinks he catches a glimpse of his daughter-in-law getting on to the boat-train, and though his secretary tells him he is mistaken he sees her again at Boulogne. Why should she be on the train? Why hasn't he heard of her intentions of travelling south? And where is her husband, Jack, Alan's son? Alan gets his answers soon enough. He meets up with Pearl on the express and she tells him that she and Jack are planning to separate. Jack intends to stand as a Labour candidate at the next election and Pearl in her 'calm, reasoned egotism' (chapter 5) is not prepared to put up with a husband whose conscience goads him into political activity. ' "It's his conscience" ', she tells Alan, ' "his conscience is awful" ' (chapter 12). Alan foresees a 'clash, a collision, a terrible interlocking, with most distressing consequences of all sorts' (chapter 17).

But Alan's conscience is becoming awful to him, too. It begins to chafe even before he boards the boat-train. He thinks of the cab driver who has brought him to Victoria, of the porters who tend his luggage: 'Something wrong somewhere: something wrong! . . . Society was sick' (chapter 1). And looking out of his pullman window at the crowds of working men and women getting the train and its occupants ready to leave, he wonders:

> 'Why are we going, and why are they helping us to go? . . . And why do they not storm the trains and take our places by force? All have their cares, and I have not a care in the world. These contrasts on the platform at Victoria are really too spectacular. . . . How crudely I am thinking! Still, I haven't a care in the world. But the world is my care.' He fingered the volume of Wordsworth in the pocket of his new blue overcoat. (chapter 2)

For Alan has bought *The Prelude* with him. In the words of John Stuart Mill, he wishes to find that 'real, permanent happiness in tranquil contemplation' which Wordsworth, who was Bennett's favourite poet, can bring him. Or so he hopes. But his conscience will not let him alone. As soon as the train begins to move, Alan scrutinizes his fellow passengers:

> What a cargo of opulent beings, of whom it might be said that for them the sensual world did indeed exist! What a cargo of fleshly ideals and aspirings! Thus Alan criticised.
>
> The glib young couple in the far corner lapping a drink apiece and feverishly smoking cigarettes – the youth slim and elegant, the girl's vapid, pretty, initiated face made up in rose and white and black to the last degree of artificiality! The gross middle-aged couple sunk in dailiness and in a hebetude so deep that they were unconscious even of the boredom inflicted upon them by the everlasting society of their partners. The lone, chic lady, intensely self-conscious and alert for the gaze of interest. (chapter 3)

This is the Prohack universe, stripped to its hollow bones by the terrible clarity of Alan's gaze. He is on board a train of fools. One begins to see now why it is that Mrs Lucass's nerves should be so taut, so ready to snap. Her hysteria is surely the response of a sensitive person to the opulent cargo which is clattering aimlessly across Europe, moving lemming-like to its death. She is, Alan thinks, 'incensed against the whole of God's universe'. And his own conscience, the conscience of a basically incurious, sober, common-sensical man – the conscience of a Sam Raingo, or almost – slug-gishly wakes and once awake will not go back to sleep. 'I have not a care in the world.' But his Prohackian contentment has been utterly lost:

> Why? After all, there was nothing new in these notions concerning the contrasts of existence. He had had them, vaguely, for years. Some-times they had formulated themselves as from his office-window he had watched thousands of the firm's employees hurrying, hurrying out of the yard's gates, a pathetic procession, under arc lights, at the sound of release given by a shrieking siren. But of late these notions had been growing clearer in outline, less vague, more insistent: the spirit of the age besieging, investing, the citadel of his conscience. (chapter 8)

It is worth noting that shortly after these reflections we hear rumour of the first accident. The spirit of the age may well lead to collisions: 'Why were they humbled, and why was he, Alan, among

the salt of the earth. . . . What had he done to gain his paradise?'
(chapter 8).

Why, why, why? The questions keep coming:

> He had a superfluity of money, and he was squandering it on an in-
> excusable self-indulgence. Were his heart and brain in such a state
> that he could find no better use for riches? Were there not hospitals,
> educational schemes, the advancement of science? He was getting
> gross and ostentatious, after the style of a plutocrat who by chicane
> has made a fortune in a moment, and is too ignorant and coarse to
> employ it with decency. (chapter 9)

Alan is now guiltily aware of the fact that he can't avoid being
identified with the opulent cargo which had so disgusted him.
Never mind that his notion of benevolence is hopelessly inadequate; what matters is his sense of guilt, a sense of which
Wordsworth cannot rid him. Waking from sleep, he:

> heard some object slip down between the bed and the wall. He sur-
> mised that it must be the Wordsworth which he had been trying, with
> ignominious lack of success, to read for the steadying of his soul amid
> the storms of life.
> 'Let the damned thing go!' he reflected negligently. (chapter 15)

Jack joins the Rome express at Aix-les-Bains. He wants to clear
matters up with Pearl. But Pearl is adamant. She will not continue
to live with him if he persists in his plan to enter politics. Alan can
do nothing to help either of them. He feels and knows himself to
be useless. And then the express crashes.

Up to this point, and leaving out of account one or two blemishes,
Accident reads like a masterpiece in the making. True, the blemishes are worrying – just why will become much clearer by the time
we have finished the book – but on the whole it looks as though we
are confronted by a taut, wonderfully suggestive and economically
handled poetic novel, in which character and incident go well
beyond the merely individual and gather to themselves large possibilities. As we read the first half of *Accident* we feel that it is
surely about the 'vast smug surface' of society, below which are
obscure, persistent and increasingly powerful rumblings that at any
moment will erupt into violent destructiveness. Even more than the
1890s the spirit of the age at the end of the 1920s must have

seemed *fin de siècle*. *The Waste Land* had already been written, Waugh's brilliant and troubling *Vile Bodies* would soon make its appearance, as would the early poems of Auden; and in between are, for example, Huxley's atrabilious satires, Upward's strange and haunting story 'The Railway Accident' (written in 1928, though not published until later) and Bennett's novel, with its hallucinatory, heightened rendering of a world about to go smash. Not that in terms of style or manner Bennett owes anything to the younger men of the twenties. If anything, it is the long shadow of Chekhov which lies over the pages of *Accident*. The Chekhov of whom Bennett said he would never tire, of *Ward No. 6* and, perhaps, *The Cherry Orchard* (having attended a production of that play in 1925, Bennett told Beaverbrook that it had been 'one of the greatest theatrical evenings of my life', *Letters*, vol. III, p. 243). But Bennett is not derivative. The 'new manner' is very much his own and it is at its finest in the first half of *Accident*.

Sadly, it does not survive into the second half of the novel. After the crash Bennett more or less throws his own subject away. *Accident* becomes positively Prohackian in its cheery resolution of all difficulties. The Lucasses are reunited with each other and with the rest of the passengers, and Pearl and Jack are also reunited. Alan is hurt – but only slightly. The train driver alone dies. It is as though Bennett has taken us to the edge of an abyss and then rapidly backtracked and made pretence that it never really existed. The catastrophe turns out to be in no way symbolic of the train of fools over which Alan's conscience has been so active. Indeed, all the larger issues and questions are lost sight of in the second half of the novel. We are asked to consider that the crucial question is whether Pearl will return to Jack. The whole book does an abrupt about-turn. What had been a novel dealing allusively but powerfully with contemporary society now becomes a novel operating on a purely domestic level.

There would be little point in showing how disastrous this is. But I do need to say that Bennett fatally compromises his own sense of catastrophe by exposing Jack's politics to Pearl's scorn. This is partly because when Jack actually gets round to voicing his ideas they prove to be naïve in the extreme, and partly because Pearl's reaction to them is equally naïve. Yet there is no indication that Bennett himself thinks that either of them is to be criticized for what they say. Conscience and egotism, yes, we are asked to see these as dictating Jack and Pearl's actions. But naïvety, no. Yet I do not see how else we can respond to Jack's speeches about 'the under-dog'. The problem is twofold. On the one hand it is clear that Bennett expects us to be shaken, as Alan is, by Jack's remarks: ' "*Our* consciences have wakened up. No one's easy in his mind about things. It wasn't like that forty years ago. Our lot didn't trouble themselves then. I expect they took everything for granted." ' But not now. For now there is a Labour Party which cares about poverty and injustice, and that is why Jack has joined it. His words make Alan feel uncomfortable:

> He hated to feel uncomfortable: he disliked and feared an excess of uncompromising honesty: he feared what might happen to himself if the habit grew of uncompromising honesty; but he personally could not answer the phrases. . . . Yes, he was afraid of his son's simplicity and sincerity and directness, which induced in him a mood of uneasy social guilt and responsibility evaded. But he was intensely proud of the surprising Jack. (chapter 27)

Now that is perfectly acceptable. Alan's conscience has once more been opened up. Good. He is troubled by Jack's words. Good.

Except that Jack's words hardly get to the root of the matter. Of itself that needn't bother us. Jack's 'simplicity and sincerity and directness' can obviously function as motives at least as well as the tough political reasonableness which he notably lacks. He is *all* simplicity. But then why should so intelligent a man as we are asked to believe Alan is be taken in by that? The answer must be that once Bennett has put the issues in Jack's terms he has reduced them to a level at which Alan, having recovered from his shock at Jack's having any ideas at all, will be able to cope with them (and therefore with his conscience); and that Pearl can be used to show that she has right on her side.

It is Pearl who is allowed decisively to floor Jack's arguments:

> 'As if all politics weren't class war! And if there isn't a class war, who's going to begin one? Not us. It's Labour that's out for a class war. Not that I care so much about class. What I care about is my family, and yours too. When you really get down to bedrock, the family's the most important thing.'

Of this ineffable speech Alan thinks that

> He might have seen the defects clearly, but he deliberately would not.
> For Pearl had captured the whole of his sympathy by her appeal for
> the institution of the family. The family for him was more sacred than
> anything else in the social structure. It was the main article of his
> religion. And, though she had slighted marriage to him, how she had
> defended the family! She cared tremendously for the ornaments of
> existence; she was without doubt luxurious. But her preoccupation
> with powder and rouge, the cut of frocks, manners, the arts of elegance,
> did not prevent her from having basic ideas about life. . . .
>
> She had gone deeper and risen higher than Jack with his resounding
> abstractions, his limited vision, his cruel fanaticism. (chapter 28)

No use pretending that Alan isn't thinking Bennett's own thoughts.
The passage desperately attempts to cover up the cracks of the two
Pearls: Pearl of the first half of the novel, all 'calm, reasoned
egotism', and Pearl of the second half who in spite of slighting
marriage has 'basic ideas about life' which are much finer than
Jack's.

What then of Alan's conscience? It is quietly buried under the
main article of his religion. But it revives at the very end of the
novel. Jack decides to renounce political ambitions for Pearl and
family life:

> But what about political ideals and aims? What about the boy's zeal
> for what he deemed to be the welfare of his country? What about the
> under-dog? Abandoned, all abandoned, in favour of passion for a
> woman! . . . Alan was amazed and depressed by [his wife's] apparent
> total failure to perceive the secret tragedy underlying her son's return
> to sanity. Better madness and disaster than this sanity based on
> emotion. (chapter 34)

But this is a last and vulgar attempt to rescue a theme which by
now has been sunk without trace. Madness and disaster had
applied to the train of fools, to the 'opulent cargo' heading towards
death. Now, it applies to the individual who has anyway turned
from it to a sanity based on emotion.

It is easy enough to show how *Accident* goes wrong. But it is not
so easy to say why it does, or to explain why Bennett should back
away from his own subject. Yet some explanation is called for,

simply because the mystery of *Accident*'s sudden collapse from brilliance to bathos is so extraordinary. My own guess is that Bennett did not quite realize where his novel was leading him, and that when he came to understand its direction he decided to call a halt. In other words, the subject of *Accident* proved altogether too uncomfortable for him to handle, perhaps because it raised any number of troubling questions about its author's conscious stance as apolitical man, determined to keep apart. The novel breaks down because Bennett wasn't prepared to face up to the vision of catastrophe which for half its length *Accident* subtly and discomposingly assembles. There may, of course, be very good reasons for not wanting to be identified with such a vision, but that is not the point. Or rather, if Bennett had wished to show that such a vision is mistaken or rashly apocalyptic he should have done something very different from what he does – which is merely to turn his back on it.

What one realizes is that the first half of *Accident* is markedly at odds with the way Bennett handles potentially disruptive forces in earlier novels of the 1920s. Elsie and Joe, Geoffrey and Gwen, are finally to be seen as representative not of breakdown but of continuity, survival, renewal. But the view of society in *Accident* is an altogether blacker affair.

Yet even in the brilliant first half of the novel there are hints that all is not well with Bennett's imaginative control over his material. One tends not to notice them, or be worried by them, because one is absorbed in the novel's seemingly assured drive towards accident. But with the last page read it is possible to feel that all along Bennett may have been worried about where his novel was taking him and have been quietly planning to subvert his own imaginative powers. Pearl is of crucial importance here. She seems to be the embodiment of a particularly heartless, egotistic and emotionally sterile personality. But when she breaks the news of Jack's intentions to Alan, he reflects:

> Of what use her loveliness, her charm, her remarkable intelligence, her powder, her paint her circlet of brilliants, her chic? The deep, incurable sadness of the universe had seized her, bowed her down. But she would not yield. . . . Again the inexplicable, touching pathos of the car, of the whole train rushing and grinding along in the darkness

222 Arnold Bennett : a study of his fiction

from nowhere to nowhere, wrung his heart. . . . He thought of
Wordsworth. He *was* Wordsworth, mute, drenched in the heavenly
melancholy wonder of life. (chapter 13)

It is fustian. And it is also plain silly. Pearl hasn't been bowed down
by anything so grand as the deep, incurable sadness of the universe.
She's been thwarted in her plans to be a fine society lady by a
husband who wants to enter politics. Nor will it do to pretend that
the passage is meant to show us

> strained time-ridden faces
> Distracted from distraction by distraction
> Filled with fancies and empty of meaning.

Elsewhere in the first half of *Accident* Eliot's words fit perfectly.
But not here. And though when Alan considers himself to be
Wordsworth, 'drenched in the heavenly melancholy wonder of
life', he is indeed filled with fancies and empty of meaning, that is
not what Bennett means at all. On the contrary, we are to understand that Alan has discovered a true meaning in Pearl's resistance
to Jack's plans and in her own femininity, which is that of all
women. 'These strange beings, with their marvellous qualities,
were entitled to forbearance and loving kindness. They were
oppressed, by the very nature of things. They were caught in life
like rats in a trap' (chapter 19). This thought occurs to Alan just
before the train crashes, and although I have no very clear idea
what he means – nor, I suspect, has Bennett – it very plainly marks
the re-emergence of the clubman. And from now on the clubman
takes control. He is well to the fore when Alan feels that he must
comfort his wife over Jack and Pearl's threatened separation: 'He
wanted to comfort Elaine, who was perhaps mentally incapable of
argument on the high philosophic male plane, but who had the
robust sense to see the folly of all irony' (chapter 31). And his
appearance in the book means an end to *Accident*'s powerful fable
and a return to consoling fiction, to 'cheeriness and manliness, beer
and cricket, briar pipes and monogamy'.

Pearl is not the first of Bennett's fictional studies of what, for
want of a better word, I have to call the flapper – that particular
kind of brittle, cynical-minded woman of the 1920s, intent on the
good life and bright lights, music and champagne. There had been

Mr Prohack's daughter, Sissie, there is Cora the heroine of the title story in the volume *The Woman Who Stole Everything* (1927), and there is Myrtle of 'Myrtle at 6 a.m.', in *The Night Visitor and Other Stories* (1932). All these young women have a positive hunger for excitement, they lead slightly risqué private lives and have a habit of endangering their marriages – present or future – because of their indifference to or ignorance of their menfolk's needful attention to public affairs. But they are all recalled to true values: love, the family, private life. None of them is particularly convincing and one has the feeling that Bennett goes on writing about them because although they fascinate him he is also bewildered and slightly alarmed by their apparent decision not to be 'oppressed by the very nature of things'. It is as though he is determined to tame them in his fiction, even if they can't be tamed in real life.

Cora is typical. She is married, can't bear her husband's dragging her away from parties early, and won't understand that he does so in order to get a night's sleep so that he may put in a good day's work earning the money they need if she is to continue to go to parties. Cora has a lover, whom she takes down to what she imagines is her uncle's deserted country cottage. But the uncle unexpectedly turns up and after some clubman's philosophizing persuades her to renounce the lover and return to her husband.

'The Woman Who Stole Everything' is an inept tale, but it has a claim on our attention. Cora's lover is 'Sweeney' Todd, 'a muscular man of thirty-nine or forty at least, with hairy hands, arms and chest' (chapter 5). Ape-like Sweeney. The allusion is, I think, quite conscious. Bennett and Eliot had known each other for a number of years, and in September 1924 Eliot had paid a call on Bennett to ask him about theatre craft. In his *Journal*, Bennett recorded that Eliot had told him that he was now

> centred on dramatic writing. He wanted to write a drama of modern life (furnished flat sort of people) in a rhythmic prose 'perhaps with certain things in it accentuated by drum-beats.' And he wanted my advice. We arranged that he should do the scenario and some sample pages of dialogue.

I do not know whether Bennett saw much or anything of what was to be *Sweeney Agonistes* before a portion of it, 'Wanna Go Home,

Baby?' was published in *Criterion* in January 1927, but it is at least possible that he did. In June of that year he wrote to Eliot, 'I should very much like to see you. I have often wondered what happened to that Jazz play' (*Letters*, vol. III, p. 286). But even if he hadn't seen the sample pages which Eliot had promised him it is very likely that they had discussed together the characters who would be in Eliot's play. Bennett's Sweeney Todd is either a private joke between himself and Eliot or it suggests that his mind was running along lines that reminded him of his conversation with the poet. 'The Woman Who Stole Everything' is, after all, about disruptive tendencies and forces in 'modern life', and it picks on social values that Bennett clearly regarded as threateningly decadent. Cora is the focus for them here, just as Pearl is a partial focus for them in the first half of *Accident*. And in both story and novel Bennett copes with his sense of disaster by coping with the woman. The 'flapper' is reduced to some essential femininity, she is conventionalized and sentimentalized; and the threat to civilization recedes.

Perhaps Bennett himself felt that his study of Pearl left a good deal to be desired. At all events, he tried again and this time he got much closer to success. Certainly *Imperial Palace* (1930) owes much of its distinction to his handling of Gracie Savott.

IV

Gracie is the daughter of Sir Henry Savott, a financial wizard who has set his heart on buying the Imperial Palace, the 'unique hotel' managed by Evelyn Orcham. Much of this longest of all Bennett's novels is taken up with the dealings between Evelyn and Sir Henry, rather less with the relationship between Evelyn and Gracie; but it is the latter which is the more interesting. Not that there is anything wrong with Bennett's handling of the relationship between the two men. Indeed, I would say that *Imperial Palace* is the least flawed of all Bennett's novels. But it marks a return to a more limited kind of realism. It has nothing of the 'new manner'. I suspect that the near disaster of *Accident* made Bennett decide to go back to what he knew he could do well and without risk. And in this novel he does it superbly. *Imperial Palace* is solidly realized

and its style, though slightly mandarin, is noticeably chaster than
is usual with Bennett. There is very little overblown rhetoric in its
600 pages. And in spite of the novel's great length, the writing
rarely flags. It may well be that Bennett was determined to do
better than Dreiser, whose *American Tragedy* he had been reading,
and of which he noted in the *Journal* that 'taken as a whole it is very
fine and impressive', though 'the mere writing is simply bloody –
careless, clumsy, terrible'. 'Seems ordinary at first', he added, 'but
after 40 pages it does begin to hold you. The fellow has a large
sense of form, and an eye for things that count with the imagination.' It would not be inaccurate to apply those words to *Imperial
Palace*. Which is not to say that Bennett's novel is in any way an
attempt to outdo *An American Tragedy* it is merely to point out
that *Imperial Palace* also has a large sense of form, is full of
details that count with the imagination, and is packed with 'lots and
lots' of those 'original, true psychological observations', which
Bennett noted and admired in Dreiser.

Imperial Palace certainly seems ordinary at first. But it begins to
hold one because of Bennett's success in making Evelyn Orcham
an impressive and sympathetic character. It is a matter for some
astonishment. Evelyn is a man of means and very little thought.
His imagination rarely stretched further than visions of himself as
owner of more and better hotels:

> He was thinking:
> 'What am I alive for? What is my justification for being alive and
> working? I cannot keep on creating the Palace. I have created it. The
> thing is done. I can't do it again.'
> For the first time he was addressing to his soul the terrible compre-
> hensive question, which corrodes the very root of content in the
> existence of millions of less fortunate people, but which had never
> presented itself to Evelyn until the previous night:
> 'Why?' (chapter 25, iii)

But these reflections are casual and soon dropped. 'Why?' is not
really a question that greatly bothers Evelyn. And though on one
occasion he finds himself examining his conscience about the
merger that Savott is offering him, the examination is soon over:

> 'In a place like this [Evelyn tells Savott] you get some very melo-
> dramatic contrasts, and they make you think. And when I think for

instance of you in your suite, or me here, and then of some of the fellows and girls down in the basements, I get a sort of notion that there must be something wrong somewhere. And your mergers aren't likely to do such a devil of a lot to put it right.' (chapter 24, ii)

'There must be something wrong somewhere.' Alan Frith-Walter's very words. But after all Evelyn signs the merger and is excited at the prospect of managing the other European hotels which Savott has bought. Bennett takes care to keep this novel apart from the issues which had prompted *Accident*, and ended by wrecking it.

Yet Evelyn is not a complacent man. There is nothing of Prohack about him. If he reminds one of any of Bennett's earlier heroes it is of Edwin Clayhanger. He has something of Edwin's mixture of hard-headed common sense and decent considerateness. But Evelyn is a bigger man than Edwin, in the sense that he has responsibility for more people and that more depends on his way with them. And it is here that *Imperial Palace* becomes so impressive. For Bennett is simply excellent at showing how and why Evelyn is a successful manager. His ability to delegate authority, his quick-wittedness, his genuine passion for the hotel, his informed delight in every part of its workings, his acute knowledge of and feeling for his staff – Bennett brings all this out with great ease and assurance. The result is that what looks at first glance to be a subject of quite spectacular dullness becomes one of absorbing interest. One is prepared to be bored by *Imperial Palace*. But one isn't.

From the start of his career Bennett had been fascinated by the intricate and difficult working of hotels. When in September 1929 he was beginning work on the novel he noted in his *Journal* that he had all the material he needed in a notebook:

I would sooner lose fifty pages of the manuscript than that of the notebook. If I did lose it, I think I should be capable of abandoning the novel forever. . . .

I have been fighting for years against the instinct to write this particular novel. About thirty years ago I was taken to the Savoy Hotel for tea, came out, went home, and wrote 'The Grand Babylon Hotel' in three-weeks of evening work. 'The Grand Babylon Hotel' was a mere lark. The big hotel de luxe is a very serious organization; it is in my opinion a unique subject for a serious novel; it is stuffed with human nature of extremely various kinds. The subject is characteristic of the age; it is as modern as the morning's milk; it is tremendous, and worthy of tremendous handling. I dare say it's beyond me.

He needn't have worried. As the novel progresses one comes to know the Imperial Palace as one had known the Baines and Clay-hanger houses and the streets and squares of Bursley. And one also comes to know the ways of big business. If *Lord Raingo* had been masterly at showing us life inside the corridors of power, *Imperial Palace* is every bit as impressive when it shows us life among directors, tycoons and shareholders. No one but Bennett could have made such drama out of the merger by means of which Savott gets control of the hotel.

But *Imperial Palace* is not only about the workings of a big hotel. It is also about Evelyn's private life. Which is where Gracie Savott comes in. She comes into the hotel, indeed, at the very opening of the novel, early in the morning, demanding that Evelyn take her to Smithfield. He does so and we get one of Bennett's most con-vincing pieces of descriptive writing. The writing about Gracie is not nearly so convincing, however. We are told that she has been a champion racing driver, that she is now beginning to write seriously, and that she likes slumming. She takes Evelyn into a pub and later makes him take her to a cheap steak bar. 'I suppose this is the modern girl', Evelyn reflects (chapter 14, ii). But her modernity seems a bit forced at this stage, a desultory catalogue of uncon-ventionalities:

> She had fallen into sloth and self-indulgence, aimless, restless, un-happy. Her formidable engine-power was wasting itself. She had rejoined her smart friends, formed the habit of never wanting to go to bed and never wanting to get up, scattered her father's incalculable affluence with both hands, eaten, drunk, gambled, refused herself no fantastic luxury . . . lived the life furiously. And the life was death. Against his inclination, her father had taken her with him to America. She had had hopes of the opportunities and the energy of America. They were frustrated. In New York she had lived the life still more furiously. And it was worse than death. (chapter 5, ii)

Gracie is the modern woman in search of 'the meaning of life'. She isn't a heartless cynic. At one particularly unfortunate moment we are told that in speaking to Evelyn 'her tone had more than solemnity; it was religious; it vibrated with the formidableness of mystical passion' (chapter 50, i). We've been here before, and it isn't good.

But Gracie in Paris is a very different matter. She and Evelyn meet there by chance, since after the merger he has to visit various European cities, to check up on the workings of Savott's hotels. Gracie tells him she is in love with him. Chapters 55 to 61 are about their affair, and they are among the best that Bennett wrote. Certainly he never more convincingly caught the feeling of sexual passion and the prickly hostilities and brief reconciliations of lovers than when writing about Evelyn and Gracie.

He had earlier flirted with the idea of a middle-aged man being seduced by a younger girl, but had always turned away from it, either in the interest of 'briar pipes and monogamy', or because he preferred to make the relationship a vicarious one – as in the cases of Cora and her uncle and Alan and Pearl. But there is nothing vicarious in the relationship of Evelyn and Gracie. It is a fully sexual one and Bennett emphasizes the fact. He needs to do this because he wants to show that although Evelyn isn't really in love with Gracie he is powerfully attracted to her. And he brings it off triumphantly – a fact which I have to offer as mere assertion since only by pages-long quotations could I hope to show just how well Bennett establishes the nature of their relationship, in its twists and turns, moments of accord and distrust.

On the other hand, I think I can show how Bennett succeeds in making Gracie a fully credible figure in the Paris section of the novel. Her moods change quixotically, from passion, to delight, to gloom, to anger. They do so because she knows that Evelyn doesn't love her. As she tells him:

> 'I've been happy today too. But I've been happy in *my* love, not yours. It is happiness to be in love. But it's misery as well, if you're the only one who's in love. Now you've heard. I'm a beast. But I'm honest. At any rate I've been honest with you. And I'm not going to cry, or whine, or anything of the sort. I'm going to be terribly nice, because it isn't a bit your fault.' (chapter 58, iii)

But in fact she turns terribly nasty. Rightly, too, because Evelyn tries to condescend to her; he wants to treat her in the way that

Bennett had too often approvingly let his fictional heroes treat their women. Not here, however:

> 'Now I wonder whether it would be asking you too much to make the tea,' said Evelyn. The formula was ceremonious, but the tone commanded.
>
> 'Hadn't I better do the flowers first?' Gracie suggested.
>
> 'Men before flowers,' said Evelyn. 'Organise your energy, my dear. You can see to the flowers while the water is boiling for the tea. And give me your mackintosh, will you?' (chapter 59, i)

Evelyn's patronizing tone is that of Hoape's with Christine, Prohack's with his wife, Raingo's with Delphine. But what happens to Evelyn never happened to them. Gracie turns on him. He wants her to wear a certain dress, and she refuses. Evelyn says:

> 'I always thought women liked to dress to please men, and—'
>
> 'You thought wrong then. . . . Do you imagine I can't read you like the front page of a newspaper? If you do you're mistaken. You just made up your mind to come the grand over me. You said to yourself you'd force me to keep on wearing that dowdy thing. You thought you'd show me who was the master here. Just because I've been fool enough to tell you and show you how I've gone crazy about you.'
>
> 'Not at all,' he protested unconvincingly.
>
> 'I say yes!' she cried.
>
> He saw that she was inexplicably losing her temper. 'Oh, very well!' he thought superiorly, and waited.
>
> 'The truth is,' she cried, louder and louder, 'and you may as well know it, you're conceited. You always were conceited, and I've made you more conceited. You show it the whole time! You simply can't move without showing it. You're taking advantage of me every minute, that's what you're doing!'
>
> He sat down, near the door, thinking what a brilliant idea it was to sit down.
>
> 'Now, come here! Please!' he begged her. If only she would obey, he could restore her to his knee, and soothe and fondle her into being rational.
>
> 'There you are again!' she cried. 'I'm in love with you. So I'm to be your slave. Finger up, I come. Finger down, I go . . . you just don't know what love is. You take everything for granted. Men generally do. And you're worse than most. I'm an idiot, but I'd sooner be an idiot than a conceited ass like you are . . .'

At which point, his male complacency finally shattered, Evelyn loses his temper and accuses her of being a rotten writer: ' "And now you *can* go!" she shouted. "I've listened to you. Most women would have shut you up. But I'm different. Off you go." Her hands were clenched' (chapter 59, iii). And go he must.

It is a brilliant scene and particularly arresting because Bennett manages to get inside Gracie's mind so that her sense of outrage at Evelyn's behaviour comes out suddenly, dramatically and convincingly. Reading this section of the novel one realizes yet again how utterly inaccurate Virginia Woolf's criticism of the best of Bennett is, and how generously understanding he can be of a range of characters and temperaments about which, by comparison, she knows or can say nothing.

Gracie and Evelyn make up, but it is clear that their affair is doomed. He returns to London, still much involved with her, but she sends him a letter saying that she's not prepared to continue their relationship. It is a good letter, typical of her fearless truth-telling, and of her refusal to sell herself short. In reply, Evelyn sends her a note: 'DEAR GRACIE. Thank you for your letter. Good-bye. Yours, E.O.' He is, we sense, relieved rather than sorry that the affair should be closed, because he has been alarmed and briefly thrown badly off course by Gracie's ways. For Evelyn is a conventional man. Early on in the novel he had idly speculated on the possibility of Gracie becoming his mistress, and like Sam Raingo he thinks of his mistress as a trivially furtive possession. The actual affair shakes him up. He can't cope with Gracie, she won't be a dream-mistress. By the end of the novel he is engaged to marry one of his staff, Violet Powler, a conventional woman who will minister to his sense of male superiority. Violet is inevitably far less interesting than Gracie and though she is well enough done and Bennett skilfully establishes Evelyn's growing sense of her indispensable usefulness to him, he sensibly doesn't waste much time on their relationship.

The Paris episode is almost a novel in itself. I wish it had been. For it shows that Bennett was capable of writing well about sexual passion and that he could dramatize it with an intensity and credibility for which his earlier work doesn't prepare us. Gracie Savott emerges as one of his most convincing females, infinitely more believable in her sexuality than the ineffable Carlotta or thoroughly conventional Christine. And Evelyn, too, is treated in the Paris section with the kind of ironic ruthlessness that comes as a welcome relief after Bennett's earlier contentment with his heroes' typical attitude to women. This is not to deny that there are moments when the Paris episode comes perilously close to slipping into sentimentality and condescension. But the flaws are faint. 'He saw that she was inexplicably losing her temper.' It isn't meant to be inexplicable to us, and that it should be so to Evelyn tells us much about him. Decent and considerate man though he usually is, he is egotistically obtuse when it comes to Gracie. I regret only that Bennett didn't spend more time analysing the seismic upset which Evelyn carries back to London with him. But to have done so would, I suppose, have thrown the entire novel out of kimber.

It is, of course, always possible that had he lived longer Bennett would have gone on to write a full-length study of sexual passion. There are hints that *Dream of Destiny*, the novel he left unfinished at his death, might have developed in this direction. Unfortunately, too little of it was completed for us to have much sense of how he would have treated the relationship between Roland Lane-Smith, a comfortably off, early middle-aged bachelor, and the young American actress, Phoebe Friar. As it is, we have to be content with what he had found room to include in the Paris section of *Imperial Palace*. But that is a good deal, especially when coupled with the novel's absorbed and detailed study of hotel business, management of men. I do not think that the novel ranks with Bennett's very best work, yet although it retreats from the 'new manner' it is a considerable achievement and marks a further stage in that recovery which *Riceyman Steps* had begun.

Bennett of course hadn't planned that *Imperial Palace* should be his last work. But as matters turned out that was what it proved to be. 'Everything is going wrong, my girl', Bennett said to Dorothy, as he lay on his deathbed. It is high time that things began to go right for so fine a novelist.

Index